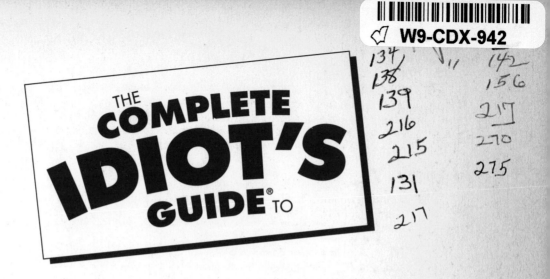

THE COMPLETE IDIOT'S GUIDE® TO

Low-Sodium Meals

by Shelly Vaughan James and Heidi McIndoo, R.D.

ALPHA

A member of Penguin Group (USA) Inc.

To Savannah, who was a constant presence in the kitchen and never a food critic. —Shelly
To my beautiful baby girl, Laila, who surprised us by coming early and spent several hours sleeping on my shoulder as I finished work on this book. And to my wonderful husband, Sean, and my mom, Sandy Swadley, who helped and supported me so much in those first few weeks of new motherhood and always. —Heidi

ALPHA BOOKS

Published by the Penguin Group

Penguin Group (USA) Inc., 375 Hudson Street, New York, New York 10014, U.S.A.

Penguin Group (Canada), 10 Alcorn Avenue, Toronto, Ontario, Canada M4V 3B2 (a division of Pearson Penguin Canada Inc.)

Penguin Books Ltd, 80 Strand, London WC2R 0RL, England

Penguin Ireland, 25 St Stephen's Green, Dublin 2, Ireland (a division of Penguin Books Ltd)

Penguin Group (Australia), 250 Camberwell Road, Camberwell, Victoria 3124, Australia (a division of Pearson Australia Group Pty Ltd)

Penguin Books India Pvt Ltd, 11 Community Centre, Panchsheel Park, New Delhi—10 017, India

Penguin Group (NZ), cnr Airborne and Rosedale Roads, Albany, Auckland 1310, New Zealand (a division of Pearson New Zealand Ltd)

Penguin Books (South Africa) (Pty) Ltd, 24 Sturdee Avenue, Rosebank, Johannesburg 2196, South Africa

Penguin Books Ltd, Registered Offices: 80 Strand, London WC2R 0RL, England

Publisher: *Marie Butler-Knight*
Editorial Director/Acquisitions Editor: *Mike Sanders*
Senior Managing Editor: *Jennifer Bowles*
Development Editor: *Christy Wagner*
Production Editor: *Megan Douglass*
Copy Editor: *Nancy Wagner*

Cartoonist: *Jody Schaeffer*
Book Designer: *Trina Wurst*
Cover Designer: *Kurt Owens*
Indexer: *Julie Bess*
Layout: *Ayanna Lacey*
Proofreading: *Mary Hunt*

Contents at a Glance

Contents

Appendixes

Introduction

When you picked up this cookbook, you were probably looking for a few delicious recipes you could prepare knowing that the meals you were eating fit into your sodium-restricted diet. Naturally, we've included hundreds of mouth-watering recipes, all of them low in sodium. But we believe that the best test of a great cookbook is if you, the reader, can take away what you've learned and put into practice the measures and methods you need to live a more healthful life.

We've tried to share sodium-mindful recipes for the foods you love, as well as to intrigue your taste buds with new flavors and combinations. Beyond the appetizing recipes, we've shared the information you need to know for cooking in a sodium-sensible kitchen.

If you've felt a bit lost in your own kitchen, not knowing what to do or how to do it without salt or other high-sodium seasonings, we're here to help. You'll discover the bright tastes of herbs, spices, and many other flavorings that bring out the great flavors of your foods. None of the recipes in these pages depends on any of the potassium chloride salt replacements, although some of the special low-sodium ingredients use these in their processing. You should always check with your doctor before using a potassium chloride salt substitute.

Equipped with essential information, you can cook and eat with confidence. Food will always take on more significance for you now that you need to be mindful of your sodium-restricted diet. But you should never feel restricted in great taste and great company. With flavorful recipes, you can eat with your family and friends, communing over delicious dishes for everyday meals and all your special occasions.

Here's to your health!

How This Book Is Organized

This book is divided into seven parts:

Part 1, "In the Lo-So Know," provides the indispensable information on salt and sodium you need to know to eat and cook low-sodium meals. You'll learn how to read nutrition labels and find the sodium in your diet. We introduce you to salt alternatives and how to add flavor to foods without using salt and other high-sodium seasonings and flavorings.

Part 2, "For Starters, Snacks, and Sippers," features tempting recipes for appetizers, dips, snacks, and beverages. You'll find recipes to serve for parties and everyday munching.

Part 3, "Breakfast, Brunch, Lunch, and Lighter Fare," offers foods for your early morning rush, your leisurely weekends, your midday meal, and any time you need a less heavy meal. We give dozens of recipes for hearty salads, filling soups and stews, and sodium-responsible sandwiches.

Part 4, "The Meat of the Matter … or Not," highlights your needs for main dish recipes from simple to spectacular. You'll find everything from fish and seafood, chicken, turkey, beef, pork, and even meatless meals.

Part 5, "Side by Side," is packed with recipes for all your favorite go-withs— breads, side salads, vegetables, and other side dishes that make your meals complete.

Part 6, "The Sweet Spot," pleases your sweet tooth with recipes for scrumptious delights. Treat yourself to cookies, brownies, bars, fudges, sauces, puddings, cakes, cheesecakes, pies, tarts, crisps, and cobblers.

Part 7, "'Tis the Seasoning," gives you plenty of recipes to boost the flavor of your foods. Classic condiments, salad dressings, salsas, relishes, slathers, spreads, and seasoning blends help you add that bit of taste to make your meals memorable.

Garnishes

You'll see many sidebars throughout the book that offer you a little something extra. Here's what to look for:

Lo-So Lingo

These boxes give definitions that provide you with helpful vocabulary in cooking low-sodium foods.

Pinch of Sage

These boxes contain valuable information to help you in the kitchen and with specific recipes.

Salt Pitfall

Warnings in these boxes tell you how to avoid eating or cooking with too much sodium.

Acknowledgments

Although only two names appear on the cover of this cookbook, we are all too aware of the contributions made by many others to make this book possible.

The authors would like to thank their families for their patience, for picking up some of the slack at home, for their baby-sitting services, and for their willingness to taste-test everything.

We thank Marilyn Allen of the Allen O'Shea Literary Agency for her support and guidance in this project. Thank you, Mike Sanders, our acquisitions editor at Alpha, whose tolerance and instruction excelled in the face of a premature arrival into the world. And we thank our development editor Christy Wagner, production editor Megan Douglass, and copy editor Nancy Wagner for whipping our manuscript into shape for accuracy and readability. Shelly would like to thank JoAnna M. Lund for her guidance and confidence in her abilities that culminated in this project.

Trademarks

All terms mentioned in this book that are known to be or are suspected of being trademarks or service marks have been appropriately capitalized. Alpha Books and Penguin Group (USA) Inc. cannot attest to the accuracy of this information. Use of a term in this book should not be regarded as affecting the validity of any trademark or service mark.

Part 1

In the Lo-So Know

With just a little helpful information, you can easily prepare sodium-sensible meals everyone will love—even people not specifically watching their sodium intake. When you learn how to replace the salt shaker (and other high-sodium seasonings and sauces) with herbs and spices, veggies, fruits, and other seasoning secrets, you'll feel great about your reduced sodium levels and be savoring what you've cooked.

Additionally, you need to know which foods have naturally occurring sodium and in what amounts. More important, you should learn where sodium is hiding and which foods are available in a spectrum of reduced-sodium versions (and how to find them). Once you've mastered this information—and it's easy, really it is—you'll have the confidence to step into your kitchen and create flavorful, mouthwatering meals to fit everyone's needs.

Chapter 1

The Shakedown on Salt

In This Chapter

- ◆ Losing your taste for salt
- ◆ Making sure your water isn't foiling your low-sodium efforts
- ◆ Deciphering food-label nutrition information
- ◆ Identifying sodium-related terms

Salty—it's one of the four basic tastes. Sodium, which salt can provide, is an essential mineral every body needs for regulating fluid balance. The amount of sodium the body requires, though, is very small—exceptionally less than the average person's intake.

If you're trying to cut back on salt and other sources of sodium, gathering some knowledge will help you obtain your goal. You need the basics. What is salt? Where does sodium come from? How can I cook without it? With answers to these questions, you can begin serving sodium-responsible meals that are not only healthful but delectable besides.

What's Shakin'?

Common table salt is the chemical compound sodium chloride (NaCl); by weight, it's about 40 percent sodium and 60 percent chloride. Salt is a major source of the sodium most people consume. But the average person doesn't need the amount of sodium that he eats. Do you know that you can ingest all the sodium your body needs to maintain healthy functioning without eating a grain of salt? You can, because sodium occurs naturally in meats, dairy products, poultry, eggs, seafood, fruits, vegetables, and cereal products.

Salt at Work

The popularity of salt has endured throughout the ages because of its usefulness. Its preserving properties were vital before civilizations had readily accessible refrigeration. Adding salt to a food dehydrates the cells, including any bacteria cells present, which in turn retards bacterial growth that results in spoilage.

Salt is also the muscle behind the flour in bread making. The salt strengthens the gluten in the dough, thereby enabling the dough to expand with a uniform texture. You'll find that salt-free breads are coarser and denser in texture than typical fluffy white breads.

And salt provides a means for curing meats, pickling vegetables and other foods, and making cheese. But now, with today's technologies, manufacturers have developed alternative methods to making lunch meats, pickles, and cheeses without using salt. That means many of your favorite foods are available without the sky-rocketing sodium contents.

More important to you on a personal level, salt is the enduring flavor enhancer. In simple terms, your tongue tastes salt and sends a message to your brain. Your brain now knows you're eating, so it lets your nose in on the information. Your nose starts to smell the food. The flavor of the food comes from your tongue tasting and your nose smelling the food.

Retraining Your Taste Buds

You've probably spent any number of years honing your taste for salt. But the good news is that your taste for salt is developed and not innate! Because you've learned to like salty foods, you can *unlearn* your love of salt, too.

If you have the luxury, try cutting back on salt gradually. Take the salt shaker off the table, replace salt in recipes with herb-and-spice seasoning blends or other appropriate salt substitutes, and opt for the unsalted versions of snacks such as nuts and crackers. Over time, your taste for salt will diminish.

Keep following the tips for reducing sodium in your diet until you reach a comfortable level for you that falls within your doctor's or nutritionist's guidelines, if necessary:

- Season foods without salt at the table and when cooking; try herbs, spices, and other low-sodium seasonings.
- Substitute low-sodium forms of seasonings and sauces, such as Worcestershire sauce, soy sauce, and bouillon.
- Purchase ingredients with the lowest sodium content possible, by carefully reading the nutrition labels.
- Use fresh or frozen fruits and vegetables or no-salt-added canned foods.
- Prepare pasta, noodles, rice, and hot cereals without the optional salt.
- Opt for no-salt-added condiments, such as mustard, ketchup, barbecue sauce, and salsa.

 Pinch of Sage _____

Now that you're not seasoning with salt, don't throw out the salt shaker! Check out some of these alternative uses for salt:

Blot wine spilled on a tablecloth and then cover the stain with salt to absorb the remainder. Rinse the tablecloth with cold water. If the spill is on carpet, vacuum up the salt after it has absorbed the spill.

To keep cut flowers fresh longer, add a dash of salt to the water.

Sprinkle salt into canvas shoes to absorb moisture and odors.

Rub tea- or coffee-stained cups with salt to remove the stains.

Soak new candles in a strong salt solution for several hours and then dry well to keep them from dripping when they burn.

It's Something in the Water

Did you know the water you drink contains sodium? Depending on the source, the sodium content of water varies greatly. If you're using tap water, the source of your water is your local water department. You can contact them for information on the sodium levels in your tap water. One way to bypass your tap is to purchase a water filtration system. You can choose either a pitcher that filters out sodium, to keep it in

Salt Pitfall

We have based the recipes in this book on the use of sodium-free bottled water. Therefore, the nutrition analysis given for any recipe calling for water does not account for any water-supplied sodium.

your refrigerator for drinking and cooking needs, or you can install a filter on your kitchen tap that removes a percentage of the sodium from the tap water.

If you have a water softener in your home, the chemicals used to condition your water are likely raising its sodium content. Bypass your softener whenever you use water for drinking or cooking.

If your water's sodium content is too high for your needs, consider buying sodium-free bottled water for use in cooking and for drinking.

Navigating the Nutrition Analysis

The nutrition analysis accompanying each recipe in this book can help you plan your daily meals and snacks to fall within your recommended sodium intake. You'll also be able to track your calories, protein, carbohydrates, fat, and so on. The amounts you'll find listed with each recipe refer to an individual serving.

Each recipe provides the number of servings and the serving size for you. Should a recipe provide a range of servings along with a range in an ingredient amount, the information offered for each serving is based on the first serving size given in conjunction with the first ingredient amount listed. If a recipe offers an alternative ingredient, it's not considered in the nutrition analysis. We have used those ingredients listed first for the calculations. Likewise, the analyses do not take into account any suggested serving accompaniments, as you may or may not choose to use these suggestions.

The following nutrients are included in the analyses provided in this book:

Calories. How many calories you need to consume each day depends on your gender, age, height, and physical activity level. Check with your doctor or nutritionist for the appropriate amount of calories you should eat. For additional information, visit www.mypyramid.gov. Per gram, protein and carbohydrate contain 4 calories while fat carries 9 calories.

Sodium. The recommended sodium intake for healthy adults on a 2,000-calorie diet is 2,300 milligrams (about 1 teaspoon). If your doctor or nutritionist has indicated a modified amount for you, follow those instructions.

Protein. The recommendation ranges from 44 to 63 grams per day.

Fat. Your total fat grams should not exceed 65 if you consume a 2,000-calorie diet. Try to favor monounsaturated and polyunsaturated fats.

Saturated fat. Only 10 percent or less of your daily calories should come from saturated fat. For the 2,000-calorie diet, that calculates to 20 grams.

Cholesterol. Keep your intake under 300 milligrams per day. If you're at risk for heart disease, try to restrict your consumption. Check with your doctor or nutritionist as needed.

Carbohydrate. The recommended level is 300 grams for a 2,000-calorie diet.

Dietary fiber. Eat at least 25 grams a day.

Calcium. Get at least 1,000 milligrams daily for a 2,000-calorie diet. You may need more calcium, for example, if you are an adolescent girl (1,300 mg) or a post-menopausal woman (1,200 mg).

Potassium. Recommendations suggest you should consume 4,700 milligrams per day. Found in every cell in your body, potassium helps balance your body fluids, as does sodium from outside your cells. Check with your doctor or nutritionist for the potassium level that is right for you.

Please use these nutrition analyses as guidelines. Differences in your exact ingredients and preparation methods may result in altered nutrient amounts. A food's nutritional values can vary by season, grower, and location. Thereby, the provided figures cannot be exact. Still, you can trust that the numbers are close and use them for tracking your intake.

What's more, you may need to substitute various ingredients to follow the recommendations given to you by your doctor or nutritionist. Or you may be unable to find a particular ingredient, such as salt-free whole-wheat bread, and need to substitute the available salt-free white bread. Likewise, you may enjoy experimenting with ingredient substitutions for herbs and spices, vinegars, oils, or vegetables. These adaptations may tweak a recipe to fall within your family's eating habits, provide needed variety, or use available ingredients without significantly altering the nutritional value of the recipe.

Reading Food Labels

Nutrition labels contain the information you need to know about the foods you buy. The best place to start sleuthing through nutrition labels is in your own pantry and refrigerator. You'll usually find the nutrition facts for a product on the back or side of a food package. At the top or beginning of the box, you'll find the serving size for that food. If you scroll down or over a little, you'll see sodium listed. The number of sodium milligrams in each serving follows. To the far right is a percentage. The percentage of sodium given is based on a 2,000-calorie diet for a healthy adult. (This number may not be of value to you.)

Going through the foods already in your home can prove to be eye-opening. You may discover foods high in sodium that you never would have suspected. You'll certainly discover some staples you need to replace with low-sodium alternatives.

When searching for low-sodium products, you'll need to compare nutrition labels. Unfortunately, you can't just glance at the number of sodium milligrams.

Salt Pitfall

When you're shopping for low-sodium food, beware of the following top 10 salty terms which might appear on food labels:

(1) *Pickled*, (2) *Brine*, (3) *Cured*, (4) *Smoked*, (5) *Corned*, (6) *Seasoned*, (7) *Breaded*, (8) *Au gratin*, (9) *Barbecued*, (10) *Canned*

When you evaluate similar foods, first note the serving sizes. If they're the same, you can simply compare the amount of sodium in each. If the serving sizes differ, you'll have to do some math. A product with a serving size of 1 cup containing 100 milligrams of sodium is actually lower in sodium than a similar product with a serving size of 6 ounces containing 80 milligrams of sodium.

Finding appropriate foods to eat that allow you to comply with your low-sodium needs takes time and patience. The good news is that after a short time, you will find suitable replacements for the foods you normally eat. Then, you'll only have to play sleuth again when you require a new ingredient.

Understanding FDA Guidelines

The U.S. Food and Drug Administration (FDA) has guidelines in place for food manufacturers that can help you more easily identify sodium sensible foods. Labels can carry specific terms based on their sodium content. Unfortunately, it isn't always cut and dried. Some products use "low-sodium" generically, even though they may be "very low-sodium" according to the guidelines. Labels that read "reduced sodium" may be reduced by more than 25 percent; these labels typically indicate the higher percentage. Use the sodium-related label terms to locate the products on store shelves or in online catalogs. Then, read those labels for exact information.

Sodium Guidelines Set by the FDA	
Sodium free	Less than 5 milligrams per serving
Very low sodium	35 milligrams or less per serving
Low sodium	140 milligrams or less per serving
Reduced sodium	Usual sodium level is reduced by 25 percent
Unsalted, no-salt-added, or without added salt	Made without the salt that's normally used, but still contains the sodium that's a natural part of the food itself

Salt by Any Other Name

When you're in the thick of reading an ingredients list, you need to keep an eye out for all forms of sodium. These may be listed as sodium, sodium alginate, sodium sulfite, sodium caseinate, disodium phosphate, sodium benzoate, sodium hydroxide, monos-odium glutamate (*MSG*), sodium citrate, baking powder, baking soda, sodium bicarbonate, Na, and more.

Reality check! You are not going to memorize every sodium-containing compound that may be listed on a food label. So just keep it simple. Look for the word *sodium*. It may be listed individually or within another word. The other ingredients you need to watch for are *salt*, *baking powder*, and *baking soda*. MSG is also troublesome, as the abbreviation keeps you from spotting the sodium portion of the ingredient, but that's what that "S" stands for.

Regardless of how any sodium-rich ingredient is listed, you can always refer to the nutrition facts. Every milligram of sodium will be accounted for in that amount.

Lo-So Lingo

MSG is an acronym frequently used to note the ingredient monosodium glutamate. MSG occurs naturally in many foods, but the manufactured version is used as an added flavor enhancer. MSG contains about one-third the amount of sodium found in table salt. You should be particularly vigilant when eating Chinese foods, which frequently contains MSG as a flavor enhancer.

The Least You Need to Know

◆ Sodium is an essential mineral, but you can easily meet your body's needs without using the salt shaker.

◆ The taste for salt is learned, so you can teach your taste buds to enjoy less salty foods.

◆ Choose sodium-free bottled water for drinking and cooking if your tap water is too high in sodium.

◆ Food labels offer clues to sodium content, but you have to read the nutrition label to get the hard facts.

Kitchen Salternatives

In This Chapter

- Deciphering commercially prepared salt substitutes
- Incorporating herbs and spices for fantastic flavor
- Seasoning with fruits, vegetables, and liquid flavorings
- Choosing the right butter or margarine for you
- Baking with sodium-free leavening agents

Your doctor or nutritionist advised you to stop adding salt to your foods during and after cooking. Now, you're standing in your kitchen empty-handed and at a loss. How do you cook without salt? Fortunately, the answer is *deliciously!* You can still create flavorful meals without adding salt. You just need a little know-how.

If your doctor or nutritionist has indicated that any of the commercially prepared salt substitutes are appropriate for you, all you have to do is simply pick some up at the supermarket. What's more, you can employ the great flavors of herbs, spices, fruits, vegetables, oils, vinegars, syrups, and sweeteners. If you think cooking without salt will result in bland, tasteless foods, hold on to your fork! Once you learn how to introduce flavor without the aid of your salt shaker, you'll be amazed how you can whip up delectable, sumptuous foods your family and friends will devour without saying, "Pass the salt, please"!

Close Encounters of the Three Kindas

While perusing the spice aisle at your local supermarket, you'll find—there, just below eye level—three different alternatives to salt: lite salt, salt substitute, and herb and spice blends. And you will find each type in several different brands. Check with your doctor or nutritionist to learn which one(s) is suitable for you.

Worth Half Its Salt

As the name implies, *lite salt* does contain salt. You can use the half-and-half mixture of salt (sodium chloride) and potassium chloride in cooking and baking as well as for seasoning at the table.

Lite salt may contain potassium iodide, as do some regular salts. Salt is often iodized for dietary purposes. Iodine deficiency can cause a condition of the thyroid gland called goiter.

> **Lo-So Lingo**
>
> **Lite salt** is a blend of sodium chloride and potassium chloride in equal parts. Because salt makes up only half of the mixture, lite salt contains 50 percent less sodium than regular salt. Consult your doctor before using any salt replacement containing potassium chloride.

Potassium Imposters

Salt substitute is the term applied to the potassium chloride product for use in place of ordinary salt. A salt substitute contains no sodium. You can use it in cooking and for seasoning at the table.

Some people dislike potassium chloride salt alternatives because of a bitter aftertaste. Some salt substitutes claim to have no bitter aftertaste. As the proof is in the pudding, you'll have to taste-test them yourself.

> **Lo-So Lingo**
>
> **Salt substitute** is a product intended for people on sodium-restricted diets. Comprised of potassium chloride, salt substitutes are sodium free. Check with your doctor before using any salt substitute.

Herb and Spice Blends

Another alternative for those trying to reduce their sodium intakes are herb and spice blends. These salt-free salt substitute seasoning blends are available in a wide range of flavors to season any number of dishes. You can use them in place of the salt called for in recipes, as well as for at-the-table seasoning.

Because herbs and spices contain trace amounts of sodium, these seasoning blends are not entirely sodium-free. However, the slight amount of sodium in the portions used should not cause concern. Many foods naturally contain sodium. As a matter of fact, your body requires sodium to function properly. Your doctor or nutritionist can recommend the proper sodium intake for you.

Flavor Savers

Preparing flavorful, mouthwatering foods without added salt—and even without a potassium chloride salt substitute—is possible. You can infuse flavor into recipes through a plethora of ingredients. Herbs, spices, fruits, vegetables, oils, vinegars, syrups, and sweeteners can all perk up the taste of food.

Herb Insight

Use herbs in cooking in either their fresh or dried forms. Dried herbs pack a more concentrated flavor. A good rule is 1 tablespoon fresh herb equals 1 teaspoon dried herb. You can adjust the amounts to taste, of course.

Many people prefer the bright flavor of fresh herbs. Fresh herbs must be treated gently, though. You may store them in the refrigerator for up to 5 days. If you need to hold fresh herbs longer, place them stem end down in a tall glass of cold water in the refrigerator and change the water every other day.

High-moisture fresh herbs such as basil, mint, tarragon, and chives can be frozen to preserve their fresh taste—although freezing makes them limp. Wash and pat the herbs dry before spreading individual leaves on a baking sheet. Place the sheet in the freezer until the leaves are frozen solid. Transfer them to a resealable freezer bag to store in the freezer. When needed, use the same amount of frozen herbs as you would fresh herbs.

Dried herbs offer the convenience of a long shelf life; most can be stored for up to 6 months. For a quick test of your herb's freshness, open the jar. If you can't identify the herb by its pungent aroma, it needs to be replaced. Keep your herbs in a cool, dark place because sunlight and heat cause dried herbs to deteriorate more quickly. Don't store your herb jars next to the stove.

Herbs offer a wide variety of aromas and flavors. Experiment to discover your own favorite food-herb pairings. Here are some traditional uses for common herbs:

Basil enhances the taste of tomato dishes and sauces, as well as soups, salads, pastas, and meats. It's frequently used in Italian and Mediterranean cuisines.

Bay leaves infuse flavor into soups, stews, and marinades. Discard these large, brittle leaves before serving.

Cilantro, the leaf of the coriander plant, is a traditional ingredient in Mexican and Indian dishes, as well as in Caribbean and Asian cooking. Try it in salsas, sauces, soups, stews, salads, and meats. It is sometimes referred to as Chinese parsley, as it resembles flat-leaf parsley.

Dill weed's feathery green leaves liven up vegetables, salads, eggs, light meats, fish, mustards, and other sauces. It's used extensively in Scandinavian cooking.

Marjoram is sweeter than oregano and widely used in French, Italian, North African, and Middle Eastern cuisines. It seasons meats, poultry, fish, beans, breads, cheese dishes, eggs, tomato dishes, soups, and salad dressings.

Mint is available in a variety of types, with peppermint and spearmint being the most common. Use mint in beverages, candies, baked goods, desserts, vegetables, salads, jellies, and lamb sauce.

Oregano is more savory than marjoram and used regularly in Italian cooking. Use oregano to enhance pizzas, sauces, salads, eggs, meats, and vegetables.

Parsley is available in curly and flat-leaf varieties, with the latter being more flavorful. Parsley is mild enough to be added to nearly any recipe. It's often used for color.

Rosemary's gray-green, piney leaves complement Italian, Greek, and Provencal recipes. Use it in breads, eggs, meats, potatoes and other vegetables, soups, and stews. It is often called for in its ground form.

Sage is a strong-flavored herb, so use its green-gray leaves or dried form in moderation. Breads, dressings, sausages, and pork all benefit from its distinctive taste.

Tarragon is prized in French cuisine. Use it in sauces, salads, and fish and poultry dishes.

Thyme is called for in herbes de Provence, bouquet garni, Zahtar (a Middle Eastern spice blend), jerk seasonings, and curry blends. Try it in pizzas, potatoes and other veggies, salads, soups, stews, eggs, meats, and dressings.

Spice It Up

Spices can kick up the flavor of any number of dishes. Commonly available in their ground forms, store spices in a cool, dry place. If heat and moisture are kept at bay, ground spices will stay fresh for about 6 months. If you prefer to grind your own whole spices, you can store the whole spices for a year or longer, as you can dry mustard. If you have slightly older spices and you just can't be wasteful, add a bit more than the recipes call for.

Spice blends are readily available for purchase. Some of your favorites may contain salt as an ingredient, though. Whether you choose to mix your own spice blends because you need to avoid the salt or because it's more economical, store them as you would any other spice or herb. Glass jars with tight-fitting lids are your best option. Keep them in the same cool, dry, dark place you store the remainder of your collection.

The heady aromas and sharp tastes of spices can invigorate your cooking. Use the following common spices to expand the flavor of your foods. But don't feel you have to work within these perimeters. Feel free to experiment with your favorite flavors.

Allspice has an aroma that hints of cloves, nutmeg, and cinnamon, hence the name. Use it in baked goods, beverages, meats, poultry, grains, egg dishes, soups, and stews.

Anise seeds taste and smell like licorice. They flavor baked goods, candies, breads, cheeses, fish and shellfish, sausages, and condiments.

Caraway seeds give rye bread its distinctive flavor. You can use them to season cabbage, potatoes, soups, stews, sausages, and cheeses.

Cayenne is sometimes labeled as ground red pepper. Its hot zing can add flavor to beans, meats, chilis, soups, stews, sauces, and dips.

Celery seeds are tiny brown seeds with a celerylike flavor and aroma that you should use in moderation. Sprinkle them on eggs, poultry, dressings, salads, salad dressings, tomato dishes, stews, and sauces.

Chili powder is a spice blend of ground chilies, paprika, cumin, and garlic. Watch for salt as an ingredient in many blends. As its name implies, it's most often used in chilis, but you may also add it to dips, sauces, corn breads, beans, meats, and chicken.

Chinese five-spice powder is made of star anise, fennel or anise seeds, Szechwan or black peppercorns, cinnamon, cloves, or ginger. Use it to season Asian dishes, meats, poultry, and stir-fries.

Cinnamon is used in traditional Mexican cooking. You'll also find it useful for baked goods, beverages, sweet potatoes, pumpkin and squash dishes, sauces, and curries.

Cloves in their whole form resemble small spikes and should be discarded before serving. Use whole or ground cloves to enhance baked goods, fruits, sweet vegetables, pork, sauces, and ketchup.

Coriander seeds' sweet-tart citrus taste can spice up meats, eggs, dips, sauces, marinades, grains, and cream soups.

Cumin, prized in Indian, Thai, Vietnamese, and Mexican cuisines, can be used in seed or ground form. Try it in beans, chilis, and curries.

Curry powder is a spice blend that may consist of cumin, turmeric, coriander, fennel, cinnamon, cloves, and so on. The flavors range from mild to fiery hot. You can add a blend to chicken or tuna salad, soups, eggs, and vegetables.

Dry mustard allows you to make your own low-sodium mustards. It's also good for eggs, cheese dishes, meats, and salad dressings.

Ginger can be added to Asian dishes in its fresh form. Ground ginger is commonly used in baked goods, beverages, and curries.

Nutmeg and its more intense lacy outer covering, mace, are typically added to baked goods. Nutmeg lends flavor to sauces, beverages, custards, and puddings as well. You can also try it for savory dishes of meat, chicken, fish, vegetables, soups, and stews.

Paprika is ground from the pimiento, the pepper used to stuff green olives. Most commercial paprika is mild, but hot versions do exist. What you find on your supermarket shelf and what's called for in most recipes is the mild version unless otherwise noted. Use it to liven up goulashes, chicken, fish, eggs, potatoes, soups, and stews.

Pinch of Sage

When purchasing any spice blends such as chili powder, curry powder, and poultry seasoning, read the labels and ingredient lists carefully. They may, and many do, use salt or even MSG as an ingredient. If the labels aren't clear, you may have to contact the manufacturer for details.

Pepper is available in white, green, and black peppercorns, whole or ground. It's a staple spice around the world, and you can use it in nearly every savory dish.

Poppy seeds are tiny, round, blue-gray seeds from the opium poppy flower. (They do not contain opium.) Sprinkle them onto breads, rolls, and noodles or into salad dressings and dips.

Poultry seasoning is a blend of spices and herbs, such as sage, thyme, rosemary, marjoram, parsley, black pepper, onion powder, garlic powder, and nutmeg. Watch for blends that contain salt. Its use is evident from it name.

Sesame seeds are valued in Asian and Middle Eastern cuisines. Embed these seeds atop breads, rolls, and crackers, or scatter them in salads or stir-fries.

Turmeric is a golden yellow spice that easily stains. Try it in rice, chutneys, relishes, and curry powders.

Good Ol' Fruits and Veggies

What could be more basic than flavoring foods with other foods? At times, it's difficult to distinguish whether an ingredient is a main ingredient or a flavoring, but don't fuss too much over it. As long as the eatin's good, go with it. However, if you're looking for a new depth of flavor for a recipe, try adding a seasoning fruit or vegetable such as the following:

Bell peppers are available in a rainbow of colors. Green bell peppers are immature and have a more raw taste. Red, orange, and yellow bell peppers are milder and sweeter tasting. Use minced, diced, and chopped bell peppers in egg dishes, meats, chicken, fish, beans, cheese dishes, tomato dishes, potatoes and other vegetables, soups, stews, chilis, grains, pastas, salads, sauces, and dips.

Celery is commonly added to dishes for flavor, but it's fairly high in sodium, as vegetables go. One large rib of celery has about 50 milligrams sodium, so add it in moderation. Sliced, diced, and chopped celery enhances the taste of egg dishes, cheese dishes, fish, beans, soups, stews, tomato dishes, potatoes and other vegetables, grains, pastas, dressings, salads, sauces, dips, and more.

Chili peppers pack a heat that can kick up the flavor for fiery food lovers. The heat of a chili pepper is measured in Scoville units of heat:

Pepper	Scoville Units
Bell	0
Pepperoncini	100 to 500
Poblano	1,000 to 2,000
Jalapeño	2,500 to 8,000
Serrano	8,000 to 22,000
Scotch bonnets	150,000 to 325,000
Red savina habañero	up to 577,000

The capsaicin that accounts for the heat of a chili pepper is concentrated in the white ribs as well as the seeds, so removing these veins from the inside of the pepper, along with the seeds, reduces the burn factor. *Most important:* thoroughly wash your hands after handling hot peppers or consider wearing gloves. You won't want to rub your eye with the essence of the pepper still on your fingers!

Garlic is a pungent but delicious addition to many dishes. Buy fresh garlic bulbs or prepared garlic cloves, chopped garlic, minced garlic, and crushed garlic. The flavor of fresh garlic is stronger, but prepared garlic is very convenient. You can use garlic powder in cooking, but don't substitute it for fresh garlic.

Lemon juice and zest adds a bright, citrus-y zing to recipes. Fresh lemon juice and zest are superior in flavor, but you can substitute bottled lemon juice and grated lemon peel from the spice aisle if convenience is a priority. Of course, other citrus juices and zests are just as valuable, including lime, orange, and grapefruit.

Mushrooms come in large variety and a wide price range. Button mushrooms with their small white caps are common in supermarkets. Portobello mushrooms, including the baby portobellos (also known as crimini mushrooms), are becoming largely available as well. You may also find shiitake, oyster, morel, and other mushrooms offered in their fresh or dried forms. (Unless you're an expert, do not gather wild mushrooms for cooking.)

Pinch of Sage

The age-old question: how do you keep your eyes dry when cutting an onion? Try chilling your peeled onion for a bit before chopping it. You should also cut into the root end last.

Onions introduce an array of flavors from pungent to sweet, mild to sharp. Scallions, green onions, shallots, red onions, yellow onions, white onions, sweet onions—your choices are plentiful. You can enhance almost any savory recipe with the addition of onions—from breads to soups, salads to sauces, and meats to grains.

Raisins come in two basic varieties: golden and dark. You're probably most familiar with the dark raisins your mom gave you as a snack, but both are made from Thompson seedless grapes, so use whichever type you prefer. Raisins can sweeten up breads, baked goods, desserts, grains, salads, and meats.

Tomatoes can be utilized in either their fresh or dried forms. They lend their flavor to an array of recipes. Try them in egg dishes, meats, poultry, fish, dips, beans, vegetables, soups, stews, chilis, chowders, breads, grains, pastas, salads, and sauces.

Making a Splash

Liquid flavorings give you another option for great taste in place of salt. Try these:

Honey is often thought of as a replacement for sugar. But honeys range in colors and flavors based on which flowers the bees visited. Generally, light-colored honey is milder and darker honeys have a bolder taste. Honey can add flavor to sauces, salad dressings, marinades, beverages, breads, desserts, and baked goods.

Maple syrup comes in light, medium, and dark ambers, with the tastes ranging from delicate to mapley to robust. Keep a good-quality maple syrup in your refrigerator to enhance meats, chicken, beans, vegetables, baked goods, and desserts.

Molasses adds a distinct taste to meats, poultry, fish, vegetables, sauces, and baked goods.

Oil comes in a wide variety. Olive, peanut, sesame, walnut, and avocado oils provide great tastes. Salad dressings will have subtle flavor changes if you substitute another oil. Stir-fries and vegetables may also benefit from oil experimentation.

Salt Pitfall

Do not give honey to children younger than 12 months of age because botulism spores can be present in honey. Adults and toddlers older than 1 year old can ingest these spores without concern. However, infants' digestive systems may be too immature to digest the bacterial spores, which can make the babies sick.

Vanilla extract, along with the various other extracts found in your spice aisle, quickly flavors baked goods, sauces, vegetables, and beverages.

Vinegar comes in varieties as well, including white, cider, red wine, balsamic, rice, and numerous other flavored vinegars. Splash it in marinades, salad dressings, potato salads, egg dishes, seafood, cabbage, leafy greens, tomato sauces, mustards, and pastas.

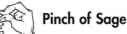

Pinch of Sage

Be careful which rice vinegar you pick up, as the regular type is loaded with sodium. Be sure to choose the sodium-free version.

The Better Butter

We've used unsalted butter in preparing the recipes in this book. It's widely available and always sodium free; look for it in your grocer's dairy case. Butter packages are marked "salted" or "unsalted." Salted and unsalted butters are interchangeable in most recipes. You'll want to purchase the unsalted type for your dietary needs.

If those needs include watching your saturated fat and cholesterol intake as well, you can choose to substitute a sodium-sensible margarine. Talk to your doctor or nutritionist about sodium content, saturated fat, cholesterol

Salt Pitfall

Baked goods should be prepared with a margarine that contains at least 60 percent fat. Spreads lower in fat cannot be used for baking purposes.

amounts, trans-fatty acids, and other concerns that may affect your butter or margarine choice. He or she can recommend the right butter or margarine for you.

If you do substitute for the unsalted butter, calculate the additional sodium, decreased fats, and change in calories. You can compare nutrition labels at the supermarket or go to www.nutritiondata.com for the nutrition facts.

Leavening Agent Awareness

Two of the most common leavening agents used in baked goods are baking powder and baking soda. They work great in giving your baked goods the rise they need. The bad news: both are high-sodium products. The good news: sodium-free substitutions are available. If you can't find them locally, order them from a reputable online store.

One option is Featherweight sodium-free baking powder, which is a blend of monocalcium phosphate, potato starch, and potassium bicarbonate. Add this product to a recipe just as you would regular baking powder.

If your doctor or nutritionist indicates you shouldn't have the 70 milligrams potassium in the ⅛-teaspoon serving of the Featherweight brand, try Ener-G sodium-free baking powder. It's a calcium carbonate and citric acid blend. A note of warning: Ener-G sodium-free baking powder is a single-acting product, unlike the standard double-acting regular baking powder you may be used to. The single-acting baking powder requires nearly twice as much of the product as called-for regular baking powder. Additionally, you may have to tweak the recipe to add the baking powder at the end of mixing and get your pan into the oven quickly. Read the label carefully for specific instructions.

Ener-G also sells a sodium-free baking soda that's simply calcium carbonate. Its label calls for using twice the amount of regular baking soda called for in a recipe.

You may have recipes that call for cream of tartar. Frontier makes a cream of tartar product that has just 1 milligram sodium in a ½-teaspoon serving. It's marketed as an activator for the Featherweight sodium-free baking powder.

Salt Pitfall

Recipes in this book that call for sodium-free baking powder or sodium-free baking soda call for the equivalent of the original measurement of regular baking powder and baking soda. If your ingredient is Featherweight sodium-free baking powder, simply add the amount indicated in the recipe. If you choose Ener-G sodium-free baking powder, nearly double the measurement. When using Ener-G sodium-free baking soda, double the measurement. Carefully read the label directions for any other sodium-free substitutions you may use.

The Least You Need to Know

- Seasoning without salt can create delicious dishes.
- Herbs and spices infuse flavor to make mouthwatering recipes.
- Kick up the taste of foods by seasoning with other foods, such as onions, garlic, and lemon juice.
- Low-sodium liquid flavorings, such as vinegars and concentrated extracts, are smart options for great taste.
- Unsalted butter reduces the sodium count in dishes, but your doctor or nutritionist may recommend a sodium-sensible margarine substitute.
- Read the label of a sodium-free leavening agent carefully for special directions on how to use that particular product.

Part 2

For Starters, Snacks, and Sippers

In addition to eating three nutritious meals a day, you're going to want to nosh. Whether you're hosting a cocktail party, throwing a shower for a friend, or just lounging in front of the TV, you'll need some sodium-responsible options for you, your family, and your guests to enjoy.

Appetizers, snacks, and beverages add variety to your diet in smaller portions. Plus, they fit the occasion, whatever it may be. Hot hors d'oeuvres, snick-snacks, frosty drinks—they're delicious and refreshing when you need that between-meal pick-me-up.

Chapter 3

All-Occasion Appetizers

In This Chapter

- Preparing appetizers lower in sodium
- Keeping the serving size in mind
- Entertaining with small bites
- Snacking on tasty tidbits

Most everyone loves nibbling on bite-size noshes, sampling a wide array of tasty tidbits. If appetizers do their job well, your appetite is whet for the coming meal, and you're still hungry enough to eat it.

Of course, you may enjoy an entire meal made of an assortment of scrumptious little bites, Spanish *tapas* style. Keep in mind that all sodium and other nutritional tallies apply, even if the food's eaten while you're standing.

Dainty delights also make great snacks. With their small size, appetizers naturally lend themselves to between-meal nibbling. And they're so versatile, you'll want to make them all the time!

Entertaining Ideas

Appetizers are such great all-around foods, what *can't* you do with them? From first-course offerings to cocktail party noshes, these little bites delight guests at every gathering.

Pinch of Sage ⎯⎯⎯⎯

If you're hosting a hot, hot, hot party—and we mean *al fresco* in temperatures above 90°F—don't leave any foods out at room temperature more than 1 hour. Throw away any perishable foods you've held unrefrigerated for an hour.

If you'll be offering appetizers over a long period of time, keep safe-handling in mind. Keep cold foods cold and hot foods hot. You can set cold dishes in bowls or trays filled with chipped ice to keep them at or below 40°F. Chafing dishes, warming trays, and slow cookers can help keep cooked foods hot—at or above 140°F. Another option is to serve a small amount at a time. Exchange the plates instead of adding fresh morsels to those already sitting out. Any food left at room temperature for more than 2 hours you must discard. You want your guests to remember your fabulous party, not a resulting trip to the hospital.

Eyer Beware

Standing before a buffet spread with dozens of delectable tidbits may tempt you to pig out. So after you tuck your dangling tongue back in your mouth, survey the choices. Your stomach will be just as delighted with the noshes that are lower in sodium. Plus, you'll be proud of yourself for keeping your sodium level in check. Choosing hors d'oeuvres lower in sodium keeps you from feeling deprived.

If you just try each appetizer, you've probably reached the serving size. Eating more than one helping (and thereby more sodium) is easy to do. Remember, a single helping of any appetizer is petite. They don't call them tidbits for nothing!

To Snack or Not to Snack?

Snacking is no longer a bad word. Eating a small serving between meals provides needed energy and keeps your blood sugar levels more consistent throughout the day. Also, you're less likely to grow hungry enough to binge when next you eat.

Appetizers are a convenient way to provide modest snacks. Choose wisely, and you can include a variety of foods for a well-balanced diet.

Flaming Pineapple Shrimp Skewers

½ lb. (about 20) medium cooked or uncooked cocktail shrimp (tails intact)

1 (20-oz.) can pineapple chunks in their own juice, drained (2 TB. juice reserved)

1 tsp. Firehouse Chili Powder (recipe in Chapter 26) or other salt-free chili powder

2 TB. extra-virgin olive oil

2 cloves garlic, minced

Makes 10 servings
Prep time: 10 minutes
Cook time: 2 minutes
Serving size: 1 skewer
Each serving has:
81.4 calories
52.3 mg sodium
5.2 g protein
3.1 g total fat
0.4 g saturated fat
44.6 mg cholesterol
9.2 g carbohydrate
0.8 g dietary fiber
16.5 mg calcium
115.3 mg potassium

1. Place shrimp and pineapple chunks in a medium bowl. Drizzle in reserved pineapple juice, and toss to coat. Sprinkle on Firehouse Chili Powder, and toss to coat.

2. In a large skillet over medium-high heat, heat olive oil and garlic. Add shrimp mixture, and sauté for 1 minute. Turn shrimp and sauté for 1 minute more. Return to the bowl.

3. When cool enough to handle, thread pineapple and shrimp onto small wooden skewers, alternating pineapple and shrimp.

 **Pinch of Sage** _____

To skewer shrimp, push the point of the skewer through the shrimp just above the tail and again near the head.

Ricotta-Stuffed Cherry Tomatoes

Makes 1½ dozen
Prep time: 15 minutes
Chill time: 30 minutes
Serving size: 2 tomatoes
Each serving has:
30 calories
13.9 mg sodium
1.8 g protein
1.9 g total fat
1.2 g saturated fat
7 mg cholesterol
1.7 g carbohydrate
0.3 g dietary fiber
31.5 mg calcium
74.4 mg potassium

18 cherry tomatoes

½ cup *lite* ricotta cheese

2 TB. chopped fresh basil

1 clove garlic, crushed

¼ tsp. freshly ground black pepper

1. Slice off tops of cherry tomatoes, about ¼ the way down, with a sharp knife. Scoop out seeds using a small melon baller or a round ¼-teaspoon measuring spoon.

2. In a small bowl, combine lite ricotta cheese, basil, garlic, and black pepper. Stir until evenly distributed. Spoon into a snack-size sealable plastic bag, seal bag, and snip off a small piece of 1 corner. Pipe ricotta mixture into cherry tomatoes. Chill for 30 minutes before serving.

Lo-So Lingo

Lite, when used in reference to sodium, refers to a product that has less sodium than the regular version of that food—usually 50 percent less. Check the nutrition label for actual sodium amounts.

Sweet and Creamy Strawberry Swoops

½ cup fat-free sour cream

1 TB. firmly packed light brown sugar

Pinch ground cinnamon

32 large whole strawberries, rinsed

1. In a small bowl, stir together sour cream, brown sugar, and cinnamon until well combined. Cover and chill for at least 1 hour before serving.

2. Hull strawberries as desired, and serve with dip.

Salternative: For a large gathering, you can double this recipe, using ⅛ teaspoon cinnamon to 1 cup sour cream. You can even double it again, if needed.

Salt Pitfall _____
Choose your fat-free or reduced-fat sour creams carefully. Many manufacturers add sodium as they reduce fat. Compare the nutrition labels closely. We've found Breakstone's Free fat-free sour cream has just 25 milligrams sodium per 2 tablespoon serving.

Makes ½ cup dip
Prep time: 5 minutes
Chill time: 1 hour
Serving size: 2 tablespoons dip with 8 strawberries
Each serving has:
85 calories
25.8 mg sodium
2.4 g protein
1 g total fat
0.3 g saturated fat
2.9 mg cholesterol
18.3 g carbohydrate
3.3 g dietary fiber
68.6 mg calcium
321.2 mg potassium

Creamy Mustard Deviled Eggs

Makes 1 dozen
Prep time: 20 minutes
Cook time: 25 minutes
Serving size: 1 egg half
Each serving has:
52.1 calories
35.2 mg sodium
3.7 g protein
3 g total fat
0.9 g saturated fat
110.5 mg cholesterol
2.3 g carbohydrate
0 g dietary fiber
21 mg calcium
34.7 mg potassium

6 large eggs

Cold water

¼ cup fat-free plain yogurt

2 TB. Make-Your-Own Mustard (recipe in Chapter 23)

2 TB. white vinegar

Dash paprika

1. Place eggs in a medium saucepan, and cover with cold water. Cover the saucepan, and bring water to a boil. When water boils, remove the pan from heat. Let stand, covered, for 20 minutes. Immediately rinse eggs under cold water until cooled. Leave eggs immersed in cold water as you peel them.

2. Cut eggs in half lengthwise. Remove yolks to a small bowl, and mash with a fork until fine crumbs form. Add yogurt, Make-Your-Own Mustard, and white vinegar. Mix thoroughly.

3. Spoon yolk mixture into a snack-size sealable plastic bag, seal bag, and snip off a small piece of 1 corner. Pipe yolk mixture into egg whites. Lightly sprinkle paprika over tops for color. Chill before serving.

Pinch of Sage

Deviled eggs make great carry-in dishes as you can prepare them the night before. For a pretty presentation, pipe the egg yolk mixture into the egg whites using a pastry bag with a fluted tip.

Icy Avocado Sorbet

2 ripe avocados

Juice of 1 lemon

Juice of 1 lime

2 TB. water

Makes 6 servings
Prep time: 5 minutes
Freeze time: 2 hours
Serving size: 3 small scoops
Each serving has:
112 calories
6.9 mg sodium
1.4 g protein
10.3 g total fat
1.6 g saturated fat
0 mg cholesterol
6.2 g carbohydrate
3.4 g dietary fiber
8.5 mg calcium
418 mg potassium

1. Scoop avocado pulp into a food processor. Add lemon juice, lime juice, and water. Process for 20 seconds or until color is even and mixture is smooth.

2. Spoon mixture into a shallow dish. Cover with plastic wrap, and freeze for 30 minutes. Stir and then freeze again, covered, for 30 minutes more. Stir and then freeze again, covered, until frozen.

3. Remove from the freezer at least 30 minutes before serving time. Use a small scoop or a melon baller to serve.

Pinch of Sage

Avocados discolor quickly. Don't cut into an avocado until you're ready to prepare it. The lemon and lime juices in this recipe help to keep the avocado from browning.

Easy Cheddar Melt Potato Skins

Makes 4 servings
Prep time: 10 minutes
Cook time: 15 minutes
Serving size: 2 potato halves
Each serving has:
214.9 calories
7.2 mg sodium
10.9 g protein
9.2 g total fat
5.9 g saturated fat
28.3 mg cholesterol
27 g carbohydrate
3.3 g dietary fiber
218.6 mg calcium
769.1 mg potassium

4 all-purpose potatoes

1 cup shredded *low-sodium* cheddar cheese

¼ cup chopped green onion tops

1. Preheat the oven to 400°F. Spray a baking sheet with nonstick cooking spray.

2. Wash potatoes and prick all over with the tines of a fork. Arrange potatoes in a circle on a microwave-safe plate. Cook on high for 10 to 12 minutes or until potatoes are tender. Remove potatoes from oven, cover with a paper towel, and let stand for 5 minutes.

3. Cut potatoes in half lengthwise. Using a spoon, scoop out pulp, leaving a thin ¼- to ½-inch shell.

4. Arrange potato skins on the prepared baking sheet. Sprinkle on cheese, and scatter green onions over top. Bake for 5 minutes or until cheese is melted and bubbly.

Salternative: You can serve these potato skins with your favorite tasty toppers, such as Fresh-Taste Tomato Salsa (recipe in Chapter 25), Great Guacamole (recipe in Chapter 4), and/or fat-free sour cream. Just remember to calculate in the additional sodium from the nutrition analysis or the nutrition facts label.

Lo-So Lingo

Low-sodium denotes foods that contain 140 milligrams of sodium or less per serving. Low-sodium cheddar cheese can actually be very low sodium with only 5 milligrams sodium per ounce. Because salt (sodium chloride) is integral in the production of cheese, low-sodium cheeses are made with the salt substitute potassium chloride instead, keeping the sodium content to a minimum.

Cheddar Rice–Stuffed Mushrooms

1½ TB. unsalted butter

12 button mushrooms, stems removed and wiped with a damp paper towel

3 TB. sliced green onions

1 clove garlic, minced

½ cup cooked long-grain brown rice (about 3 TB. uncooked)

½ cup finely shredded low-sodium cheddar cheese

⅛ tsp. ground white pepper

Makes 1 dozen
Prep time: 10 minutes
Cook time: 15 minutes
Serving size: 2 mushroom caps
Each serving has:
88.1 calories
4.7 mg sodium
3.4 g protein
6.2 g total fat
3.8 g saturated fat
17.2 mg cholesterol
5.2 g carbohydrate
0.7 g dietary fiber
70.7 mg calcium
103.3 mg potassium

1. Preheat oven to 350°F. Melt ½ tablespoon butter in a small saucepan over medium heat. Add mushrooms, and cook, stirring, for 1 minute. Transfer mushrooms to a baking sheet, placing them gill side up.

2. Melt remaining 1 tablespoon butter in a skillet. Sauté green onions for 1 minute. Add garlic, and sauté for 1 minute. Turn off heat, and stir in cooked rice. Turn mixture into a small bowl, and let cool for a few minutes.

3. Stir cheese and white pepper into rice mixture, combining thoroughly. Spoon mixture into mushroom caps, mounding above hollows. Bake for 10 minutes or until cooked through and mushrooms start to exude liquid.

Pinch of Sage

If you have some extra stuffing mixture, you can spoon it into a few extra mushroom caps. Sautéing the mushroom caps helps them sit flat on the baking pan, but raw mushroom caps will cook up during the baking time, too.

Grilled Pizza-Parlor Quesadillas

Makes 6 servings
Prep time: 10 minutes
Cook time: 16 minutes
Serving size: 2 wedges with 4 teaspoons sauce
Each serving has:
262.6 calories
122.2 mg sodium
10.6 g protein
12.6 g total fat
4.6 g saturated fat
14.6 mg cholesterol
26.2 g carbohydrate
3.3 g dietary fiber
175.3 mg calcium
220.4 mg potassium

Pinch of Sage

Use a pizza cutter to make quick work of slicing the quesadil-

1 (8-oz.) can no-salt-added tomato sauce

¼ tsp. dried basil

⅛ tsp. dried oregano

⅛ tsp. garlic powder

⅛ tsp. onion powder

⅛ tsp. freshly ground black pepper

⅓ cup halved, sliced yellow onions

¼ cup diced green bell peppers

4 button mushrooms, trimmed, wiped with a damp paper towel, and sliced

4 Fresh Tortillas (recipe in Chapter 16) or other low-sodium tortillas

1⅓ cups shredded fresh mozzarella cheese

1. In a small bowl, combine tomato sauce, basil, oregano, garlic powder, onion powder, and black pepper. Stir to blend.

2. Spray a large, nonstick skillet with nonstick cooking spray. Add onions, green bell peppers, and mushrooms, and cook over medium heat for 3 to 4 minutes or until softened. Remove vegetables from the skillet and set aside.

3. Spray the skillet with nonstick cooking spray again. Spoon 2 tablespoons sauce over ½ of each tortilla. Sprinkle ⅓ cup cheese over sauce on each tortilla. Scatter onion mixture over top, evenly distributing. Fold over tortillas. Cook, 1 at a time, over medium heat for 2 minutes on each side or until toasted and cheese is melted. Let each quesadilla stand briefly before cutting into 3 wedges to serve.

4. Heat remaining sauce to serve as a dip for the quesadillas.

Chapter 4

Dips and Scoops

In This Chapter

- Making dips lower in sodium
- Serving the hit of the party
- Snacking responsibly
- Following the serving size

One sure way to draw a crowd is to bring out a dip. Everyone gathers 'round, and conversation and laughter are sure to follow.

Dips may also be a snacking solution. You know you should eat more fruits and vegetables, but plain-Jane slices don't do it for you. A dip can get you munching and crunching your fruits and veggies with delight. With the dips and scoops recipes in this chapter, you can get a great fresh taste without excessive sodium. Let the dipping begin!

Throwing a "Scooper" Party

What's a party without a dip or two—or three? To throw a "scooper" party, you just need to eye the dip from a guest's perspective.

Make the dip easily accessible in bowls close to where the action is—your guests won't have to stretch to reach the dip, and you'll have less mess to clean up after the party. Refill the dip, as well as the dippers, for happy guests and safety purposes. Foods shouldn't sit out for more than 2 hours; putting out smaller portions more frequently is a good idea. And if your dippers require toothpicks, provide a place for your revelers to dispose of them. You don't even want to think of what they may do with them otherwise.

Smart Dipping

When you're browsing the dip spread or making yourself a snack, remember, dips are intended to complement the dippers, not overpower them. Be aware of serving size, and don't use a full serving on just one apple slice! If you decide to eat more, remember to count the additional sodium, calories, fat, and so on.

Dips do make good snacks and many times enable you to eat more good-for-you fruits and vegetables. But you don't want to munch thoughtlessly in front of the TV. Hitting the bottom of the bowl is not a good indicator of when to stop eating. If you're apt to eat your way through a whole bowl of dip, place just one portion on a plate.

> **Salt Pitfall** _____
>
> Many great dips are traditionally served with high-sodium dippers such as salted chips, pretzels, crackers, and breads. Be sure your dippers don't spoil the reduced sodium of the dip. Fresh fruits and veggies make great dipping vehicles. Otherwise, try unsalted chips, pretzels, crackers, and low-sodium breads.

The High Price of Convenience

Picking up a carton of chip dip at the supermarket seems so easy. Now that you know the importance of reading nutrition labels, though, you'll notice the high sodium content of most commercially prepared dips and envelopes of dip mixes. But that doesn't mean you have to throw down your carrot stick or resign yourself to eating everything plain and dry from now on.

If you crave the convenience of a commercial dip mix, you can buy a small selection of low-sodium packets. But making homemade dips and scoops that are lower in sodium is so easy. You can readily purchase ingredients at most supermarkets, and preparation is, many times, quick and simple. Plus, the taste is fresher. Easy, better-tasting, and good-for-you: get ready to plunge that carrot stick into a concoction of luscious proportion!

Lemon Lover's Poppy Seed Dip

⅔ cup fat-free sour cream

4 tsp. honey

1 tsp. finely grated lemon zest

1 TB. fresh lemon juice

1 TB. poppy seeds

Makes 14 tablespoons
Prep time: 5 minutes
Chill time: 30 minutes
Serving size: 2 tablespoons
Each serving has:
41 calories
18 mg sodium
1.4 g protein
0.9 g total fat
0.3 g saturated fat
2.2 mg cholesterol
7.4 g carbohydrate
0.1 g dietary fiber
52.1 mg calcium
66.5 mg potassium

1. In a small bowl, stir together sour cream and honey. Stir in lemon zest and lemon juice and then stir in poppy seeds until evenly distributed.

2. Cover and chill for at least 30 minutes before serving. Serve with apple slices, seedless green grapes, or other favorite fruits.

 Pinch of Sage _____

To keep honey from clinging to your measuring spoon, first spray the measuring spoon with a little nonstick cooking spray. The honey will slide right out, especially if your measuring spoon is metal.

Creamy Strawberry Fruit Dip

Makes 3½ cups
Prep time: 5 minutes
Serving size: 2 tablespoons
Each serving has:
32 calories
5.5 mg sodium
0.4 g protein
2.1 g total fat
1.8 g saturated fat
0.4 mg cholesterol
3.1 g carbohydrate
0 g dietary fiber
7.2 mg calcium
1.5 mg potassium

1 (8-oz.) container frozen whipped topping, thawed

1 (6-oz.) container low-fat strawberry yogurt or other favorite flavor

1. In a medium bowl, stir together whipped topping and yogurt until thoroughly combined.

2. Serve with your favorite fresh fruits.

Salt Pitfall

You may substitute low-fat or fat-free whipped topping in this recipe. It will add a small amount of sodium to each serving, though. Check the nutrition labels for specific information.

Crisp and Creamy Waldorf Dip

Makes 3 cups
Prep time: 15 minutes
Serving size: ¼ cup
Each serving has:
70.7 calories
11.7 mg sodium
1.7 g protein
3.4 g total fat
0.3 g saturated fat
0.4 mg cholesterol
10 g carbohydrate
0.9 g dietary fiber
32.7 mg calcium
68 mg potassium

1 cup fat-free plain yogurt

2 TB. honey

1 TB. fresh lemon juice

1½ cups finely diced McIntosh apples (about 1 very large)

1 cup sliced seedless red grapes

½ cup chopped unsalted walnuts

1. In a medium bowl, combine yogurt, honey, and lemon juice. Stir until blended.

2. Stir apples into yogurt mixture to coat. Add grapes and walnuts, and stir to distribute evenly. Serve immediately, or chill for up to 4 hours.

Favorite Fiesta Black Bean Dip

1 (15-oz.) can *no-salt-added* black beans, rinsed and drained

2 TB. fresh lime juice

1 clove garlic, crushed

½ cup diced tomatoes, seeded as desired

¼ cup sliced green onions

½ cup fat-free plain yogurt

¼ tsp. ground cayenne

Makes 3 cups
Prep time: 10 minutes
Chill time: 1 hour
Serving size: 2 tablespoons
Each serving has:
13.7 calories
39.7 mg sodium
1 g protein
0 g total fat
0 g saturated fat
0.1 mg cholesterol
3.2 g carbohydrate
1 g dietary fiber
12.4 mg calcium
63.7 mg potassium

1. In a medium bowl, mash beans, lime juice, and garlic with a fork. Add tomatoes, green onions, yogurt, and cayenne. Stir until blended.

2. Cover and chill for at least 1 hour before serving. Serve with carrot sticks, bell pepper strips, or unsalted baked tortilla chips.

Lo-So Lingo

Foods with **no-salt-added** labels have been processed without introduced salt where they typically would be prepared with salt. Nutrition labels will list sodium amounts for individual servings.

Mediterranean Roasted Eggplant Dip

Makes 3½ cups
Prep time: 10 minutes (plus 40 minutes rest time)
Cook time: 1 hour
Serving size: 2 tablespoons
Each serving has:
22.2 calories
4.7 mg sodium
1 g protein
0.9 g total fat
0.1 g saturated fat
0.1 mg cholesterol
3.1 g carbohydrate
1.1 g dietary fiber
16.3 mg calcium
88.2 mg potassium

2 medium eggplants

⅔ cup fat-free plain yogurt

4 cloves garlic, minced

½ jalapeño pepper, minced

1 tsp. ground cumin

1½ TB. fresh lemon juice

⅛ tsp. freshly ground black pepper

4 tsp. dried mint

½ cup toasted and chopped unsalted almonds

1. Preheat the oven to 400°F. Place eggplants on a baking sheet, and prick through skins all over with the tines of a fork. Bake for 1 hour or until tender, turning occasionally. Let cool. Peel eggplants and place pulp in a colander over the sink to drain for 30 minutes.

2. Transfer eggplants to a food processor. Pulse for 10 seconds or until puréed. Add yogurt, garlic, jalapeño pepper, cumin, lemon juice, black pepper, and mint. Pulse for 15 to 20 seconds or until thoroughly blended.

3. Cover and chill eggplant mixture for up to 8 hours, if needed. Just before serving, fold in almonds. Serve with low-sodium pita chips, your favorite veggies, or unsalted crackers.

 Pinch of Sage _____

To toast almonds, place them in a dry skillet over medium heat for 2 to 5 minutes, watching them carefully and shaking occasionally to avoid burning.

Green Herbed Veggie Dip

½ cup fat-free plain yogurt

2 cloves garlic, minced

4 tsp. dried parsley flakes

¼ tsp. dried marjoram

¼ tsp. freshly ground black pepper

¼ tsp. onion powder

Makes ½ cup
Prep time: 5 minutes
Serving size: 2 tablespoons
Each serving has:
16.6 calories
18.7 mg sodium
1.5 g protein
0 g total fat
0 g saturated fat
0.6 mg cholesterol
3.3 g carbohydrate
0.2 g dietary fiber
46.6 mg calcium
20.3 mg potassium

1. In a small bowl, combine yogurt, garlic, parsley flakes, marjoram, black pepper, and onion powder. Stir until blended.

2. Serve with your favorite veggie dippers.

Great Guacamole

1 ripe avocado

1 TB. fresh lemon juice

1 TB. fresh lime juice

1 clove garlic, minced

1 small tomato, finely diced

1 jalapeño pepper, seeds and ribs discarded, and minced

Makes 1⅓ cups
Prep time: 10 minutes
Serving size: 2 tablespoons
Each serving has:
33.6 calories
2.7 mg sodium
0.5 g protein
2.9 g total fat
0.5 g saturated fat
0 mg cholesterol
2.2 g carbohydrate
1.1 g dietary fiber
3.4 mg calcium
138.7 mg potassium

1. Using a metal spoon, scoop avocado pulp out of peel. Stir and chop avocado into lemon juice and lime juice in a medium glass bowl.

2. Add garlic, tomato, and jalapeño pepper to avocado mixture. Stir until blended and desired consistency is reached. Serve immediately or chill briefly.

Pinch of Sage

To remove the pit from an avocado, cut the avocado in half. Embed the middle of the knife blade into the pit. Then slowly turn the knife, releasing the pit.

Zippy Jalapeño Hummus

Makes 1 cup
Prep time: 5 minutes
Serving size: 2 tablespoons
Each serving has:
53.8 calories
0.5 mg sodium
3 g protein
0.7 g total fat
0 g saturated fat
0 mg cholesterol
8.8 g carbohydrate
2.3 g dietary fiber
28.4 mg calcium
122.8 mg potassium

1 (15-oz.) can no-salt-added garbanzo beans, drained (2 TB. liquid reserved)

3 fresh jalapeño peppers, seeds and ribs discarded, and chopped

3 cloves garlic, minced

½ tsp. ground cumin

2 TB. fresh lemon juice

1. In a blender or food processor, combine garbanzo beans, jalapeño peppers, garlic, cumin, lemon juice, and reserved garbanzo bean liquid.

2. Blend on high speed for 1 minute or until smooth, stopping to scrape down sides as necessary. Serve with low-sodium pita bread, crackers, or your favorite veggies.

Salt Pitfall

After seeding and chopping the jalapeño peppers, be sure to wash your hands. If you forget and then touch your eyes or lips, you'll find out the hard way that the essence carries the heat of the peppers.

Snack Time Finger Foods

In This Chapter

♦ Choosing snacks lower in sodium
♦ Snacking without feeling deprived
♦ Satisfying your between-meal hunger
♦ Fitting snacks into your daily eating plan

Now that you're all grown up and following a low-sodium diet, you have to behave appropriately—eat bland foods, shun anything that tastes good, always use utensils. Not so! If you make good snack choices—and plenty of delicious options are out there—food can still be fun.

Getting the munchies is inevitable, so plan accordingly. Have your favorite snacks on hand, and toss that silverware! These hunger-busters are for fingers only.

Snack Attack Flak

Once upon a time, snackers were thought to be weak creatures who lacked the willpower of prudent eaters who held fast to the institution of three meals a day. Fortunately, now snacking is not only an accepted but also an encouraged affair.

Naturally, you can't run rampant with this newfound notion. Try these tips for fitting snacks into your daily eating plan:

◆ Portion control is essential for everyone, and sodium control is especially crucial for you. If you're a bottom-of-the-bag muncher, take out only a single serving. Dividing recipe yields into single portions helps you keep a snack attack from overpowering your low-sodium efforts.

◆ Plan your snacks if you're apt to hit the vending machine. A little preparation keeps you in control of your sodium consumption.

◆ Sensible snacks can add essential variety to your diet. Look at your snack as a little pick-me-up that offers nutrition and fuel to push you on to your next full meal.

Of course, if you don't have time to whip up any of these snacks, fresh fruits and veggies always make a smart snack choice. You can't go wrong with a banana or carrot sticks.

Pinch of Sage _____

Just a glance at the nutrition label on many bagged snacks tells you they're swimming in sodium. Potato chips, corn chips, pretzels, popcorn, crackers, and the rest aren't intended for the lo-so crowd. Rather than totally cut out snacking, however, buy reduced-sodium alternatives. Be sure to check the labels for sodium amounts. Or you can prepare your own alternatives with some of the recipes in this chapter.

Sugar-and-Spice Pecans

6 TB. unsalted butter

3 cups unsalted pecan halves

1½ cups confectioners' sugar

1 TB. ground cinnamon

1 TB. ground cloves

1 TB. ground nutmeg

Makes 3 cups
Prep time: 10 minutes
Cook time: 20 minutes
Serving size: ¼ cup
Each serving has:
328 calories
2.5 mg sodium
3.2 g protein
27.1 g total fat
5.8 g saturated fat
15.5 mg cholesterol
20 g carbohydrate
2.6 g dietary fiber
13.3 mg calcium
12.7 mg potassium

1. In a large, heavy skillet, melt butter over low to medium-low heat. Stir in pecans to coat. Cook, stirring occasionally, for 20 minutes or until heated through and lightly toasted. Remove with a slotted spoon to a plate lined with paper towels.

2. Meanwhile, measure confectioners' sugar, cinnamon, cloves, and nutmeg into a large, sealable plastic bag. Seal the bag, and shake until blended.

3. Pour pecans into the bag, and shake until evenly coated. Turn pecans into a colander over the sink; shake to remove excess confectioners' sugar mixture. Spread pecans in a single layer on a sheet of waxed paper. Cool completely before storing in an airtight container.

Pinch of Sage _____

If you don't have a colander, you can remove the coated pecans from the bag with a slotted spoon, shaking off the excess confectioners' sugar mixture.

¡Olé! Taco Popcorn

Makes 4 servings
Prep time: 5 minutes
Cook time: 5 minutes
Serving size: 2 cups
Each serving has:
148.2 calories
2 mg sodium
1.7 g protein
12.2 g total fat
7.2 g saturated fat
31.1 mg cholesterol
9.3 g carbohydrate
1.6 g dietary fiber
5.6 mg calcium
44.4 mg potassium

¼ cup popcorn kernels

¾ tsp. Taco Seasoning Mix (recipe in Chapter 26)

¼ cup unsalted butter, melted

1. Pour popcorn kernels into a hot-air popcorn machine and pop.
2. Stir Taco Seasoning Mix into melted butter. Drizzle over popcorn, and toss to mix.

Salternative: If you don't have a hot-air popcorn machine, prepare the popcorn as you usually do. If you add oil, remember to add that information to the nutritional analysis.

Pinch of Sage

The recipe for Taco Seasoning Mix has a bit of a kick to it. If you prefer the milder taste of another salt-free taco seasoning mix, you may substitute it in this recipe. The same goes for a more fiery blend. Read the ingredients list carefully, though; most commercial blends contain sodium.

Italian-Seasoned Popcorn

¼ cup popcorn kernels

3 TB. unsalted butter

½ tsp. dried basil

½ tsp. dried oregano

¼ tsp. garlic powder

¼ tsp. onion powder

Makes 4 servings
Prep time: 5 minutes
Cook time: 5 minutes
Serving size: 2 cups
Each serving has:
123.4 calories
1.4 mg sodium
1.7 g protein
9.3 g total fat
5.4 g saturated fat
23.3 mg cholesterol
9.5 g carbohydrate
1.7 g dietary fiber
9.8 mg calcium
50.1 mg potassium

1. In a hot-air popcorn machine, pop popcorn kernels.

2. Meanwhile, melt butter. Stir in basil, oregano, garlic powder, and onion powder. Drizzle over popcorn, and toss to coat.

Salternative: If you don't have a hot-air popcorn machine, prepare the popcorn as you usually do. If you add oil, remember to add that information to the nutritional analysis.

Pinch of Sage

If you're watching your fat or caloric intake, you can spray the popcorn with a sodium-free buttery spray and then toss with the seasonings.

Ants on a Log

2 TB. no-salt-added natural peanut butter

4 (3-inch) celery sticks

2 TB. raisins

Makes 1 serving
Prep time: 5 minutes
Serving size: 4 logs
Each serving has:
262 calories
63.6 mg sodium
9.3 g protein
16.5 g total fat
3.4 g saturated fat
0 mg cholesterol
24.9 g carbohydrate
3.8 g dietary fiber
48.7 mg calcium
551.6 mg potassium

1. Spread peanut butter on celery sticks.

2. Push raisins into top of peanut butter.

Salt Pitfall

Celery is one vegetable that is comparatively high in sodium. Try to limit it in your diet.

Sweet Crunch Trail Mix

Makes 2 cups
Prep time: 5 minutes
Serving size: ½ cup
Each serving has:
364 calories
5 mg sodium
8.5 g protein
21.2 g total fat
4.5 g saturated fat
0.9 mg cholesterol
38.9 g carbohydrate
4.7 g dietary fiber
51.6 mg calcium
361.9 mg potassium

¼ cup unsalted dry-roasted peanuts

¼ cup unsalted whole almonds

¼ cup unsalted cashew pieces

¼ cup unsalted sunflower seeds

¼ cup raisins

¼ cup dried cranberries

¼ cup dried cherries

¼ cup semi-sweet chocolate chips

Combine peanuts, almonds, cashew pieces, sunflower seeds, raisins, cranberries, cherries, and chocolate chips in a large, sealable plastic bag.

 Pinch of Sage _____

Substitute any of your favorite unsalted nuts, seeds, or dried fruits to find your own best mix. Try walnuts, pecans, macadamia nuts, soy nuts, pumpkin seeds, dried pineapple, dried papaya, dates, banana chips, and more. Stored tightly sealed in a cool, dry place, your mix will keep until the earliest "best by" date stamped on your individual ingredients.

Pan-Fried Zucchini Rounds

1 large egg

¼ cup whole-wheat flour

¼ tsp. freshly ground black pepper

3 TB. extra-virgin olive oil

1 medium zucchini, sliced

¼ tsp. garlic powder or to taste

Makes 1 cup		
Prep time: 10 minutes		
Cook time: 20 minutes		
Serving size: ¼ cup		
Each serving has:		
145.9 calories		
17.3 mg sodium		
3.4 g protein		
11.6 g total fat		
1.8 g saturated fat		
53.1 mg cholesterol		
7.8 g carbohydrate		
1.6 g dietary fiber		
14.2 mg calcium		
140.2 mg potassium		

1. Beat egg in a small bowl. In another small, shallow bowl, stir together whole-wheat flour and black pepper.

2. In a nonstick skillet over medium to medium-low heat, heat 1 tablespoon extra-virgin olive oil.

3. Dip zucchini slices into egg and then dredge in seasoned flour to coat, shaking off excess. Fry for 3 minutes or until browned. Turn and fry for 3 minutes more or until underside is browned. (You may have to cook zucchini in batches. Add more extra-virgin olive oil to the skillet as necessary.) Remove zucchini with a slotted spoon to a plate lined with paper towels. Sprinkle on garlic powder.

Salternative: If you think these zucchini slices need a bit more seasoning, sprinkle on a favorite salt-free salt substitute seasoning blend.

Pinch of Sage

If you have leftover tomato sauce from the Individual Lasagna Casseroles recipe in Chapter 15, use it as a dipping sauce for these Pan-Fried Zucchini Rounds.

Peanut-Butter-Banana Swirls

Makes 16
Prep time: 5 minutes
Serving size: 4 swirls
Each serving has:
65.2 calories
0 mg sodium
1.6 g protein
3.6 g total fat
0.6 g saturated fat
0 mg cholesterol
6.7 g carbohydrate
0.9 g dietary fiber
0.6 mg calcium
1.1 mg potassium

¼ cup no-salt-added natural peanut butter

2 Fresh Tortillas (recipe in Chapter 16) or other low-sodium tortillas

1 ripe banana

1. Spread peanut butter over tortillas.

2. Mash banana with a fork and then spread over peanut butter.

3. Roll up tortillas tightly. Cut 1-inch slices on the diagonal.

 Pinch of Sage _____
Keep the tortilla whole, and this recipe also makes a delicious lunchtime sandwich.

Vinegared Cucumbers

Makes 2 cups
Prep time: 5 minutes
Chill time: 30 minutes
Serving size: ½ cup
Each serving has:
14 calories
2.6 mg sodium
0.4 g protein
0.1 g total fat
0 g saturated fat
0 mg cholesterol
4 g carbohydrate
0.5 g dietary fiber
10.6 mg calcium
110.4 mg potassium

1 large cucumber, peeled and sliced

1⅓ cups water

⅔ cup white vinegar

1. Place cucumber in a medium bowl. Pour water and vinegar over top.

2. Cover and chill for at least 30 minutes.

Salternative: You may add onion slices to the mixture, if you like.

Cheddar and Jalapeño Nachos

1 tsp. cornstarch

¼ cup fat-free milk

¼ cup finely shredded low-sodium cheddar cheese

3 doz. small *unsalted* baked tortilla chips (2 servings)

1 jalapeño pepper, seeds and ribs discarded, and thinly sliced

Makes 2 servings
Prep time: 5 minutes
Cook time: 3 minutes
Serving size: 18 tortilla chips with 3 tablespoons cheese sauce and ½ jalapeño pepper
Each serving has:
224.5 calories
19.1 mg sodium
8.7 g protein
6.1 g total fat
3 g saturated fat
14.7 mg cholesterol
36.2 g carbohydrate
2.9 g dietary fiber
137.7 mg calcium
81.8 mg potassium

1. In a small saucepan, whisk cornstarch into milk until blended. Heat over medium heat just until bubbles form around edge of the pan and then reduce heat to low. Slowly whisk in cheese until melted and smooth. Remove from heat.

2. Pour cheese sauce over tortilla chips. Scatter jalapeño pepper slices over top, and serve.

Lo-So Lingo

When a food's labeled **unsalted**, it means no salt was added during processing, where it typically would have been. As with the term *no-salt-added*, foods labeled *unsalted* may contain sodium. Read the nutrition label to find out how much.

Chapter 6

Wetting Your Whistle

In This Chapter

- ◆ Recognizing sodium in beverages counts
- ◆ Making healthful beverage choices
- ◆ Celebrating with party punches
- ◆ Indulging in weather-appropriate drinks

Reducing the sodium in your diet affects not just your food choices but your beverage consumption as well. Liquid-served sodium counts just as much as food-served sodium or liquid calories—and can be just as overlooked.

Soda pop, some fruit drinks, even your tap water can add to the sodium intake you're trying to limit. Still, you're unlikely to drink only sodium-free bottled water day-in and day-out. But don't worry, you can easily prepare flavorful beverages that won't wreck your daily sodium limits. For all the occasions when you want something special to drink, the recipes in this chapter offer a number of tasty options. Cheers!

Punch Bowl Pleasers

We often celebrate special occasions with festive punches and other mingled drinks. But the base ingredients can be sodium-rich soda pops, drink mixes, and ice creams.

Whether a wedding, anniversary, baby shower, graduation, bridal shower, or other happy occasion, you, too, can toast its significance while still meeting your low-sodium requirements. You'll want to monitor your number of servings, though. It's easy to keep refilling your cup from the punch bowl that seems never to drain.

Punches made with large measures of teas, coffees, low-sodium fruit juices, club soda, and sherbets are often good picks. Alternating a punch with other beverages such as black coffee, tea, and bottled water will keep you from feeling deprived while keeping your sodium count in check.

Front-Porch Sippers and Cozy Slurps

Whether you have a front porch or not, the dog days of summer will have you begging for a cold, frosty beverage. The hot-weather classics—old-fashioned lemonade and homemade iced tea—are not only satisfying on a sweltering day, but they're also very low in sodium. Of course, commercial mixes and prepared teas and lemonades may contain sodium; check the nutrition labels.

Pinch of Sage

If you can't live without soda pop, you can find a small selection of sodium-free and very low-sodium alternatives. Check out Appendix B for more information.

When you're craving something thicker, try whipping up a smoothie instead of a milkshake. The recipes in this chapter are lower in sodium and taste great. Or fill a frosty, tall mug with a float, using sodium-free seltzer water instead of the traditional soda pop. You'll have it made in the shade!

When the air turns crisp and you just want to curl up inside with a good book, a soothing, hot beverage is in order. A mug of hot cocoa made with a cup of fat-free milk produces a drink with up to 145 milligrams of sodium, though—and that's not allowing for any marshmallows. The version in this chapter uses nondairy creamer, which is a useful sodium-free alternative.

Tea and coffee are good sodium-free choices. Just be sure you aren't adding too much sodium with your additions. And remember that many flavored tea and coffee mixes do include some sodium; check the labels.

Splash of Sunshine Punch

2 qt. apricot nectar

2 qt. pineapple juice

1 qt. unsweetened orange juice

6 cups ginger ale, well chilled

Makes 6½ quarts
Prep time: 5 minutes
Chill time: 1 hour
Serving size: 1 cup
Each serving has:
119 calories
15.2 mg sodium
0.3 g protein
0.1 g total fat
0 g saturated fat
0 mg cholesterol
30 g carbohydrate
0.5 g dietary fiber
5.4 mg calcium
257.1 mg potassium

1. In a 2-gallon container, stir together apricot nectar, pineapple juice, and orange juice. Chill for at least 1 hour before serving.

2. Just before serving, pour in ginger ale.

Salternative: You may increase or decrease this recipe as needed.

Pinch of Sage _____

If other large containers are unavailable for mixing, use a clean 1-gallon milk jug.

Warm Orange Blossom Tea Punch

Makes 2 quarts
Prep time: 5 minutes
Cook time: 2 hours, 5 minutes
Serving size: 1 cup
Each serving has:
102 calories
8.9 mg sodium
0.2 g protein
0 g total fat
0 g saturated fat
0 mg cholesterol
25.3 g carbohydrate
0.4 g dietary fiber
9.1 mg calcium
181.9 mg potassium

6 cups boiling water

6 individual green tea bags

1½ cups pineapple juice

1½ cups unsweetened orange juice

⅓ cup granulated sugar

2 TB. honey

1 navel orange, halved and sliced

1. Pour boiling water over green tea bags in a large slow cooker. Let steep for 5 minutes. Discard tea bags.

2. Stir in pineapple juice, orange juice, sugar, and honey. Add orange slices, cover, and cook on low heat for 2 to 3 hours or until heated through and flavors have mingled. Serve warm.

Salternative: You may also chill and serve punch over ice, if you prefer.

Pinch of Sage _____

Ladle this pretty punch right from the slow cooker, if you like. After it's heated, the punch will stay hot for some time, so turn off the slow cooker.

Mocha Latté Punch

¼ **cup granulated sugar**   **6 TB. lite chocolate syrup**

2 cups strong coffee   **4 cups fat-free milk**

1. In a large container, stir sugar into coffee until completely dissolved. Stir in lite chocolate syrup, and add milk, stirring until well blended. Chill for at least 2 hours before serving.

2. Stir again before serving. Pour into a punch bowl, and serve over ice.

Salternative: You may increase or decrease this recipe as needed.

Salt Pitfall _____
Be aware of serving size. This rich punch has a ½ cup serving. If you drink more, be sure to count the additional sodium content.

Makes 1½ quarts
Prep time: 5 minutes
Chill time: 2 hours
Serving size: ½ cup
Each serving has:
58 calories
52.1 mg sodium
2.9 g protein
0.2 g total fat
0.1 g saturated fat
1.6 mg cholesterol
11.3 g carbohydrate
0.1 g dietary fiber
102 mg calcium
165.7 mg potassium

Old-World Christmas Wassail

Makes 3 quarts
Prep time: 5 minutes
Cook time: 10 minutes
Serving size: 1 cup
Each serving has:
184.6 calories
22.2 mg sodium
0.1 g protein
0 g total fat
0 g saturated fat
0 mg cholesterol
46.4 g carbohydrate
0.1 g dietary fiber
2 mg calcium
130.8 mg potassium

2 qt. apple cider

2 cups pineapple juice

1½ cups unsweetened orange juice

¾ cup fresh lemon juice

1 cup granulated sugar

2 cinnamon sticks

¾ tsp. ground cloves

1. In a large pan, combine apple cider, pineapple juice, orange juice, lemon juice, sugar, cinnamon sticks, and cloves. Stir. Bring to a boil and then remove from heat.

2. Discard cinnamon sticks, and stir again before serving.

 Pinch of Sage _____

If you need to keep this beverage hot during a holiday party, transfer it to a slow cooker on low heat.

Coffee-Laced Eggnog Punch

½ cup strong coffee

⅓ cup granulated sugar

1 cup hot water

4 cups cold water

1 cup light whipping cream

2 tsp. pure vanilla extract

4 large pasteurized eggs, beaten

1 qt. reduced-fat creamy vanilla ice cream, softened

2 TB. imitation rum extract or to taste

1 tsp. ground nutmeg

Makes 2½ quarts
Prep time: 10 minutes
Chill time: 1 hour
Serving size: ¾ cup
Each serving has:
179.8 calories
56.9 mg sodium
4.4 g protein
8.9 g total fat
4.9 g saturated fat
92.4 mg cholesterol
18.7 g carbohydrate
0.7 g dietary fiber
86.9 mg calcium
47.9 mg potassium

1. In a large pitcher, combine coffee, sugar, and hot water. Stir until sugar dissolves and then stir in cold water. Stir in light whipping cream and vanilla extract. Stir in pasteurized eggs. Add ice cream, rum extract, and nutmeg, and stir together until ice cream blends into beverage. Chill for at least 1 hour before serving.

2. Stir again before serving. Serve from a chilled punch bowl, and garnish individual servings with an additional sprinkle of nutmeg, if desired.

 Pinch of Sage _____

You must use pasteurized eggs in this recipe because the eggs are not cooked. Regular eggs—even if they have clean, uncracked shells—will put you and your guests at risk for illness caused by salmonella bacteria that can cause an intestinal infection.

Old-Time Lemonade

Makes 5 cups
Prep time: 10 minutes
Serving size: 1 cup
Each serving has:
128 calories
6.2 mg sodium
0 g protein
0 g total fat
0 g saturated fat
0 mg cholesterol
34 g carbohydrate
0.8 g dietary fiber
18.2 mg calcium
0.6 mg potassium

4 lemons

¾ cup granulated sugar or superfine sugar

4 cups water

1. Juice lemons, removing seeds. (You should have about 1 cup lemon juice.) Pour into a pitcher.

2. Stir in sugar. Add water, stirring until sugar is completely dissolved. Chill. Serve in tall glasses over ice.

Tropical Breeze Smoothie

Makes 4 cups
Prep time: 5 minutes
Serving size: 1 cup
Each serving has:
78 calories
39.8 mg sodium
2.8 g protein
0.1 g total fat
0.1 g saturated fat
1.3 mg cholesterol
18 g carbohydrate
1 g dietary fiber
79.4 mg calcium
124 mg potassium

1 cup fat-free plain yogurt   **1 ripe banana**

¾ cup light lemonade   **12 ice cubes**

½ cup crushed pineapple in its own juice

1. Combine yogurt, lemonade, pineapple, banana, and ice cubes in a blender.

2. Blend on high speed for 15 to 20 seconds or until smooth. Serve immediately.

Salt Pitfall

Read nutrition labels carefully. Many yogurts go up in sodium as they go down in fat. We found that our store brand actually fell in sodium as it went from regular to low fat to fat free. Don't dismiss store brands and generics when choosing ingredients.

Spiced Peach Smoothie

¾ cup frozen peach slices

3 ice cubes

½ cup fat-free plain yogurt

¼ cup fat-free milk

⅛ tsp. ground cinnamon

Dash ground nutmeg

Dash ground allspice

1 tsp. honey

Makes 1 serving
Prep time: 5 minutes
Serving size: 1½ cups
Each serving has:
271 calories
112.9 mg sodium
8.4 g protein
0.4 g total fat
0.1 g saturated fat
3.7 mg cholesterol
63.5 g carbohydrate
3.6 g dietary fiber
237.3 mg calcium
350.8 mg potassium

1. In a blender, combine peach slices, ice cubes, yogurt, milk, cinnamon, nutmeg, allspice, and honey.

2. Blend on high speed for 45 to 60 seconds or until smooth and well blended, scraping down sides as necessary. Serve immediately.

Pinch of Sage _____

Cinnamon is actually the inner bark of a variety of ever-green trees. After the bark is stripped, it's dried in the sun, curling into its recognizable stick form.

Banana Bread Smoothie

Makes 1 serving
Prep time: 5 minutes
Freeze time: 2 hours
Serving size: 1½ cups
Each serving has:
181 calories
102.5 mg sodium
8.3 g protein
0.7 g total fat
0.3 g saturated fat
3.7 mg cholesterol
40.3 g carbohydrate
2.8 g dietary fiber
233.7 mg calcium
569 mg potassium

1 ripe banana

3 ice cubes

½ cup fat-free plain yogurt

¼ cup fat-free milk

¼ tsp. pure almond extract

1. Peel and cut banana into 1-inch chunks. Freeze for 2 hours or until firm.

2. In a blender, combine frozen banana chunks, ice cubes, yogurt, milk, and almond extract. Blend on high speed for 15 to 20 seconds or until smooth and well blended. Serve immediately.

Salt Pitfall _____

Milk manufacturers boost its taste by adding sodium as they remove fat. The amount of sodium added is minimal, though. Ask your doctor or nutritionist which type of milk is best for you.

Frosty Chocolate Raspberry Float

Makes 1 serving
Prep time: 5 minutes
Serving size: 2 cups
Each serving has:
80 calories
40 mg sodium
3 g protein
0 g total fat
0 g saturated fat
0.4 mg cholesterol
18 g carbohydrate
0 g dietary fiber
100 mg calcium
120 mg potassium

½ cup fat-free vanilla chocolate swirl frozen yogurt

1 cup raspberry-flavored seltzer

1. Scoop frozen yogurt into a tall glass.

2. Pour in seltzer. Serve with a straw and a long-handled spoon.

Salternative: To keep your taste buds happy, try varying the flavors of both the seltzer and the frozen yogurt.

 Pinch of Sage _____

Flavored seltzer waters are a good alternative to soda. You get the fizz of the carbonation without the sodium.

A Cup of Hot Cocoa

1 TB. cocoa powder

2 TB. granulated sugar

1 cup boiling water

2 TB. nondairy creamer

¼ tsp. pure vanilla extract

Makes 1 serving
Prep time: 5 minutes
Serving size: 1 cup
Each serving has:
160 calories
3.3 mg sodium
1.3 g protein
2.5 g total fat
0.3 g saturated fat
0 mg cholesterol
31.8 g carbohydrate
1.4 g dietary fiber
11.7 mg calcium
150.5 mg potassium

1. Measure cocoa powder and sugar into a mug.

2. Pour boiling water over top, and stir to dissolve. Stir in nondairy creamer and vanilla extract. Serve immediately.

Salt Pitfall _____

If you love to float marshmallows in your cocoa, remember to factor in the additional sodium. You can find the milligrams per serving listed on the nutrition label.

Hot Mulled Cider

1 qt. apple cider

2 TB. firmly packed light brown sugar

Pinch nutmeg

4 lemon slices, seeded

8 whole cloves

4 cinnamon sticks

Makes 4 servings
Prep time: 5 minutes
Cook time: 10 minutes
Serving size: 1 cup
Each serving has:
147.5 calories
27.8 mg sodium
0 g protein
0 g total fat
0 g saturated fat
0 mg cholesterol
37.2 g carbohydrate
0 g dietary fiber
6.3 mg calcium
31.2 mg potassium

1. In a medium saucepan, stir together apple cider, light brown sugar, and nutmeg. Stud each lemon slice with 2 cloves and then add cloved lemon slices to saucepan.

2. Bring mixture to a boil. Reduce heat, cover, and simmer for 5 minutes. Discard lemon slices.

3. Pour cider into mugs. Garnish each serving with a cinnamon stick.

Salternative: You may double this recipe, if needed. Use a saucepan large enough to hold the mixture comfortably.

Autumn Spiced Coffee

Makes 1 serving
Prep time: 5 minutes
Serving size: 1 cup
Each serving has:
76.2 calories
5.7 mg sodium
0.3 g protein
1.1 g total fat
0 g saturated fat
0 mg cholesterol
16.3 g carbohydrate
0.6 g dietary fiber
17.2 mg calcium
160.4 mg potassium

¼ tsp. plus ⅛ tsp. ground cinnamon

Scant ⅛ tsp. ground cloves

1 cup hot black coffee

1 TB. granulated sugar

1 TB. nondairy creamer

1. Stir cinnamon and cloves into coffee.

2. Stir in sugar until dissolved. Stir in creamer until blended.

Salternative: Nondairy creamer is a good, sodium-free substitute for real dairy cream. But if you prefer to use cream, just calculate in the bit of sodium it adds, using the information on the nutrition label. You can also adjust the amounts of spices, sugar, and creamer given in this recipe to perfect your personal, pleasurable cup of coffee.

Lo-So Lingo _____

When a measurement is labeled **scant,** don't overfill the measure. Leave it just a tad short.

Part 3

Breakfast, Brunch, Lunch, and Lighter Fare

Breakfast: it's the most important meal of the day. It can start your day off right with high energy and good nutrients. Taking the time to eat breakfast or brunch can boost your metabolism and help maintain your good health, all without tallying up too much sodium.

At midday or whenever you want a lighter meal, a salad, soup, or sandwich—or any grouping—can fill the bill. The combination of proteins, carbs, and vegetables or fruits keeps your diet well-balanced and your stomach satisfied.

Fast-Fix Breakfasts

In This Chapter

- Starting your day off right
- Planning for the most important meal of the day
- Being sodium wise in a time crunch
- Preparing quick, low-sodium breakfasts

From the moment your morning wake-up alarm sounds to the time you arrive at work or school, you're playing the beat-the-clock game. You may think you've tricked the clock, shaving off time by skipping breakfast. But the trick's on you.

Without a nutritious start to your day, your energy level languishes, your attention span shrivels, your blood sugar level crashes, and your metabolism rebels. The best trick you can learn is how to squeeze good nutrition into your morning rush.

The recipes in this chapter offer you some possibilities for doing just that. You may need a fast-fix, quick-eat breakfast. Or maybe you're really pressed for time and need a speedy breakfast that can travel with you. Either way, get ready to be a breakfast believer!

Getting a Breakfast Plan

You plan for the future; you plan for a rainy day; you even plan what to have for dinner. But when it comes to the meal that jump-starts your day, do you have a strategy? You don't need a spreadsheet or a computer-generated, color-coded bar chart. All you may need is a scrap of paper and a pen to write out a grocery list. If you have the necessary ingredients on hand, you can whip up a sodium-sensible breakfast faster than you can say "hitting the drive-thru."

If your idea of fitting breakfast into the whirlwind you call morning is grabbing a prepared pastry or greasy breakfast sandwich through your car window, you're going to have to rethink your routine. And don't weep over the astronomical sodium content of those tastiest of morning temptations because they are all-around lacking in nutrition.

Pinch of Sage

If you don't care for the mainstream, ready-to-eat cereals that fit your sodium-restricted diet, check your supermarket's cereal aisle for a few low-sodium and very low-sodium alternatives (these cereals tend to have healthy-sounding brands and names). Also, check out Appendix B for more information.

You and your body deserve better. Plus, in the time you spend repeating your order into a crackling speaker, you can prepare a hot (or cold if you like), homemade, sodium-mindful meal. And if you just don't feel like cooking first thing in the morning, you do have a few ready-made options. Choose shredded wheat, puffed wheat, or puffed rice cereal over other regular ready-to-eat cereals. Avoid instant hot cereals that soar in sodium. Instead choose quick oats, creamy hot wheat cereals, or farina (ground wheat berries). With these you have all the time and options you need for a fast, healthful breakfast.

Crunch Berry Parfait

1 TB. unsalted sliced almonds

1 TB. flaked coconut

½ cup fat-free plain yogurt

¾ tsp. confectioners' sugar

2 drops pure almond extract

½ cup granola

⅔ cup fresh raspberries (or your choice of other berries or fruit)

Makes 1 serving
Prep time: 10 minutes
Serving size: 1 parfait
Each serving has:
247 calories
86.2 mg sodium
9.7 g protein
6.1 g total fat
1.7 g saturated fat
2.5 mg cholesterol
44 g carbohydrate
8.6 g dietary fiber
187.1 mg calcium
80.6 mg potassium

1. In a dry skillet over medium heat, toast almonds and coconut for 2 to 5 minutes. Shake the skillet often and watch carefully, as they toast suddenly and can be quick to burn.

2. In a small bowl, stir together yogurt, confectioners' sugar, and almond extract.

3. In a tall parfait glass or other dessert dish, layer yogurt mixture, granola, and raspberries 2 or 3 times, as glass allows. Sprinkle toasted almonds and coconut on top.

Salt Pitfall

Granola, like many prepared foods, varies in sodium content from brand to brand. Read nutrition labels carefully.

Maple Syrup and Brown Sugar Oatmeal

Makes 1 serving
Prep time: 3 minutes
Cook time: 1 minute
Serving size: 1 bowl
Each serving has:
413 calories
18.5 mg sodium
13.7 g protein
5.5 g total fat
1 g saturated fat
0.3 mg cholesterol
79.3 g carbohydrate
8.3 g dietary fiber
87.8 mg calcium
448.4 mg potassium

½ cup quick oats

¾ cup water

1 TB. firmly packed light brown sugar

1 TB. pure maple syrup

1 TB. fat-free milk

1. Pour oats into a microwave-safe bowl. Add water, and microwave on high for 1 to 1½ minutes or until oats are softened and liquid is absorbed. Stir.

2. Stir in light brown sugar and maple syrup. Then stir in milk until well mixed.

Salternative: This recipe makes a thick oatmeal. If you prefer a thinner oatmeal, add ¼ to ½ cup more water, increasing the cooking time as necessary.

Salt Pitfall

Commercial instant oatmeals boast convenience, but they're loaded with sodium. Quick oats are a smart alternative—all but as fast as instant with just a fraction of the sodium. Plus, you can create your own favorite flavors.

Peach Melba Oatmeal

½ cup quick oats

1 cup water

⅓ cup chopped frozen peach slices

¼ cup frozen raspberries

1 TB. granulated sugar

1 tsp. fat-free milk

Makes 2 servings
Prep time: 4 minutes
Cook time: 1½ minutes
Serving size: ¼ cup
Each serving has:
201 calories
3.6 mg sodium
7.2 g protein
2.7 g total fat
0.5 g saturated fat
0.1 mg cholesterol
37.5 g carbohydrate
5.1 g dietary fiber
27.5 mg calcium
171.7 mg potassium

1. Pour oats into a medium microwave-safe bowl, and add water. Add peaches and raspberries, and microwave on high for 1½ to 2 minutes or until oats are softened and liquid is absorbed. Stir to combine.

2. Stir in sugar and milk, and mix well.

Salternative: If you prefer to use fresh fruit, you may follow this recipe or, for a crisper texture, stir the fresh peaches and raspberries into the oatmeal after it's cooked.

Honey Nut Multi-Grain Cereal

Makes 1 serving
Prep time: 3 minutes
Cook time: 1½ minutes
Serving size: 1 bowl
Each serving has:
305 calories
11.4 mg sodium
6.6 g protein
11.8 g total fat
1.2 g saturated fat
0.3 mg cholesterol
49.2 g carbohydrate
6.2 g dietary fiber
45.8 mg calcium
261.5 mg potassium

¾ cup water

½ cup sodium-free multi-grain hot cereal (rye, barley, oats, and wheat)

1 TB. honey

1 TB. fat-free milk

2 TB. chopped unsalted pecans

1. In a microwave-safe bowl, pour water over cereal. Microwave on high for 1½ to 2 minutes or until done.

2. Stir in honey, milk, and pecans until blended.

Salternatives: Save a little sodium by replacing the milk with nondairy creamer, if you like. You can substitute your favorite unsalted nuts for the pecans; try walnuts, peanuts, or even hazelnuts.

Pinch of Sage

If you're unsure whether a container is suitable for microwave use, test it first. Place 1 cup tap water and the container in your microwave oven, and microwave on high for 1 minute. The water should get warm and the container should be cool or lukewarm. If it's hot, it's not microwave-safe.

Sugar and Spice Rice

1 cup cooked long-grain
brown rice (about ⅓ cup
uncooked)

½ cup fat-free milk

1 TB. firmly packed light
brown sugar

¼ tsp. ground cinnamon

½ cup blackberries, raspberries, blueberries, or sliced
strawberries

Makes 1 serving
Prep time: 3 minutes
Cook time: 5 minutes
Serving size: 1 bowl
Each serving has:
350 calories
79 mg sodium
9.8 g protein
2.3 g total fat
0.5 g saturated fat
2.5 mg cholesterol
73.7 g carbohydrate
7.6 g dietary fiber
212 mg calcium
478.8 mg potassium

1. Stir together rice, milk, light brown sugar, and cinnamon in a
   small saucepan. Bring to a boil. Immediately reduce heat to
   medium and cook, stirring occasionally, for 3 to 4 minutes or
   until thick and creamy.

2. Spoon into a serving bowl and let cool slightly. Add blackberries, stirring in as desired.

Pinch of Sage

If you have rice left over from last night's dinner, this
breakfast is a delicious use for it. If you don't have leftover rice,
substitute instant brown rice that cooks in 10 minutes. Remember that instant rices do contain a little sodium, from about 5 to
20 milligrams. Check the nutrition label.

Wild Rice and Berries

Makes 1 serving
Prep time: 3 minutes
Serving size: 1 bowl
Each serving has:
136 calories
36.6 mg sodium
5.6 g protein
0.5 g total fat
0.1 g saturated fat
1.2 mg cholesterol
28.5 g carbohydrate
2.5 g dietary fiber
81.9 mg calcium
219.2 mg potassium

½ cup cooked wild rice, chilled

¼ cup fresh blueberries

½ tsp. honey

Pinch ground cinnamon

¼ cup fat-free milk

1. In a cereal bowl, combine wild rice, blueberries, honey, cinnamon, and milk.

2. Stir to mix well.

Salternative: You may serve this as a warm cereal, if you prefer. Warm the mixture in a small saucepan over low heat or in the microwave on reheat for 1 to 2 minutes or until heated through.

 Pinch of Sage

With leftover wild rice, breakfast is as easy as stirring. Be sure to cook extra wild rice whenever you prepare it and then store it in the refrigerator for a quick breakfast the next morning.

Breakfast Stir-Fry Scramble Pita

Makes 1 serving
Prep time: 3 minutes
Cook time: 3 minutes
Serving size: 1 pita pocket
Each serving has:
303.4 calories
372.5 mg sodium
17.8 g protein
13.7 g total fat
3.6 g saturated fat
425 mg cholesterol
28.5 g carbohydrate
4.2 g dietary fiber
64.7 mg calcium
288 mg potassium

2 large eggs

2 TB. cold water

¼ cup leftover Asian-Flavored Carrot Crunch Salsa (recipe in Chapter 25)

1 no-salt-added whole-wheat pita pocket

1. Spray a small skillet with nonstick cooking spray. Heat over medium heat.

2. In a small bowl, whisk eggs with cold water. Stir in Asian-Flavored Carrot Crunch Salsa, and cook for 3 minutes or until eggs are set. Spoon into pita pocket.

Salternative: The pita pocket allows you to eat this breakfast on the go. Of course, eat the eggs from a breakfast plate, if you prefer.

Peanut Butter and Pineapple Burrito

2 TB. no-salt-added natural
peanut butter

2 TB. crushed pineapple

1 Fresh Tortilla (recipe in
Chapter 16) or other low-
sodium tortilla

Makes 1 serving
Prep time: 3 minutes
Serving size: 1 burrito
Each serving has:
483.7 calories
2.9 mg sodium
12.5 g protein
28.8 g total fat
5 g saturated fat
0 mg cholesterol
43 g carbohydrate
5.7 g dietary fiber
4.5 mg calcium
8.6 mg potassium

1. In a small bowl, stir together peanut butter and pineapple.

2. Spread mixture down center of Fresh Tortilla. Fold up tortilla burrito-style.

 Pinch of Sage _____

Oil separation is normal in natural peanut butter, so don't pour it off! Stir the oil back into the peanut butter. You also need to refrigerate natural peanut butter after opening it to prevent rancidity because it doesn't contain preservatives. Tightly closed, you can store it for up to 3 months.

Peanut Butter Stacked Apple

1 large eating apple

2 TB. no-salt-added natural
peanut butter

Makes 1 serving
Prep time: 3 minutes
Serving size: 1 apple
Each serving has:
325.1 calories
0 mg sodium
7.4 g protein
16.8 g total fat
2.1 g saturated fat
0 mg cholesterol
39.3 g carbohydrate
7.7 g dietary fiber
14.8 mg calcium
243.8 mg potassium

1. Core apple, and slice horizontally into 4 or 5 sections.

2. Spread peanut butter between apple sections, and reassemble apple.

Pinch of Sage _____

Good eating apples to try are Gala, McIntosh, Red Delicious, and Empire.

Very Berry Tofu Breakfast Smoothie

Makes 1 serving
Prep time: 5 minutes
Serving size: 2 cups
Each serving has:
341.6 calories
16.9 mg sodium
9.4 g protein
5.1 g total fat
0.6 g saturated fat
0 mg cholesterol
69.2 g carbohydrate
4.2 g dietary fiber
78.9 mg calcium
521.8 mg potassium

6 oz. soft tofu, drained and chopped

6 ice cubes

3 TB. honey

¼ tsp. vanilla extract

¼ cup blueberries

¼ cup blackberries

4 medium strawberries, hulled

1. In a blender, combine tofu, ice cubes, honey, vanilla extract, blueberries, blackberries, and strawberries.

2. Blend on high speed for 1 minute or until smooth, stopping to scrape down sides as necessary.

 Pinch of Sage _____

This healthful drink starts your morning off right with lots of protein, calcium, and antioxidants—all enjoyed from your commuter cup.

Chapter 8

Weekend Morning Indulgences

In This Chapter

- ◆ Enjoying unhurried weekend morning breakfast
- ◆ Cutting the sodium in breakfast foods
- ◆ Making brunch an event
- ◆ Serving breakfast—at dinner!

Leisurely weekend mornings provide time for relaxing, connecting with family, and indulging in flavorful breakfast foods. Although the goal of the weekday breakfast may be to get you going, weekend morning meals allow you to savor the flavor and the company.

With the recipes in this chapter, you'll find alternatives to some of the sodium explosion of leisurely breakfasts. Good ingredient choices can help, such as preparing your own sausage with ground turkey and spices. Sodium-conscious substitutions also play a role. Low-sodium cheeses, low-sodium breads, and sodium-free baking alternatives can bring you back to breakfast.

With a few good choices, you can prepare tempting breakfasts that are lower in sodium than traditional breakfast fare. Plus, you can easily accompany any of the dishes here with a selection of fresh fruits for a healthful, heart-warming gathering. So put the kettle on, set the breakfast table, and indulge!

> **Pinch of Sage** _____
>
> Sodium-free alternatives are available for baking powder and baking soda. You can use them to prepare your favorite pancakes, waffles, breakfast breads and muffins, and more. If you can't find Featherweight sodium-free baking powder, Ener-G sodium-free baking powder, or Ener-G sodium-free baking soda near you, turn to Appendix B for more information about where to order them. Or enter the brand names into your favorite search engine and see what you can find.

Breakfast: Good *Any* Time

Leisurely breakfasts and the foods served are memorable because they only happen occasionally. When you have the time, use it to treat yourself and your loved ones to the eye-opening aromas and irresistible flavors of breakfast.

If your family prefers to lounge in bed on a Saturday morning, start cooking just before they normally awaken. The tantalizing smells wafting from the kitchen are sure to arouse them. If it's later than breakfast, call it brunch and enjoy it just the same.

You may also fill a lazy morning with extended family and friends. Serve a collection of dishes buffet style to make it easier on you if cooking for many people seems a daunting task. Most everyone loves brunch, and catching up with each other over enjoyable food is a great way to start the weekend.

Perhaps you just can't find the time for a long, luxurious weekend morning breakfast. Don't fret. You can serve these mouth-watering recipes just as easily for dinner any day of the week. Breakfast foods are simply wonderful, day or night.

Good Start Sausage Patties

¼ tsp. plus ⅛ tsp. rubbed sage

¼ tsp. dried basil

¼ tsp. dried oregano

¼ tsp. freshly ground black pepper

¼ tsp. garlic powder

⅛ tsp. dried dill weed

⅛ tsp. ground allspice

⅛ tsp. ground nutmeg

Pinch Firehouse Chili Powder (recipe in Chapter 26) or other salt-free chili powder

2 TB. water

1 large egg white

¾ lb. ground turkey

Makes 4 servings
Prep time: 10 minutes
Cook time: 13 minutes
Serving size: 1 patty
Each serving has:
119.1 calories
74.1 mg sodium
17.5 g protein
5.3 g total fat
1.5 g saturated fat
48.8 mg cholesterol
0.6 g carbohydrate
0.2 g dietary fiber
7 mg calcium
22.8 mg potassium

1. Preheat the broiler, and spray the rack of a broiler pan with nonstick cooking spray.

2. In a medium bowl, combine sage, basil, oregano, black pepper, garlic powder, dill weed, allspice, nutmeg, Firehouse Chili Powder, water, egg white, and ground turkey. Mix well, and shape into 4 (3-inch) patties. Arrange on the broiler rack.

3. Broil 3 to 4 inches from heat for 10 minutes. Turn patties over, rotate, and then broil on other side for 3 to 4 minutes or until done.

 Pinch of Sage

The first time you try these breakfast patties, follow the recipe. Then, experiment with the seasonings until they taste just perfect to you.

Veggie Confetti Frittata

Makes 1 serving
Prep time: 5 minutes
Cook time: 10 minutes
Serving size: 1 frittata
Each serving has:
168.2 calories
131.3 mg sodium
13.3 g protein
10.2 g total fat
3.1 g saturated fat
425 mg cholesterol
5.7 g carbohydrate
1.3 g dietary fiber
64.3 mg calcium
275.7 mg potassium

1 green onion, trimmed and thinly sliced

2 TB. finely diced red bell pepper

2 TB. finely diced green bell pepper

1 TB. cold water

2 large eggs

2 TB. finely diced tomatoes

1. Preheat the broiler. Generously spray an 8-inch ovenproof skillet with nonstick cooking spray. (If you don't have an ovenproof skillet, cover your skillet's plastic handle completely with foil. Remember when handling the skillet that the handle will be hot from the broiler.)

2. Sauté green onion, red bell pepper, and green bell pepper over medium-low heat for 3 minutes or until softened.

3. Meanwhile, lightly beat cold water into eggs.

4. Stir tomatoes into the skillet. Arrange vegetable mixture in a single layer over bottom of the skillet. Pour egg mixture into the skillet. Cook, without stirring, for 4 to 6 minutes or until eggs are *soft-set* on top.

5. Place the skillet under the broiler about 4 inches from heat. Broil for 1 minute or until top is golden brown.

Salternative: You may mix and match the sautéed ingredients in this frittata to suit individual tastes. Try mushrooms or sweet onions, or even add fresh herbs with the tomatoes. Prepare each diner's frittata to order.

> **Lo-So Lingo**
>
> **Soft-set** refers to a stage when the eggs have started to firm, with some movement still, but they aren't set yet in this case on the top.

Crisp Home Fries

1 TB. extra-virgin olive oil

2 medium all-purpose potatoes, scrubbed and diced

½ tsp. onion powder

½ tsp. garlic powder

¼ tsp. chipotle chili powder
or cayenne

¼ tsp. freshly ground black
pepper

1 TB. minced yellow onions

Makes 2 servings
Prep time: 5 minutes
Cook time: 25 minutes
Serving size: ½ cup
Each serving has:
167.4 calories
4 mg sodium
4.3 g protein
6.8 g total fat
0.9 g saturated fat
0 mg cholesterol
27.7 g carbohydrate
3.4 g dietary fiber
25.5 mg calcium
750 mg potassium

1. In an 8- to 10-inch nonstick skillet, heat extra-virgin olive oil over medium to medium-low heat. Add potatoes, stirring to coat evenly. Cook for 5 minutes, stirring frequently.

2. Add onion powder, garlic powder, chipotle chili powder, and black pepper. Stir. Cook for 15 minutes, stirring frequently.

3. Stir in onions, reduce heat to low, and cook, stirring often, for 3 minutes or until onions are translucent and tender.

 Pinch of Sage

You can increase this recipe to serve the number of people you have for breakfast. Just be sure to use a skillet large enough to keep the potatoes in a single layer. If your preference is for softer home fries or if you won't be available to stir the potatoes frequently, cook them slower and longer.

Lemon Raspberry Crepes

Makes 7 servings
Prep time: 25 minutes
Cook time: 15 minutes
Serving size: 2 crepes
Each serving has:
143.2 calories
40 mg sodium
5.1 g protein
5 g total fat
2.5 g saturated fat
70.5 mg cholesterol
19.9 g carbohydrate
1.7 g dietary fiber
59.3 mg calcium
47.4 mg potassium

2 large eggs

½ cup fat-free milk

½ cup water

1 cup all-purpose flour

2 TB. unsalted butter, melted

1 (6-oz.) container fat-free lemon yogurt

½ dry pint fresh raspberries

2 tsp. confectioners' sugar

1. In a medium bowl, blend together eggs, milk, and water. Stir in flour and butter. Let batter stand for 20 minutes.

2. Heat an electric skillet to 350°F, and spray skillet generously with nonstick cooking spray. Pour 2 tablespoons batter onto the skillet for each crepe, and cook for 30 seconds or until edges are dry and underside is golden. Turn and cook for 15 seconds or until golden. Remove to a sheet of waxed paper, and repeat with remaining batter.

3. Spread yogurt down centers of crepes. Scatter raspberries over yogurt. Fold over sides of crepe, and lightly sprinkle tops with powdered sugar.

 Pinch of Sage

These basic crepes do not have sugar in the batter, so you may fill them with your choice of savory fillings as well.

Homemaker's Holiday Cranberry Coffeecake

2 cups whole-wheat flour

1 cup chopped fresh or frozen cranberries

1¼ cups chopped unsalted walnuts

1 cup unsalted butter, softened

2 cups granulated sugar

1 cup egg substitute

½ cup fat-free evaporated milk

1½ tsp. pure vanilla extract

Makes 12 servings
Prep time: 20 minutes
Cook time: 50 minutes
Serving size: 1 slice (¹⁄₁₂ coffeecake)
Each serving has:
458.4 calories
207.3 mg sodium
8.6 g protein
24.5 g total fat
10.5 g saturated fat
41.6 mg cholesterol
53.7 g carbohydrate
3.9 g dietary fiber
55.6 mg calcium
173.7 mg potassium

1. Preheat the oven to 350°F. Generously spray a fluted tube pan with nonstick cooking spray with flour or with regular nonstick cooking spray and then lightly dust with flour.

2. In a medium mixing bowl, stir together whole-wheat flour, cranberries, and walnuts.

3. In a large mixing bowl, beat butter and sugar at medium speed with an electric mixer until light and fluffy. Add egg substitute ¼ cup at a time, mixing well after each addition. Stir in evaporated milk and vanilla extract. Mix well.

4. Turn dry ingredients into wet ingredients, and blend just until moistened. Scrape batter into the prepared pan and smooth top with a rubber spatula. Bake for 50 to 60 minutes or until a cake tester inserted in the center comes out clean.

Pinch of Sage

If you're not watching calories, you can drizzle on a confectioners' sugar glaze (just mix a very small amount of liquid, such as water or fruit juice, with confectioners' sugar). This coffeecake is pleasantly sweet without it, though, and has a texture much like a quick bread.

Cinnamon Morning Apples

Makes 4 servings
Prep time: 5 minutes
Cook time: 16 minutes
Serving size: ½ cup
Each serving has:
156.3 calories
1 mg sodium
0.1 g protein
5.8 g total fat
3.6 g saturated fat
15.5 mg cholesterol
27.9 g carbohydrate
2.7 g dietary fiber
5.4 mg calcium
3.7 mg potassium

2 TB. unsalted butter

2 apples, cored, peeled, and cut into ½-inch slices

⅓ cup granulated sugar

½ tsp. ground cinnamon

Pinch ground nutmeg

1. In a medium, nonstick skillet over low heat, melt butter. Add apples, sugar, cinnamon, and nutmeg, and stir to coat.

2. Sauté mixture over medium-low to medium heat for 12 to 16 minutes or until apples are tender. Stir frequently to prevent sticking and scorching. Serve as a side dish or as a topping for pancakes, waffles, or French toast.

 Pinch of Sage _____

If you need to slice the apples ahead of time, retard browning by rubbing the apple slices with a slice of lemon. Try Braeburn, Golden Delicious, Granny Smith, or Jonagold apples for this recipe.

Sweet Curried Eggs

Makes 2 servings
Prep time: 5 minutes
Cook time: 15 minutes
Serving size: ¾ cup
Each serving has:
317.1 calories
130.8 mg sodium
13.4 g protein
21.2 g total fat
10.1 g saturated fat
455 mg cholesterol
18.2 g carbohydrate
3.8 g dietary fiber
63.7 mg calcium
304.7 mg potassium

2 TB. unsalted butter

½ cup diced sweet onions

1 apple, cored and diced

½ tsp. salt-free curry powder

4 large eggs

¼ cup *no-salt-added* tomato sauce

1. In a 10-inch nonstick skillet over medium heat, melt butter. Sauté sweet onions and apple for 8 to 10 minutes or until tender. Stir in curry powder.

2. In a medium bowl, whisk eggs. Add tomato sauce, and whisk until blended. Pour into the skillet, and cook, stirring frequently, for 5 minutes or until eggs are set.

Golden-Baked Pancake

⅓ cup unsalted butter

4 large eggs

1 cup fat-free milk

1 cup whole-wheat flour

3 TB. granulated sugar

½ tsp. ground cinnamon

Makes 6 servings
Prep time: 10 minutes
Cook time: 20 minutes
Serving size: 1 wedge
Each serving has:
259.1 calories
64.7 mg sodium
9 g protein
14 g total fat
7.5 g saturated fat
170.1 mg cholesterol
24.8 g carbohydrate
2.8 g dietary fiber
71.9 mg calcium
112.5 mg potassium

1. Preheat the oven to 425°F. Place butter in a 9-inch round cake pan, and melt it in the preheating oven.

2. In a blender, whip eggs and milk on high speed for 10 seconds or until blended. Add whole-wheat flour, and beat on high speed for 20 seconds or until thoroughly blended.

3. Remove bubbling butter from the oven. Pour batter into hot pan. Sprinkle sugar and cinnamon over top of batter.

4. Bake for 20 minutes or until raised and golden. Cut into wedges. Serve with the Cinnamon Morning Apples (recipe in this chapter), your favorite syrup, or dusted with powdered sugar.

Salt Pitfall _____

Use caution when removing butter from the oven. It's hot and bubbling, and it can spatter.

Hearty Buckwheat Pancakes

Makes 5 servings
Prep time: 10 minutes
Cook time: 15 minutes
Serving size: 2 pancakes
Each serving has:
252.4 calories
41.2 mg sodium
7.7 g protein
10.2 g total fat
1.6 g saturated fat
43.5 mg cholesterol
34.3 g carbohydrate
3.3 g dietary fiber
199.8 mg calcium
469.1 mg potassium

½ cup whole-wheat flour

¼ cup buckwheat flour

¼ cup all-purpose flour

¼ cup quick oats

3 tsp. *sodium-free* baking powder

3 TB. extra-light olive oil

2 TB. honey

1 cup fat-free milk

1 large egg, beaten

1. In a large bowl, combine whole-wheat flour, buckwheat flour, all-purpose flour, quick oats, and baking powder. Add extra-light olive oil, honey, milk, and egg. Whisk together just until blended.

2. Spray a large, nonstick skillet with nonstick cooking spray. Heat over medium heat. Pour ¼ cup batter into skillet for each pancake. Cook until bubbly on top, just firm at edges, and golden on bottom. Turn and cook until golden on underside. Repeat with remaining batter.

Lo-So Lingo

Sodium-free labeling is applied to foods that contain less than 5 milligrams sodium per serving. Sodium-free baking powder rises like regular baking powder without the high sodium content. (Read the label for any special instructions.)

Chapter 9

Fill-'Er-Up Salads

In This Chapter

◆ Eating healthfully from a single plate
◆ Choosing sodium-smart salad fixings
◆ Shoring up your veggie servings
◆ Packing a salad to go

Main-dish salads make fabulous lunches, light suppers, or even healthful snacks in smaller portions. A single dish can encompass your protein, carb, veggie, and/or fruit needs. You can even add cooked meat, poultry, or fish to vegetable-based salads if you desire.

If you keep the sodium levels of your individual ingredients in mind, you can build a fantastic, mouthwatering salad that fits into your low-sodium dietary requirements. Plus, you'll naturally be eating a serving—or two or three—of vegetables and/or fruits, helping you to more easily meet the recommended daily intake (2½ cups vegetables and 2 cups fruit per day for a 2,000-calorie diet).

Delicious, easy to prepare, and packed with nutrients—let's do salads for lunch!

Healthful Fixings

Full-meal salads offer a great opportunity for making a meal meet all your food cravings. You can mix and match your favorite vegetables, fruits, meats, toppings, and salad dressings. You do have to be smart about which ingredients you choose, though, because some traditional salad fixings are high in sodium.

At a typical salad bar, you'll find many sodium pitfalls. Bacon bits, croutons, salted nuts and seeds, frozen peas, canned beans, pickled peppers, olives, cheeses, and commercially prepared salad dressings all threaten to blow your lo-so intentions. However, you can prepare sodium-sensible salads simply by substituting appropriate ingredients. Be certain any nuts or seeds you sprinkle on top of your salad are unsalted. Substitute no-salt-added canned peas and beans, or cook dried beans for even less sodium. Purchase any pickled items only if they're no-salt-added—same with olives. Opt for low-sodium cheeses. And purchase—or prepare!—low-sodium salad dressings. With sodium-smart ingredients, you can build a perfect salad.

Smart Salad Strategies

Making a main-dish salad part of your regular menu planning provides a wealth of benefits. Preparation is easy, and cooking, if any, is oftentimes quick. Indulging in a delicious salad each day makes it almost effortless to eat a wide variety of colorful veggies and fruits, giving your body a healthy dose of vitamins, minerals, antioxidants, and fiber. Plus, you can prepare and pack your salad to take a nutritious salad with you for lunch or a midday snack.

Pinch of Sage

When tossing your salads together, try to include a rainbow of vegetables and fruits—reds, yellows, oranges, greens, blues, purples, and whites. The phytochemicals that provide the variety of colors also offer a wide range of healthful disease-deterring benefits—all without adding lots of calories or lots of sodium.

Packing a main-dish salad does require some savvy. You should always pour a salad dressing into a separate, covered container. Dressing the salad several hours before you plan on eating it will result in wilted, droopy greens. If the dressing is mixed into the salad, such as for a chicken salad, transport the salad greens in a container separate from the salad. You can quickly reheat meats in the microwave if you like. Or you can enjoy the thoroughly cooked meats cold, as long as you've kept everything below 40°F. If you have access to a refrigerator, that's your best option. If not, use a cooler to maintain the freshness and safety of your meal.

Lightly Curried Fruit and Chicken Salad

2 cups diced cooked chicken breast

1 tsp. fresh lemon juice

½ cup unsalted sliced almonds

1 papaya, seeded, peeled, and cubed

1 large banana, thinly sliced

½ cup fresh blueberries

½ cup fresh red raspberries

⅛ tsp. salt-free curry powder or more to taste

½ cup fat-free, sugar-free lemon yogurt

4 cups packed spring mix salad greens

Makes 4 servings
Prep time: 10 minutes
Cook time: 2 minutes
Serving size: 1 cup greens with 1¼ cups chicken salad
Each serving has:
339.6 calories
91.4 mg sodium
29.2 g protein
13.9 g total fat
1.7 g saturated fat
60.3 mg cholesterol
28 g carbohydrate
7 g dietary fiber
164.6 mg calcium
862.6 mg potassium

1. Turn chicken into a large bowl, and drizzle with lemon juice.

2. Toast almonds in a dry skillet over medium heat for 2 to 5 minutes, watching carefully and shaking occasionally to keep from burning; cool slightly. Stir almonds, papaya, banana, blueberries, and raspberries into chicken mixture.

3. In a small bowl, stir curry powder into yogurt until evenly distributed. Spoon into chicken mixture, and toss lightly until evenly coated.

4. To serve, place 1 cup salad greens on each of 4 plates. Mound 1¼ cups chicken mixture on top.

Salt Pitfall

Be certain your chicken was not seasoned with salt or other high-sodium seasonings or sauces when it was cooked. As long as the chicken has not been prepared with high-sodium seasonings, leftover chicken makes this recipe convenient and quick.

Wild Turkey Salad

Makes 4 servings
Prep time: 10 minutes
Serving size: ½ cup lettuce with 1 cup turkey salad
Each serving has:
247.7 calories
49.4 mg sodium
17 g protein
5.8 g total fat
0.7 g saturated fat
29.7 mg cholesterol
35.2 g carbohydrate
4.1 g dietary fiber
74.4 mg calcium
356.4 mg potassium

2 cups cooked wild rice

1 cup finely cubed cooked turkey breast

1 cup halved seedless red grapes

1 cup unpeeled diced apples

¼ cup finely diced red bell pepper

¼ cup chopped unsalted walnuts

½ cup fat-free plain yogurt

4 tsp. fresh lime juice

4 tsp. chopped fresh parsley

2 cups torn green-leaf lettuce

1. In a medium bowl, combine wild rice, turkey, grapes, apples, bell pepper, and walnuts.

2. In another small bowl, stir together yogurt, lime juice, and parsley. Stir into rice mixture until evenly coated.

3. To serve, line each of 4 plates with ½ cup lettuce. Mound salad on top.

Salt Pitfall

Wild rice—which is not really a rice at all, but an aquatic grass—can be found near the many boxes of convenience rice mixes on your grocer's shelf. Take care not to pick up one of these packages of wild rice with a high-sodium seasoning packet included. Purchase plain wild rice, which is usually sold in a smaller-size box.

Hearty Grilled Veggie Salad

2 TB. extra-virgin olive oil

1 medium eggplant, cut into 1-inch slices

1 small zucchini, cut into 1-inch slices

1 medium summer squash, cut into 1-inch slices

1 small yellow onion, cut into 1-inch slices (do not separate rings)

1 medium red bell pepper, seeds and ribs discarded, and cut into large wedges

1 lb. plum tomatoes, cored, seeded if desired, and quartered lengthwise

2 cloves garlic, minced

2 TB. chopped fresh basil

2 TB. balsamic vinegar

¼ tsp. freshly ground black pepper

Makes 6 servings
Prep time: 40 minutes
Cook time: 25 minutes
Serving size: 1 cup
Each serving has:
103.7 calories
13.1 mg sodium
2.6 g protein
5.1 g total fat
0.7 g saturated fat
0 mg cholesterol
14.5 g carbohydrate
4.7 g dietary fiber
28.9 mg calcium
545.1 mg potassium

1. Preheat a double-sided indoor grill. Lightly rub extra-virgin olive oil over cut sides of eggplant, zucchini, summer squash, and onion. Grill all for 3 to 5 minutes or until fork-tender. Grill bell pepper for 10 minutes or until tender. Grill tomatoes for 2 minutes or until just charred.

2. Remove vegetables to a large cutting board. Chop, peeling tomatoes as desired.

3. In a large bowl, combine vegetables, garlic, basil, balsamic vinegar, and black pepper. Stir to coat. Let stand for at least 30 minutes before serving. Stir again before serving. Serve warm or at room temperature. Serve vegetable mixture over mixed salad greens, if you like.

Salternative: The intense flavor of grilling is delicious, but if you feel this salad needs spiced up a bit, shake on a garlic-and-herb salt-substitute seasoning blend.

Pinch of Sage

Grill these vegetables outdoors, if you prefer. You may want to slice the eggplant, zucchini, and squash lengthwise to keep them safely atop the grilling rack. Grill the tomatoes whole and the onion and bell pepper halved so they don't slip through the grate. Or place the vegetables in a nonstick grilling basket, if you have one.

Lemon-Kissed Tuna Stuffed Tomatoes

Makes 2 servings
Prep time: 10 minutes
Cook time: 3 minutes
Serving size: 1 tomato
Each serving has:
154.7 calories
64 mg sodium
24.1 g protein
1.3 g total fat
0.2 g saturated fat
26 mg cholesterol
11.9 g carbohydrate
1.7 g dietary fiber
72.7 mg calcium
648.1 mg potassium

2 TB. fresh lemon juice

2 green onions, chopped

2 TB. diced red bell pepper

1 TB. chopped fresh parsley

1 (6-oz.) can *very low-sodium* albacore tuna packed in water, drained

3 TB. fat-free plain yogurt

2 medium tomatoes, cored

1. In a nonstick skillet over medium heat, heat lemon juice just until hot. Add green onions, red bell pepper, and parsley. Cook for 1 to 2 minutes or until softened.

2. Add tuna, flaking into the skillet. Cook 1 to 2 minutes or until heated through, and then remove from heat. Stir in yogurt, evenly coating tuna and vegetables.

3. To serve, slice tomatoes into 8 wedges each beginning at the cored top without cutting through bottoms of tomatoes. Divide tuna mixture between tomatoes.

Salternative: You can easily double this recipe as needed.

Lo-So Lingo

Very low-sodium is used on product labels to identify foods that contain no more than 35 milligrams sodium per serving.

Golden Chicken Tenders Salad

2 tsp. fresh lemon juice

1 lb. chicken tenders, rinsed and patted dry on paper towels

½ tsp. salt-free poultry seasoning

4 cups packed torn salad greens

2 small tomatoes, cored and cut into thin wedges

½ small green bell pepper, seeds and ribs discarded, and cut into thin strips

½ small yellow bell pepper, seeds and ribs discarded, and cut into thin strips

½ medium red onion, peeled and thinly sliced

4 button mushrooms, wiped with a damp paper towel, trimmed, and sliced

3 TB. unsalted sliced almonds

1 TB. unsalted sunflower seed kernels

½ cup Golden Garlic Dressing (recipe in Chapter 24)

Makes 4 servings
Prep time: 10 minutes
Cook time: 6 minutes
Serving size: 1 cup greens with 4 ounces chicken, ¼ additions, and 2 tablespoons salad dressing
Each serving has:
323.3 calories
75.9 mg sodium
30.4 g protein
19.4 g total fat
2.3 g saturated fat
67 mg cholesterol
10.8 g carbohydrate
3.5 g dietary fiber
85.2 mg calcium
449.7 mg potassium

1. Preheat a double-sided indoor grill. Drizzle lemon juice over chicken tenders, and then season with poultry seasoning. Grill chicken in batches for 3 minutes or until done.

2. Serve chicken on a bed of salad greens with tomatoes, green bell pepper, yellow bell pepper, onion, mushrooms, almonds, and sunflower seed kernels. Drizzle Golden Garlic Dressing over all.

Salt Pitfall

Make this salad your own with your favorite vegetables, salad toppings, and salad dressing. But before you start tossing, keep in mind that many traditional salad additions are higher in sodium, including bacon bits, frozen peas, canned beans, cheeses, and commercial salad dressings. You may have to forego some of your old favorites or choose sodium-smart substitutes, such as homemade salad dressings, cooked dried beans, and low-sodium cheeses.

Spring Salmon Salad

Makes 2 servings
Prep time: 15 minutes
Cook time: 10 minutes
Serving size: 1¼ cups greens with 3 ounces salmon, ½ additions, and 2 tablespoons vinaigrette

Each serving has:
424.8 calories
102.5 mg sodium
26.8 g protein
27.9 g total fat
4.3 g saturated fat
159.7 mg cholesterol
18.5 g carbohydrate
5.1 g dietary fiber
101.7 mg calcium
1,100 mg potassium

6 oz. skin-on salmon

2 cups packed torn red-leaf lettuce, rinsed and patted dry

½ cup packed baby spinach leaves, stemmed and rinsed

½ cup steamed 1-inch asparagus pieces

½ small red onion, sliced

½ yellow bell pepper, seeds and ribs discarded, and cut into thin strips

¼ cup drained no-salt-added canned peas or lightly cooked fresh peas

1 large hard-cooked egg, chopped

1 large tomato, cored and chopped

1 green onion, chopped

¼ cup Balsamic Vinaigrette (recipe in Chapter 24)

1. Preheat the broiler. Spray the rack of a broiler pan with non-stick cooking spray. Place salmon on the broiler rack, and broil 4 to 6 inches from heat for 10 minutes per inch of thickness or until done.

2. Place lettuce and spinach onto 2 plates. Flake salmon over top. Add asparagus, red onion, bell pepper, peas, egg, tomato, and green onion. Drizzle on Balsamic Vinaigrette.

Salternative: You can double this recipe as needed.

 Pinch of Sage

To hard-cook eggs, place the eggs in a saucepan and cover with cold water. Cover the saucepan and bring the water to a boil. When boiling, remove the pan from the heat. Let the eggs stand, covered, for 20 minutes. Immediately rinse the eggs under cold water until cooled, and leave them immersed in cold water as you peel them. This method will keep the surface of the yolks from developing a green cast (as does not using fresh eggs for hard-cooking). If you do find a green yolk or two, don't worry. They are perfectly safe to eat.

Veggie-Packed Pasta Salad

8 oz. whole-wheat rotini pasta

1 medium tomato, cored, diced and seeded as desired (about ½ cup)

¼ cup diced cucumber, seeded as desired

¼ cup diced yellow bell pepper

¼ cup drained, canned no-salt-added peas or lightly cooked fresh peas

1 cup Italian Dressing (recipe in Chapter 24) or other low-sodium Italian salad dressing

Makes 6 servings
Prep time: 5 minutes
Cook time: 15 minutes
Chill time: 4 hours
Serving size: 1 cup
Each serving has:
385.2 calories
4.6 mg sodium
6.1 g protein
27.7 g total fat
3.8 g saturated fat
0 mg cholesterol
31.5 g carbohydrate
3.6 g dietary fiber
24.9 mg calcium
144.9 mg potassium

1. Cook pasta according to package directions (omit salt). Drain and rinse under cold water.

2. In a large bowl, combine pasta, tomato, cucumber, yellow bell pepper, and peas. Pour Italian Dressing over top, and stir to coat all. Cover and chill for at least 4 hours. Stir again before serving.

Pinch of Sage

Use your favorite vegetables and beans in this salad—just keep the measurements the same. Choose a total of 1 cup vegetables, such as broccoli, cauliflower, zucchini, yellow squash, sweet onions, snow peas, and so on. Replace the peas with cooked dry beans or no-salt-added canned beans, such as kidney beans or garbanzo beans. You can even use your favorite low-sodium salad dressing. Serve it all on lettuce-lined salad plates for an attractive presentation.

Mexican Night Taco Salad

Makes 4 servings
Prep time: 10 minutes
Cook time: 10 minutes
Serving size: 1 salad
Each serving has:
537.9 calories
264.2 mg sodium
39.2 g protein
27.3 g total fat
10.3 g saturated fat
120.2 mg cholesterol
35.6 g carbohydrate
5.5 g dietary fiber
225.9 mg calcium
836.1 mg potassium

1 lb. 85-percent-lean ground beef

1½ tsp. Taco Seasoning Mix (recipe in Chapter 26)

4 doz. unsalted baked tortilla chips

4 cups torn salad greens

½ cup diced yellow onions

½ cup sliced black olives or no-salt-added sliced black olives

½ cup finely shredded low-sodium cheddar cheese

½ cup Fresh-Taste Tomato Salsa (recipe in Chapter 25) or other low-sodium salsa

½ cup Great Guacamole (recipe in Chapter 4) or other low-sodium guacamole

½ cup fat-free sour cream

1. In a large, nonstick skillet over medium heat, brown ground beef with Taco Seasoning Mix. Cook for 7 to 8 minutes or until browned and 160°F, stirring to break up meat. Remove with a slotted spoon to a plate lined with paper towels.

2. Line each of 4 plates with 12 tortilla chips. Spoon on ground beef mixture. Layer salad greens, onions, black olives, and cheese over top. Add dollops of Fresh-Taste Tomato Salsa, Great Guacamole, and sour cream.

Salternative: Save on a bit of sodium by substituting low-sodium black olives, which have about 8 milligrams sodium per olive.

 Pinch of Sage

This recipe calls for 85-percent-lean ground beef. If your doctor or nutritionist has indicated that you should watch your saturated fat intake by employing a leaner cut, you should use it instead. Try ground turkey breast if you're abstaining from red meat.

Pittsburgh Steak Salad

¼ cup plus 2 tsp. extra-virgin olive oil

¼ cup red wine vinegar

2 cloves garlic, minced

1 tsp. ground black pepper

½ lb. thin sandwich steak

2 cups torn salad greens

1 medium tomato, cored, seeded if desired, and chopped

¼ medium cucumber, peeled and sliced

¼ cup shredded carrots

¼ cup shredded red cabbage

1 hard-cooked egg, chopped

¼ cup shredded low-sodium cheddar cheese

2 doz. Oven-Crisped Fries (recipe in Chapter 18)

¼ cup Sweet Onion Dressing (recipe in Chapter 24) or other favorite low-sodium salad dressing

Makes 2 servings
Prep time: 15 minutes
Marinating time: 8 hours
Cook time: 4 minutes
Serving size: 1 cup greens with 4 ounces steak, ½ additions, and 2 tablespoons salad dressing

Each serving has:
895.5 calories
139.6 mg sodium
28.9 g protein
79.9 g total fat
22.8 g saturated fat
200.9 mg cholesterol
19.9 g carbohydrate
4.3 g dietary fiber
194.4 mg calcium
999.3 mg potassium

1. In a large, sealable plastic bag, combine ¼ cup extra-virgin olive oil, red wine vinegar, garlic, and black pepper. Add steak. Seal the bag, and marinate in the refrigerator for 8 hours or overnight.

2. In a large, nonstick skillet over medium heat, heat remaining 2 teaspoons olive oil. Remove steak from marinade and discard marinade. Slice steak into 2-inch strips. Cook for 2 minutes. Turn and cook for 1 minute on other side or until done. Drain on a plate lined with paper towels.

3. Line each of 2 plates with 1 cup salad greens. Top with tomato, cucumber, carrots, red cabbage, egg, cheese, and Oven-Crisped Fries. Add steak and then drizzle Sweet Onion Dressing over all.

Salternatives: If you've forgotten to marinate steak beforehand, cut it into strips and season it with ¼ teaspoon each ground black pepper, garlic powder, and onion powder. Then, cook as directed. You'll have a fast-fix lunch with great taste. If you can't find thin sandwich steak, you can substitute your favorite skillet steak cut. Just be certain to cook it as needed. The recipe can also be doubled as needed.

Salt Pitfall

Discard any uncooked marinade, as it has been in contact with raw meat and is likely to harbor illness-causing bacteria. If a recipe calls for using the marinade, be sure to bring it to a boil first.

Tex-Mex Chicken Fajita Salad

Makes 4 servings
Prep time: 10 minutes
Marinating time: up to 4 hours
Cook time: 15 minutes
Serving size: 1 cup salad greens with 4 ounces chicken and ¼ additions

Each serving has:
393.1 calories
177.2 mg sodium
29.9 g protein
17 g total fat
2.9 g saturated fat
65.5 mg cholesterol
33.7 g carbohydrate
7.2 g dietary fiber
134 mg calcium
980.4 mg potassium

Pinch of Sage

If you can't find thin-sliced chicken breast, substitute regular boneless, skinless chicken breast. Cut it into strips, and cook until no pink remains at 185°F.

Juice of 2 large limes

2 green onions, trimmed and sliced

3 cloves garlic, minced

3 TB. extra-virgin olive oil

1 TB. dried cilantro or 3 TB. chopped fresh cilantro

½ tsp. crushed red pepper flakes

¼ tsp. ground coriander

¼ tsp. anise seeds

1 lb. thin-sliced boneless, skinless chicken breast, rinsed and patted dry on paper towels

½ large green bell pepper, seeds and ribs discarded, and cut into thin strips

½ large red bell pepper, seeds and ribs discarded, and cut into thin strips

1 medium yellow onion, halved and sliced

½ cup frozen whole-kernel corn, thawed

½ cup no-salt-added black beans, drained and rinsed

4 cups torn salad greens

½ cup coarsely crushed unsalted baked tortilla chips

1 cup Fresh-Taste Tomato Salsa (recipe in Chapter 25) or other low-sodium salsa

½ cup Great Guacamole (recipe in Chapter 4) or other low-sodium guacamole

½ cup fat-free sour cream

1. In a large, sealable plastic bag, combine lime juice, green onions, garlic, 2 tablespoons extra-virgin olive oil, cilantro, crushed red pepper flakes, coriander, and anise seeds. Add chicken. Seal the bag, and marinate in the refrigerator for 4 hours, turning occasionally.

2. In a large, nonstick skillet over medium heat, heat remaining 1 tablespoon olive oil. Sauté green bell pepper, red bell pepper, and onion for 8 minutes or until onion is golden and bell peppers are tender. Turn into a medium bowl. Stir in corn and black beans.

3. Remove chicken from marinade and discard marinade. Cut chicken into large strips. In the same skillet over medium heat, cook chicken for 2 minutes on each side or until done. Remove to a plate lined with paper towels.

4. To assemble, line each of 4 plates with 1 cup salad greens. Top with chicken, bell pepper mixture, and tortilla chips. Add dollops of Fresh-Taste Tomato Salsa, Great Guacamole, and sour cream.

Chapter 10

Soups and Stews to Savor

In This Chapter

◆ Choosing sodium-sensible ingredients
◆ Benefiting from a bowlful of nutrients
◆ Slurping in moderation

Perhaps no other food is as homey as a soup or stew. The tempting aroma and delightful taste of a hot bowl warms your heart and your body. You're easily transported back to Mom's kitchen with all its comfort and care.

If you've stopped slurping up your favorite soups and stews because of the astonishing sodium counts, take heart. You can enjoy a cup of comfort by choosing low-sodium ingredients and sensible substitutions. Plus, if you've not discovered cold fruit soups, you're in for a treat.

Hot or cold, a bowl of soup or a hearty stew will supply a wealth of nutrients—and now with much less sodium. So go grab your spoon!

The Pros of Soups and Stews

If soups and stews tend to be high-sodium meals, why not just eliminate them from your diet? For one, lowering your sodium consumption shouldn't be about deprivation. You can enjoy many wonderfully delectable foods as long as you keep your portions in check.

Moreover, soups and stews are teeming with vitamins and minerals. None of the nutrients are poured down the drain because the cooking water is a vital part of the dish. Plus, soups and stews are packed with healthful ingredients—veggies, beans, herbs, spices, lean meats, even fruits. It's goodness you can eat with a spoon!

Soup Notes

If you've taken a peek at the amount of sodium in a single serving of commercially prepared soup, you probably needed a moment to catch your breath. Unfortunately, many homemade soups are typically prepared with high-sodium ingredients as well. Broths and canned tomato products are perhaps the biggest culprits.

The good news is that low-sodium alternatives are available. The recipes included in this chapter call for light, fat-free canned broths. These broths are reduced in sodium by 50 percent, but they still contain a hefty serving of sodium. We chose them because they're readily available, and if you watch your serving size, these soups and stews can easily fit into your daily, low-sodium diet. Of course, if you can buy or prepare broths lower in sodium, you can substitute those in these recipes.

Tomato-based soups should be prepared with no-salt-added canned products or fresh tomatoes. The same applies to beans. The recipes that follow call for no-salt-added canned beans for convenience. If you want to save on a bit of sodium and have time, you may prepare dried beans to substitute in any of these recipes.

Pinch of Sage

Don't get carried away when cooking dried beans by dumping the entire bag into the soaking water—unless you plan on using all those beans. One cup dried beans yields five to six cups cooked beans.

Split-Pea Soup with Mini Meatballs

1 TB. extra-light olive oil

1 medium yellow onion, finely chopped (about 1 cup)

2 celery stalks, finely chopped

1 clove garlic, minced

1½ tsp. dried crushed rosemary

1 (48-oz.) can *light* fat-free chicken broth (6 cups)

1¼ cups dried green split peas, sorted and rinsed

½ lb. ground turkey

¼ tsp. freshly ground black pepper

Makes 6 servings
Prep time: 10 minutes
Cook time: 1 hour, 50 minutes
Serving size: 1 cup soup with about 8 meatballs
Each serving has:
232.5 calories
153.9 mg sodium
19.3 g protein
6.6 g total fat
1.8 g saturated fat
25.5 mg cholesterol
25.8 g carbohydrate
9.2 g dietary fiber
45 mg calcium
460.1 mg potassium

1. In a large soup pot, heat extra-light olive oil over medium heat. Sauté onion, celery, garlic, and 1 teaspoon rosemary for 5 minutes or until softened, stirring frequently. Pour in chicken broth, add split peas, and stir. Bring to a boil over high heat. Reduce heat, cover, and simmer for 1½ hours or until split peas are tender. Remove from heat and let cool.

2. Meanwhile, combine ground turkey, black pepper, and remaining ½ teaspoon rosemary until seasonings are evenly distributed. Form into tiny ½-inch meatballs.

3. In a nonstick skillet over medium heat, brown meatballs on all sides for 7 to 10 minutes or until cooked through and no pink remains. Remove meatballs with a slotted spoon to a plate lined with paper towels to drain.

4. Ladle about ½ soup or more into a blender or food processor. Purée on high speed for 15 seconds or until smooth. Return to soup pot, add meatballs to soup, and stir. Bring to a slow simmer over medium-high heat to heat through.

Lo-So Lingo

Light, when used in reference to the sodium content, refers to a product that has at least 50 percent less sodium than the regular product. Check the nutrition label for actual sodium amounts.

Summer Garden Cream of Tomato Soup

Makes 5½ servings
Prep time: 20 minutes
Cook time: 35 minutes
Serving size: 1 cup
Each serving has:
103.3 calories
38.2 mg sodium
3.4 g protein
2.5 g total fat
0.2 g saturated fat
0 mg cholesterol
17.4 g carbohydrate
2.1 g dietary fiber
98.4 mg calcium
715.7 mg potassium

2 tsp. extra-virgin olive oil

1 medium sweet onion, thinly sliced

1 bay leaf

3 lb. fresh tomatoes, peeled, seeded, and chopped

2 tsp. cornstarch

½ cup fat-free evaporated milk

¼ tsp. freshly ground black pepper

¼ tsp. dried thyme

1. In a medium-large saucepan, heat extra-virgin olive oil over medium heat. Add sweet onion and bay leaf. Cook, stirring often, for 5 minutes or until onion is softened. Add tomatoes. Bring to a simmer over medium heat. Reduce heat to low, cover, and simmer for 20 minutes. Discard bay leaf.

2. Transfer tomato mixture to a blender or food processor. Purée to desired consistency. Return to the saucepan.

3. In a small bowl, whisk together cornstarch and evaporated milk. Stir into tomato mixture. Return to a simmer over medium heat, and simmer for 5 minutes or until thickened. Stir in black pepper and thyme until evenly distributed.

 Pinch of Sage

Don't overstir or overheat a recipe thickened with cornstarch, as it may cause thinning, defeating the purpose.

Slow-Simmered Minestrone

1 small yellow onion, diced

6 large baby carrots, halved and sliced

2 celery stalks, diced

1 cup chopped green cabbage

2 cloves garlic, minced

1 tsp. dried basil

1 tsp. dried marjoram

½ tsp. dried oregano

¼ tsp. freshly ground black pepper

2 (14.5-oz.) cans 50-percent-reduced-sodium, fat-free beef broth

1 (15-oz.) can no-salt-added tomato sauce

1 (14.5-oz.) can no-salt-added diced tomatoes

1 (15-oz.) can no-salt-added great northern beans, drained

¼ cup *pastina*

Makes 9 servings
Prep time: 10 minutes
Cook time: 4 to 5 hours
Serving size: 1 cup
Each serving has:
116.4 calories
63 mg sodium
7.2 g protein
1.1 g total fat
0.3 g saturated fat
0 mg cholesterol
19.6 g carbohydrate
4.9 g dietary fiber
57.4 mg calcium
568.9 mg potassium

1. Combine onion, carrots, celery, cabbage, garlic, basil, marjoram, oregano, black pepper, beef broth, tomato sauce, diced tomatoes, and great northern beans in a slow cooker. Cover and cook on high for 4 to 5 hours or on low heat for 8 to 10 hours.

2. Stir in pastina during last 15 to 30 minutes of cooking time. Cover and cook until pastina is tender.

Salternative: Save on a bit of sodium by substituting 2 cups cooked great northern beans.

Lo-So Lingo

Pastina is Italian for "little dough" and is simply a very small pasta. You can use any tiny pasta, such as acini de pepe and alphabets.

Down-Home Veggie Soup

Makes 12 servings
Prep time: 10 minutes
Cook time: 1 hour
Serving size: 1 cup
Each serving has:
128.2 calories
45.3 mg sodium
8.8 g protein
6 g total fat
2.3 g saturated fat
25.7 mg cholesterol
11.1 g carbohydrate
2.1 g dietary fiber
23.6 mg calcium
492.8 mg potassium

 Pinch of Sage

To easily peel tomatoes, place them in boiling water for 10 to 15 seconds. Remove with tongs. When cool enough to handle, peel with the tip of a sharp knife and your fingers.

1 lb. ground beef

2 medium yellow onions, chopped

4 cups cold water

10 baby carrots, cut on the diagonal

2 celery stalks, thinly sliced

2 medium potatoes, peeled and chopped

1 bay leaf

¼ tsp. dried basil

1 TB. garlic-and-herb salt substitute seasoning blend

6 large tomatoes, peeled, cored, and chopped

1. In a nonstick skillet, brown ground beef over medium heat. With a slotted spoon, transfer ground beef to a plate lined with paper towels to drain. Drain the skillet but do not dry.

2. In the same skillet, sauté onions over medium-low heat for 5 minutes or until just turning golden.

3. In a large soup pot, combine onions, cold water, carrots, celery, potatoes, bay leaf, basil, and garlic-and-herb salt substitute seasoning blend. Bring to a boil. Reduce heat, cover, and simmer for 30 minutes.

4. Stir in ground beef and tomatoes. Return to a boil. Reduce heat, cover, and simmer for 10 minutes or until vegetables are tender.

Honey-Kissed Strawberry Soup

1 cup sliced fresh strawberries	2 TB. fresh orange juice
1 cup fat-free plain yogurt	1 TB. honey

1. Add strawberries, yogurt, orange juice, and honey to a blender. Purée on low speed for 5 seconds. Then blend on low speed for 5 to 10 seconds, stopping to scrape down the sides if necessary.

2. Cover and chill soup for at least 1 hour before serving. Stir again before serving. Garnish individual servings with a fanned fresh strawberry or a sprig of fresh mint, if desired.

Salternative: Substitute frozen unsweetened sliced strawberries, thawed and drained, when berries are out of season.

Makes 4 servings
Prep time: 5 minutes
Chill time: 1 hour
Serving size: ½ cup
Each serving has:
57 calories
35.1 mg sodium
2.8 g protein
0.2 g total fat
0 g saturated fat
1.3 mg cholesterol
12.8 g carbohydrate
1 g dietary fiber
81.1 mg calcium
86.5 mg potassium

Pinch of Sage _____

If you pick your own fresh strawberries, pluck only plump red berries from the vines. Strawberries do not ripen after picking as other fruits do.

Tri-Colored Melon Soup

Makes 7 servings
Prep time: 20 minutes
Chill time: 1 hour
Serving size: ¼ cup
Each serving has:
98.7 calories
24.7 mg sodium
2.1 g protein
0.4 g total fat
0.1 g saturated fat
0.5 mg cholesterol
24.4 g carbohydrate
0.9 g dietary fiber
44.2 mg calcium
330 mg potassium

Pinch of Sage

You may need to adjust the honey according to the sweetness of the melons. Ripe fruit works well in this recipe.

2 cups cubed cantaloupe (about ¾ small cantaloupe)

¾ cup fat-free plain yogurt

4½ TB. honey

2 cups cubed honeydew (about ½ small honeydew)

2 cups cubed seedless watermelon

1. In a blender, combine cantaloupe, ¼ cup yogurt, and 1½ tablespoons honey. Purée on high speed for 5 seconds or until blended. Transfer to a 2-cup measuring cup or other container.

2. In the blender, combine honeydew, ¼ cup yogurt, and 1½ tablespoons honey. Purée on high speed for 5 seconds or until blended. Transfer to a separate 2-cup measuring cup or other container.

3. In the blender, combine watermelon, remaining ¼ cup yogurt, and remaining 1½ tablespoons honey. Purée on high speed for 5 seconds or until blended. Transfer to a separate 2-cup measuring cup or other container.

4. Cover and chill separate mixtures for 1 hour.

5. In each of 7 shallow bowls or deep plates, pour ¼ cup cantaloupe mixture on 1 side and then pour ¼ cup honeydew mixture on the other side. Pour ¼ cup watermelon mixture in the center. Using a wooden skewer or pick, swirl through the mixtures, circling clockwise. (Use a gentle hand to keep the colors from muddying.)

Two-Bean Turkey Chili

¾ lb. ground turkey

2 small yellow onions, chopped

1 medium green bell pepper, seeds and ribs discarded, and chopped

1 (14.5-oz.) can no-salt-added diced tomatoes, undrained

1 (15-oz.) can no-salt-added tomato sauce

1 (15-oz.) can no-salt-added pinto beans, rinsed and drained

1 (15-oz.) can no-salt-added black beans, rinsed and drained

2½ tsp. Firehouse Chili Powder (recipe in Chapter 26) or other salt-free chili powder

1½ tsp. Salt-Shaker Substitute (recipe in Chapter 26) or other salt-free salt substitute seasoning blend

¼ tsp. paprika

¼ tsp. ground ginger

Makes 7 servings
Prep time: 5 minutes
Cook time: 1 hour, 40 minutes
Serving size: 1 cup
Each serving has:
210.6 calories
226 mg sodium
16 g protein
5.2 g total fat
1.6 g saturated fat
41.7 mg cholesterol
27.6 g carbohydrate
8.6 g dietary fiber
89.6 mg calcium
765.4 mg potassium

1. In a large saucepan over medium heat, brown ground turkey with onions and green bell pepper for 7 minutes or until meat is browned and onions are translucent. Drain well.

2. Add diced tomatoes, tomato sauce, pinto beans, and black beans and stir. Add Firehouse Chili Powder, Salt-Shaker Substitute, paprika, and ginger and stir. Bring to a boil. Reduce heat, cover, and simmer for 1½ hours.

 Pinch of Sage

You can substitute any two of your favorite beans in this recipe—kidney beans, great northern beans, pink beans, and so on. Just keep them low in sodium.

One-Pot Cajun Shrimp Stew

Makes 4 servings
Prep time: 5 minutes
Cook time: 55 minutes
Serving size: 1 cup
Each serving has:
240.1 calories
198.8 mg sodium
27.7 g protein
8.5 g total fat
2.7 g saturated fat
196.2 mg cholesterol
12 g carbohydrate
1.7 g dietary fiber
83.5 mg calcium
403.4 mg potassium

2 TB. trans-fat-free soft vegetable shortening

3 TB. all-purpose flour

1 large green bell pepper, seeds and ribs discarded, and chopped

1 medium yellow onion, chopped

1 small celery stalk, diced

3 cloves garlic, minced

2 TB. no-salt-added tomato sauce

1 cup water

1 lb. peeled, deveined, cooked or uncooked medium shrimp

1. In a large saucepan over medium heat, melt shortening. Whisk in flour, and cook, whisking, for 5 minutes or until *roux* is deep golden brown. Reduce heat to low. Add green bell pepper, onion, celery, and garlic. Cover and cook for 10 minutes.

2. Add tomato sauce and water to the saucepan. Cover and simmer for 30 minutes.

3. Stir shrimp into the saucepan. Cover and gently simmer for 10 minutes. Remove from heat. Serve stew over cooked long-grain brown rice, if desired.

Lo-So Lingo

Roux is simply a French word for a fat-and-flour mixture. This recipe calls for a medium roux, which should be about the color of peanut butter. Be sure to whisk your roux constantly—that means you can't answer the phone, get the door, or chop the vegetables. You'll need to do that before you start cooking.

Farmhouse Oven Beef Stew

1½ TB. extra-light olive oil

¼ cup all-purpose flour

¾ tsp. freshly ground black pepper

¼ tsp. garlic powder

1½ lb. lean stew beef cubes

2 medium yellow onions, chopped

3 celery stalks, sliced

12 large baby carrots, sliced

2 cups low-sodium vegetable juice

1½ cups water

½ cup quick-cooking tapioca

½ tsp. dried basil

1 TB. granulated sugar

1 bay leaf

3 all-purpose potatoes, peeled and chopped

Makes 6 servings
Prep time: 10 minutes
Cook time: 2 hours, 40 minutes
Serving size: 1 cup
Each serving has:
374 calories
134.8 mg sodium
27.1 g protein
10.8 g total fat
3.2 g saturated fat
66.1 mg cholesterol
43.2 g carbohydrate
4.2 g dietary fiber
59.4 mg calcium
870.2 mg potassium

1. Preheat the oven to 325°F, and spray a deep, 3-quart casserole dish with nonstick cooking spray.

2. Heat extra-light olive oil in a large, nonstick skillet over medium heat. In a shallow dish, stir together flour, ¼ teaspoon black pepper, and garlic powder. Dredge beef cubes in seasoned flour, shaking off excess. Add beef to the skillet, and brown on all sides.

3. Transfer beef to the prepared casserole dish. Add onions, celery, and carrots.

4. In a medium bowl, combine vegetable juice, 1 cup water, tapioca, basil, remaining ½ teaspoon black pepper, sugar, and bay leaf. Stir and pour over beef mixture. Cover and bake for 2 hours.

5. Add potatoes and ½ cup water to the casserole dish. Stir. Cover and bake for 30 to 40 minutes or until potatoes are tender.

Salternative: This stew is a thick dish. If you prefer a thinner stew, reduce the amount of tapioca as desired.

Pinch of Sage

Add small whole fresh mushrooms or sliced fresh mushrooms with the potatoes, if you like. Fresh mushrooms will add just a few milligrams of sodium: 4 milligrams for 1 cup whole or 1½ milligrams for ½ cup slices.

Chapter 11

Assorted Sandwiches

In This Chapter

- Building a satisfying sandwich without soaring sodium
- Finding low-sodium breads
- Selecting sodium-responsible condiments and other fixings
- Enjoying open-face sandwiches to decrease bread amounts

Nothing says lunch like a sandwich. From the humble PB&J to a gourmet roasted eggplant and fresh mozzarella with roasted red pepper relish on focaccia, a good sandwich will hit the spot at midday.

For people on a sodium-restricted diet, eating a simple sandwich can become a complicated endeavor. Regular breads are high in sodium. Deli lunch meats contain incredibly high amounts of sodium.

And of course, we must have condiments: pickles, relish, mustard, ketchup, mayonnaise, salsa, barbecue sauce, hot pepper sauce, steak sauce, and salad dressings make building a sandwich a sodium landmine area. Should we mention the cheese?

Fortunately, you can find ingredients that will fit your low-sodium meal plan. With a little ingenuity, you can sink your teeth into a satisfying lunchtime sandwich without a care. Is that the lunch bell ringing?

It's All About the Bread

A sandwich isn't really a sandwich without the bread, right? (Well, we do have a recipe that eliminates the bread: Turkey and Swiss in a Green Blanket—it's rather tasty.) But you're at a loss as to how to find suitable breads for your needs.

We've listed a few sources in Appendix B that you can use to purchase low-sodium and even salt-free breads. Some companies will ship the breads to your home. So if you can afford slightly higher prices and shipping charges, problem is solved.

But also check out your own neighborhood for lo-so bread. You may be pleasantly surprised. Some supermarkets carry commercially made low-sodium breads, or their in-store bakeries may offer low-sodium options. You won't know until you ask. Smaller grocers often offer selections that differ from the large supermarket conglomerates. They may also be able to order low-sodium breads in small quantities from their distributors—again, ask. Local bakeries are another good place to poke around. You might have to special order low-sodium loaves, rolls, or buns but that's easy enough.

> **Pinch of Sage**
>
> Another option for a low-sodium sandwich wrap is to use a crepe from the Lemon Raspberry Crepes recipe in Chapter 8.

If you're simply unable to get your hands on low-sodium breads, you'll have to work with what's available. Perhaps the quickest solution is to make an open-faced sandwich. Using a single slice of bread automatically cuts the amount of sodium from the bread in a sandwich in half. Plus, some regularly available sandwich holders are okay in terms of sodium content. You can usually incorporate a regular corn taco shell, half an English muffin, or half a regular bun into your diet without spoiling your sodium count.

Sandwich Snafus—Avoided

Is there anything you can even put on your sandwich? Many regular condiments are too high in sodium. You can purchase most, though, in no-salt-added or low-sodium versions. If you prefer, prepare your own sodium-wise condiments from the recipes offered in Part 7.

If you'd like a classic deli meat sandwich, you'll have to be alert. Typical deli meats contain astronomical amounts of sodium. Some manufacturers, such as Boar's Head and Nonna's Kitchen, produce lower-sodium turkey, ham, or roast beef products. Ask if your deli department has lower-sodium options.

And if you top your sandwich with cheese, make it a low-sodium variety.

Turkey and Swiss in a Green Blanket

1 tsp. extra-virgin olive oil

¼ red bell pepper, seeds and ribs discarded, and thinly sliced

1 (¼-inch-thick) slice sweet onion, separated into rings

2 large leaves red-leaf lettuce

2 oz. skinless, 47-percent-lower-sodium deli turkey breast, chopped or sliced

2 to 3 tsp. Home-Style Mustard (recipe in Chapter 23)

1 (1-oz.) slice low-sodium Swiss cheese

Makes 1 serving
Prep time: 5 minutes
Cook time: 6 minutes
Serving size: 1 sandwich
Each serving has:
259.8 calories
371.9 mg sodium
20.3 g protein
13.7 g total fat
5.8 g saturated fat
68.8 mg cholesterol
13.3 g carbohydrate
1.5 g dietary fiber
324.8 mg calcium
220.5 mg potassium

1. Heat olive oil in a small skillet over medium heat. Add red bell pepper and sweet onion. Cook for 5 minutes or until softened, stirring frequently.

2. Wash and dry lettuce. Place on a plate, overlapping edges of leaves. Layer turkey over top, leaving a small margin on all sides. Spread on Home-Style Mustard and top with cheese. Scatter red bell pepper mixture over all.

3. Just before eating, wrap lettuce around filling, burrito-style.

 Pinch of Sage

Swiss cheese is naturally lower in sodium than other traditional cheeses, but you can save on some sodium if you try this sandwich without cheese.

Honey-Barbecue Chicken Breast on Toast

Makes 1 serving
Prep time: 5 minutes
Cook time: 4 minutes
Serving size: 1 sandwich
Each serving has:
337.5 calories
335.8 mg sodium
21.3 g protein
5.1 g total fat
1.1 g saturated fat
39.2 mg cholesterol
55.6 g carbohydrate
5 g dietary fiber
66.7 mg calcium
440.6 mg potassium

1½ TB. honey

1 tsp. paprika

½ tsp. dry mustard

¼ tsp. ground cayenne

1 (2.5-oz.) thin-sliced bone-less, skinless chicken breast, rinsed and patted dry on paper towels

2 slices salt-free whole-wheat bread, toasted

1 green-leaf lettuce leaf

2 thin slices tomato

1 (⅛- to ¼-inch-thick) slice sweet onion, separated into rings

1. In a small bowl, combine honey, paprika, dry mustard, and cayenne. Stir to blend.

2. Heat a small, nonstick skillet sprayed with nonstick cooking spray over medium heat. Cook chicken for 1 to 2 minutes or until browned on underside. Turn and cook for 1 minute or until done. Spoon honey mixture over chicken. Cook for 30 to 60 seconds, turning chicken to coat. Remove from heat.

3. Line 1 slice of toast with lettuce. Add tomato slices and onion rings. Place chicken with sauce over top. Close sandwich with remaining slice of toast. Cut sandwich in half, and serve immediately.

 Pinch of Sage

If you can't find salt-free bread, you can opt to serve this recipe as an open-face sandwich, using a single slice of a whole-grain bread that has the lowest sodium content you can find.

Quick and Easy Beefy Tacos

½ lb. 85-percent-lean ground beef

¾ tsp. Taco Seasoning Mix (recipe in Chapter 26)

4 sodium-free yellow corn taco shells

½ cup finely shredded low-sodium cheddar cheese

1 cup shredded lettuce

½ cup finely diced tomatoes

Makes 4 servings
Prep time: 5 minutes
Cook time: 7 minutes
Serving size: 1 taco
Each serving has:
250.7 calories
174.5 mg sodium
15.5 g protein
16.3 g total fat
6.8 g saturated fat
52.7 mg cholesterol
10.7 g carbohydrate
1.4 g dietary fiber
156.3 mg calcium
250.1 mg potassium

1. In a small, nonstick skillet over medium heat, brown ground beef with Taco Seasoning Mix. Stir, breaking up meat, until cooked through and no pink remains. Remove beef with a slotted spoon to a plate lined with paper towels.

2. Warm taco shells according to package directions. Fill each with ¼ ground beef, 2 tablespoons cheese, ¼ cup lettuce, and 2 tablespoons tomatoes.

Pinch of Sage

If you have a hard time finding sodium-free taco shells, use regular taco shells. They're fairly low in sodium and more readily available.

Turkey and Pinto Bean Soft Tacos

Makes 4 servings
Prep time: 10 minutes
Cook time: 10 minutes
Serving size: 1 taco
Each serving has:
631 calories
267.3 mg sodium
36.7 g protein
29 g total fat
9.7 g saturated fat
114.2 mg cholesterol
55 g carbohydrate
9 g dietary fiber
250.8 mg calcium
699 mg potassium

1 lb. ground turkey

1½ tsp. Taco Seasoning Mix (recipe in Chapter 26)

½ cup finely diced yellow onions

1 (15-oz.) can no-salt-added pinto beans, rinsed and drained

4 Fresh Tortillas (recipe in Chapter 16) or other low-sodium tortillas, warmed

½ cup finely shredded low-sodium cheddar cheese

½ cup finely diced tomatoes

½ cup fat-free sour cream

1. In a large, nonstick skillet over medium heat, brown ground turkey with Taco Seasoning Mix and onions. Cook for 7 to 8 minutes or until browned and no pink remains, stirring to break up meat. Stir in beans and cook for 1 minute or until heated through. Remove with a slotted spoon to a plate lined with paper towels.

2. Spoon turkey mixture down center of warmed tortillas. Sprinkle on cheese and tomatoes, spoon on sour cream, and fold over, burrito-style.

 Pinch of Sage

> You can quickly warm each tortilla in the microwave on 50 percent power for 15 to 30 seconds. Preparing the tacos while the tortillas are warm and malleable helps keep them from cracking while you're folding them.

Chunky Tuna Salad Pita Pockets

1 TB. fresh lemon juice

2 green onions, trimmed and sliced

1 (6-oz.) can very low-sodium albacore tuna packed in water, drained and coarsely flaked

¼ cup fat-free plain yogurt

3 TB. finely shredded low-sodium cheddar cheese

2 no-salt-added whole-wheat pita pockets

2 green-leaf lettuce leaves

4 thin slices tomato

Makes 2 servings
Prep time: 10 minutes
Cook time: 3 minutes
Serving size: 1 pita pocket
Each serving has:
288 calories
307.4 mg sodium
30.6 g protein
5.5 g total fat
2.6 g saturated fat
36.7 mg cholesterol
30.9 g carbohydrate
4.3 g dietary fiber
147.7 mg calcium
433.9 mg potassium

1. In a small, nonstick skillet over medium heat, heat lemon juice just until hot. Cook green onions for 1 to 2 minutes or until softened. Add tuna and cook for 1 to 2 minutes or until heated through. Remove from heat. Stir in yogurt, evenly coating tuna. Stir in cheese.

2. Line each pita pocket with 1 lettuce leaf. Spoon in tuna salad. Add 2 tomato slices to each pita pocket.

Salt Pitfall

Read those nutrition labels carefully! The tuna used in this recipe has 35 milligrams of sodium per serving, but the can lists the number of servings as 2½. The cheddar cheese that's labeled "low-sodium" has just 5 milligrams of sodium per ounce.

Salmon Swiss Melts with Avocado

Makes 2 servings
Prep time: 20 minutes
Cook time: 1 minute
Serving size: 1 English muffin half
Each serving has:
396 calories
317.5 mg sodium
34.8 g protein
19.9 g total fat
7.8 g saturated fat
85.4 mg cholesterol
21.2 g carbohydrate
5.4 g dietary fiber
637.6 mg calcium
634.1 mg potassium

1 (7.5-oz.) can no-salt-added pink salmon, drained

2 TB. finely diced green bell pepper

⅓ cup fat-free plain yogurt

1 whole-grain English muffin, split and toasted

1 lemon wedge

2 lengthwise slices avocado, halved

2 (1-oz.) slices low-sodium Swiss cheese

1. Preheat the broiler. Flake salmon flesh into a medium bowl, discarding any skin and bones. Stir in bell pepper and yogurt until evenly distributed. Spoon salmon mixture onto English muffin halves.

2. Rub lemon wedge over avocado slices to prevent discoloration. Place 2 avocado slice halves on each English muffin half, and top with cheese slices. Place sandwiches on a baking sheet, and broil for 1 to 2 minutes or until cheese is bubbly and melted.

Pinch of Sage

If you want a sandwich even lower in sodium, substitute the English muffin with 2 slices salt-free whole-wheat bread. Toast the bread and then follow the recipe as directed.

Big Beefy Burgers

1 lb. 85-percent-lean ground beef

½ small yellow onion, minced

¼ cup unsalted matzo meal

¼ cup no-salt-added tomato sauce

1½ tsp. salt-free garlic pepper blend

4 low-sodium whole-wheat rolls

Makes 4 servings
Prep time: 10 minutes
Cook time: 10 minutes
Serving size: 1 burger
Each serving has:
458.2 calories
387.5 mg sodium
27.8 g protein
20.2 g total fat
7.2 g saturated fat
77.1 mg cholesterol
41.9 g carbohydrate
5.3 g dietary fiber
89.8 mg calcium
594.1 mg potassium

1. In a medium bowl, combine ground beef, onion, matzo meal, tomato sauce, and garlic pepper blend. Mix well and form into 4 (4-inch) patties.

2. Preheat a double-sided indoor grill. Cook burgers for 10 minutes or until 160°F. Serve on rolls.

Salternative: If you prefer to prepare these burgers in the broiler, place patties on the rack of a broiler pan and broil for 6 to 8 minutes or until 160°F, turning burgers halfway through cooking time.

 Pinch of Sage

You can top your burger with your favorite additions—just be certain they aren't adding too much sodium. Use no-salt-added types of condiments, such as mustard and ketchup and any pickles or relish. If you make it a cheeseburger, choose a low-sodium slice.

Open-Face Cheese Steak Sandwiches

Makes 2 servings
Prep time: 8 minutes
Cook time: 12 minutes
Serving size: 1 sandwich
Each serving has:
555.3 calories
200.3 mg sodium
25.6 g protein
43.1 g total fat
17.2 g saturated fat
95.3 mg cholesterol
17.6 g carbohydrate
2.4 g dietary fiber
182.8 mg calcium
454 mg potassium

3 tsp. extra-light olive oil

1 small yellow onion, halved and sliced

½ lb. thin sandwich steak, trimmed of all visible fat

¼ tsp. freshly ground black pepper

¼ tsp. garlic powder

¼ tsp. onion powder

1 tsp. cornstarch

¼ cup fat-free milk

¼ cup finely shredded low-sodium cheddar cheese

1 whole-wheat hot dog bun, split and toasted

1. In a small skillet over medium heat, heat 1 teaspoon extra-light olive oil. Sauté onion for 5 minutes or until tender and golden. Remove from heat.

2. In a large, nonstick skillet over medium heat, heat remaining 2 teaspoons extra-light olive oil. Cut steak into 1-inch strips. Season steak with black pepper, garlic powder, and onion powder. Cook steak for 1½ minutes. Turn and cook other side for 1 minute or until done. Drain on a plate lined with paper towels.

3. In a small saucepan, whisk cornstarch into milk until blended. Heat over medium heat just until bubbles form around the edge of the pan. Reduce heat to low. Slowly whisk in cheese until melted and smooth. Remove from heat.

4. To assemble, pile steak onto each bun half. Top with onions, and pour cheese sauce over all.

Salternative: You can substitute thinly sliced beef sirloin or roast beef if you can't find thin sandwich steak, cooking it to 160°F to 170°F.

Pinch of Sage

If you purchase or prepare low-sodium sandwich buns—or better yet salt-free buns—feel free to enjoy this sandwich on a whole bun. Just be sure it falls within your daily dietary needs.

Broiled Cheese-Capped Salad Sandwiches

2 medium tomatoes, cored and chopped

1 large yellow onion, chopped

1 medium green bell pepper, seeds and ribs discarded, and chopped

1 medium red bell pepper, seeds and ribs discarded, and chopped

6 slices salt-free whole-wheat bread

2 tsp. extra-virgin olive oil

6 (1-oz.) slices low-sodium cheddar cheese

Makes 6 servings
Prep time: 15 minutes
Cook time: 3 minutes
Serving size: 1 sandwich
Each serving has:
226.9 calories
156.7 mg sodium
10.6 g protein
12.2 g total fat
6.4 g saturated fat
28.4 mg cholesterol
20.5 g carbohydrate
3.5 g dietary fiber
234.7 mg calcium
331.8 mg potassium

1. Preheat the broiler. In a large bowl, combine tomatoes, onion, green bell pepper, and red bell pepper.

2. Place bread slices on a baking sheet. Broil 4 to 6 inches from heat for 2 minutes or until bread is lightly toasted, watching carefully to avoid burning. Turn bread slices over.

3. Divide vegetable mixture evenly among bread slices. Lightly drizzle extra-virgin olive oil over vegetables. Top each sandwich with 1 cheese slice. Broil for 1 to 2 minutes or until cheese is melted.

Pinch of Sage

If you have trouble finding salt-free whole-wheat bread, substitute regular bread with the lowest sodium content possible. The open-face nature of this sandwich should help you stay within your sodium intake goals even with a slice of regular bread.

Classic Tomato Sandwich

Makes 1 serving
Prep time: 5 minutes
Cook time: 2 minutes
Serving size: 1 sandwich
Each serving has:
224 calories
301 mg sodium
6.5 g protein
8.6 g total fat
4.1 g saturated fat
15.5 mg cholesterol
32.9 g carbohydrate
4.9 g dietary fiber
62.6 mg calcium
504.6 mg potassium

2 slices salt-free whole-wheat bread

1½ tsp. unsalted butter

1 medium tomato, cored and thickly sliced

Pinch ground black pepper

1. Toast bread slices as desired. Spread ¾ teaspoon butter on each slice.

2. Place tomato slices on buttered side of 1 bread slice. Season with black pepper. Close sandwich, placing remaining bread slice butter-side down. Cut on the diagonal, if desired.

 Pinch of Sage

If you prefer, you may omit the black pepper. Or if you like your tomato sandwiches well seasoned, sprinkle on a salt-free salt substitute seasoning blend.

Part 4

The Meat of the Matter ... or Not

Perhaps the most repeated question, day in and day out, is "What's for dinner?" If you're new to cooking without salt or added sodium, you may dread the question each day. But you don't have to. The recipes in Part 4 give you a selection of dishes with a variety of ingredients encompassing a range of cooking times. Whether you need a fast-fix family meal or a dinner-party entrée, you'll find a recipe to prepare and savor.

Fish and seafood, poultry, beef, pork, and meatless main dishes give you the meals necessary to please your pickiest eaters, vary your dinner-time options, and keep your sodium intake at responsible levels. Moreover, the diversity of main dishes allows you to take advantage of each meal's nutrients and other health benefits. But most of your partakers will only care about the great taste. Ring the dinner bell, and watch them dig in!

Awash in Fish and Seafood

In This Chapter

- ◆ Purchasing fresh fish and seafood
- ◆ Cooking quick and nutritious meals
- ◆ Including omega-3 essential fatty acids in your diet
- ◆ Limiting certain fish

Fish and seafood are perfect for busy families because a meal from the ocean cooks up quickly. Plus, fish and seafood can carry a wide array of seasonings and flavors, so your family is sure to find a dish they savor.

You'll feel good, too, knowing you're serving your family a healthful dinner. Shellfish provide a lean protein that's low in fat and carbohydrates. The fat in oily, cold-water fish, like everyone's favorite salmon, serves up a healthful dose of omega-3 essential fatty acids. With all that going for you, what are you waiting for? Pick a recipe, and let's get cooking!

Buying the Best Catch

For the best flavor and convenience, purchase fresh fish and seafood that's properly iced or refrigerated. If you buy only from a reputable vendor, you're unlikely to see fish with a brown or yellowish discoloration or darkening around the edges—clues the fish isn't fresh. Also the flesh of a fresh fish should spring back when you press it. Don't buy fish that's soft or mushy. Finally, fresh fish and seafood smell mild and fresh with almost no odor. A fishy smell points to decomposition.

To maintain the freshness of your fish and seafood purchases, refrigerate or freeze your selections immediately when you get home. If you live any distance from the supermarket or fish market, if the weather is warm, or if you'll be storing your groceries in a hot car trunk, take along a cooler to pack your cold-storage food items in. Just be sure to separate your fish, poultry, and meats from each other and your other foods—just as you did in your shopping cart.

Cook fresh fish and seafood within a day or two. If you won't be using it in that time span, place it in the freezer, properly packaged against freezer burn. Airtight packages of heavy aluminum foil, plastic freezer wrap, and plastic freezer bags will keep your fish and seafood protected for 4 to 6 months in the freezer. Fish that was previously frozen must be identified at the supermarket or fish market. Plan on cooking any such purchases in a day or two as they should not be refrozen.

Preparation Pointers

When you prepare fish and seafood, remember to follow all safe-handling rules. Use separate utensils, dishes, and cutting boards for raw fish and seafood. Wash your hands in warm, soapy water before and after handling it. Thaw frozen fish and seafood in the refrigerator overnight. If you're in a pinch, you can thaw it in the microwave just until it's icy and malleable; then cook it immediately.

> **Salt Pitfall**
>
> Overcooking fish and seafood results in a rubbery, chewy texture, so be sure to stop cooking as soon as it's opaque.

Fish and seafood are great choices for fast meals as they typically cook in just 5 to 20 minutes. When baking or broiling, plan on cooking for a total of 10 minutes per inch of thickness. You can tell fish and seafood are thoroughly cooked when the flesh turns opaque. Fin fish will also flake easily with a fork.

> **Lo-So Lingo**
>
> **Essential fatty acids** are a type of polyunsaturated fat your body gets from foods. Your body is not able to make such fatty acids itself.

Fishing for Good Health

Oily, cold-water fish such as salmon, lake trout, tuna, herring, sardines, and mackerel contain omega-3 *essential fatty acids*. Because your body cannot make this type of polyunsaturated fat itself, you need to get it from food sources to enjoy its benefits. Research indicates that omega-3 fatty acids may promote heart health, protect against some cancers, ease depression, and facilitate improvement of some autoimmune disorders.

With the high praises of fish as a nutritional boon come the cautions of contamination. Some fish have been found to contain high levels of mercury. Therefore, it's recommended that you limit swordfish, shark, king mackerel, and tilefish to just one serving a month (for healthy adults). Check with your local extension office for up-to-date advisories as well as local fish-eating guidelines.

Tilapia Florentine

<table>
<tr><td>

Makes 4 servings

Prep time: 15 minutes

Cook time: 20 minutes

Serving size: 1 casserole

Each serving has:

179.5 calories

128 mg sodium

21.2 g protein

7.7 g total fat

1.1 g saturated fat

38 mg cholesterol

6.1 g carbohydrate

1.1 g dietary fiber

119.3 mg calcium

696.3 mg potassium

</td></tr>
</table>

2 TB. extra-virgin olive oil

4 cups packed, washed, and stemmed spinach leaves

2 green onions, trimmed and thinly sliced

½ tsp. dried marjoram

1 TB. grated lemon zest

4 (3.5-oz.) tilapia fillets, rinsed and patted dry with paper towels

1 TB. all-purpose flour

1 cup fat-free milk, divided

⅛ tsp. freshly ground black pepper

1 lemon, thinly sliced

1. Preheat the oven to 400°F. Spray 4 individual glassware casserole dishes with nonstick cooking spray.

2. In a large skillet, heat extra-virgin olive oil over medium heat. Add spinach and green onions. Sauté for 3 minutes or until spinach is wilted. Divide spinach mixture among prepared dishes, and sprinkle on marjoram and lemon zest. Place tilapia fillets on top.

3. Stir flour into ¼ cup milk. Heat remaining milk in a small saucepan over medium heat and then stir in flour mixture. Cook and stir for 3 minutes or until thickened. Stir in black pepper and pour milk sauce over fillets. Arrange lemon slices over fillets. Bake for 20 minutes or until lightly browned and bubbly.

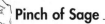

Pinch of Sage

These single-serving casseroles make a nice presentation for guests. If you don't have individual casserole dishes, bake this recipe in an 8×8×2-inch or 9×9×2-inch baking dish, alternating head-to-tail placement to fit.

Family-Pleasing Paprika-Tinged Grouper

2 TB. unsalted butter, melted

½ TB. fresh lemon juice

½ tsp. dried parsley flakes

¼ tsp. garlic powder

¼ tsp. ground white pepper

¼ tsp. paprika

1 lb. grouper fillets, rinsed and patted dry with paper towels

Makes 4 servings
Prep time: 10 minutes
Cook time: 12 minutes
Serving size: 4 ounces fish
Each serving has:
157.5 calories
61.7 mg sodium
22.1 g protein
6.9 g total fat
3.9 g saturated fat
57.5 mg cholesterol
0.5 g carbohydrate
0.1 g dietary fiber
34.6 mg calcium
557 mg potassium

1. Preheat the oven to 350°F. Position the oven rack in the upper-middle position. Cover the rack of a broiler pan with foil.

2. In a small bowl, combine butter and lemon juice. Brush about ½ tablespoon lemon-butter mixture onto the foil where fillets will be.

3. In another small bowl, combine parsley flakes, garlic powder, white pepper, and paprika. Sprinkle half on undersides of fillets. Place fillets seasoned side down on the prepared foil. Sprinkle remaining seasoning mixture over tops of fillets.

4. Bake for 12 minutes or until fish flakes easily with a fork. Brush remaining butter mixture over fillets.

 Pinch of Sage

Be sure to cover the broiler rack completely with foil, shaping it to the pan. Then you can just toss the foil—no pan scrubbing!

Lemon Cod Pockets

Makes 4 servings
Prep time: 15 minutes
Cook time: 10 minutes
Serving size: 1 pocket
Each serving has:
129.9 calories
75.3 mg sodium
18.6 g protein
4.6 g total fat
2.5 g saturated fat
47.1 mg cholesterol
3.2 g carbohydrate
1.1 g dietary fiber
26.7 mg calcium
509.7 mg potassium

4 tsp. unsalted butter

4 (4-oz.) fillets cod loin, rinsed and patted dry with paper towels

¼ tsp. freshly ground black pepper

1 lemon, sliced and seeded

1 red bell pepper, seeds and ribs discarded, and thinly sliced

4 green onions, trimmed and coarsely chopped

1 tsp. dried dill weed

1. Preheat the oven to 400°F. Place 1 teaspoon butter in the center of each of 4 large sheets of nonstick foil. Place 1 fillet on top of butter. Season fillets with black pepper, and lay lemon slices atop each fillet. Scatter red bell pepper and green onions over top. Season all with dill weed. Close foil pockets, double-sealing seams.

2. Bake for 10 to 12 minutes or until fish flakes easily with a fork.

Skillet-Sizzled Sea Scallops

Makes 4 servings
Prep time: 5 minutes
Cook time: 7 minutes
Serving size: 4 ounces scallops
Each serving has:
231.3 calories
185.2 mg sodium
19.3 g protein
15.3 g total fat
9.1 g saturated fat
76.2 mg cholesterol
3.8 g carbohydrate
0.1 g dietary fiber
35.6 mg calcium
389.6 mg potassium

5 TB. unsalted butter

1 lb. sea scallops, rinsed and patted dry with paper towels

2 cloves garlic, minced

Juice of ½ lemon

2 tsp. chopped fresh parsley

¼ tsp. paprika

1. Melt butter in a large, nonstick skillet over medium to medium-low heat. Add scallops and garlic, and cook for 4 to 5 minutes without moving scallops. Turn. Drizzle lemon juice over tops. Cook for 3 to 4 minutes or until just opaque.

2. Remove scallops to a serving platter. Sprinkle parsley and paprika over top.

 **Pinch of Sage**

Choose sea scallops that are ivory-colored or a pink-hued beige. Bright white scallops have been processed to extend their shelf-life. Avoid these, as you won't be able to brown them.

Hot and Sweet Mustard-Crusted Salmon

1 lb. skin-on salmon, rinsed
and patted dry with paper
towels

1 TB. dry mustard

1 TB. granulated sugar

1 tsp. water

¼ tsp. dried dill weed

Makes 4 servings	
Prep time: 5 minutes	
Cook time: 11 minutes	
Serving size: 4 ounces fish	
Each serving has:	
247.2 calories	
58.1 mg sodium	
25.5 g protein	
13.7 g total fat	
3.1 g saturated fat	
81.9 mg cholesterol	
3.6 g carbohydrate	
0.1 g dietary fiber	
33.1 mg calcium	
488.9 mg potassium	

1. Preheat the broiler, and spray the rack of a broiler pan with nonstick cooking spray. Place salmon skin side down on the rack. Broil 4 to 6 inches from heat for 10 minutes per inch of thickness or until salmon flakes easily with a fork.

2. Meanwhile, combine dry mustard, sugar, and water in a small bowl. Stir until thick paste forms and then stir in dill weed. Spread mixture evenly over top of salmon. Return to broiler, and broil for 1 minute or until browned and bubbly.

Pinch of Sage

To serve skin-on salmon, cut through the salmon down to, but not through, the skin for each serving. Slide a spatula between the skin and the flesh to remove each piece.

Chinese-Style Shrimp Pasta Primavera

Makes 4 servings
Prep time: 15 minutes
Cook time: 15 minutes
Serving size: 2 ounces pasta with 1 cup shrimp-vegetable mixture
Each serving has:
429.8 calories
189.5 mg sodium
27.6 g protein
10.1 g total fat
1.8 g saturated fat
0.5 mg cholesterol
57.3 g carbohydrate
3.7 g dietary fiber
82.4 mg calcium
426.7 mg potassium

8 oz. mini penne or other medium pasta

2 TB. extra-virgin olive oil

1 medium yellow onion, cut into thin wedges

3 cloves garlic, minced

½ cup *julienne-cut* carrots

½ cup trimmed Chinese snow peas (diagonally sliced if large)

1 medium red bell pepper, seeds and ribs discarded, and cut into thin strips

2 TB. lemon juice

1 TB. grated fresh ginger

⅛ tsp. crushed red pepper flakes

3 TB. cornstarch

1 (14.5-oz.) can light, fat-free chicken broth (50-percent-reduced sodium)

12 oz. peeled, deveined, cooked or uncoooked medium shrimp (about 34)

Lo-So Lingo

Julienne-cut is a technique of preparing a food, usually a vegetable, by slicing it into thin, matchstick-like pieces.

1. Cook pasta according to package directions (omitting salt) and drain.

2. In a 2-quart microwave-safe casserole dish, combine extra-virgin olive oil, onion, garlic, carrots, snow peas, red bell pepper, lemon juice, ginger, and crushed red pepper flakes. Cover, venting, and cook on high power for 3 minutes or until vegetables are tender-crisp, stirring halfway through cooking time.

3. Meanwhile, whisk cornstarch into chicken broth in a small bowl. Stir into vegetable mixture. Cover, venting, and cook on high power for 4 to 5 minutes or until sauce is a little thickened, stirring halfway through cooking time.

4. Stir shrimp into mixture. Cover, venting, and cook on high power for 1½ to 2 minutes or until heated through, stirring halfway through cooking time. Let stand for 2 minutes before serving over pasta.

Italian Shrimp Fettuccini

12 oz. fettuccini

1 lb. peeled, deveined, cooked medium shrimp

½ cup water

1 (10-oz.) pkg. frozen chopped spinach

2 TB. plus 1 tsp. extra-virgin olive oil

¼ cup fresh lemon juice

4 cloves garlic, minced

1 tsp. dried basil

¼ tsp. freshly ground black pepper

1 (14.5-oz.) can no-salt-added diced tomatoes, undrained

Makes 6 servings
Prep time: 5 minutes
Cook time: 25 minutes
Serving size: 2 ounces pasta with 1 cup sauce
Each serving has:
363.8 calories
206.5 mg sodium
24.9 g protein
7.4 g total fat
1.2 g saturated fat
114.9 mg cholesterol
49.6 g carbohydrate
4.2 g dietary fiber
103.6 mg calcium
251.3 mg potassium

1. Cook fettuccini according to package directions (omitting salt) and drain.

2. Finely chop 2 shrimp, and add to a small, microwave-safe bowl with water. Cook, uncovered, on high power for 1 minute to make a broth.

3. Unwrap frozen spinach. Place the package in the microwave on a microwave-safe plate, and cook on high for 3 minutes.

4. In a medium bowl, combine remaining shrimp, 2 tablespoons extra-virgin olive oil, lemon juice, garlic, basil, and black pepper.

5. In a 12-inch nonstick skillet over medium heat, heat remaining 1 teaspoon extra-virgin olive oil. Add spinach, tomatoes, and shrimp broth. Increase heat to high. Cook and stir for 2 minutes or until boiling. Add shrimp mixture. Cook for 2 minutes or until heated through.

6. To serve, line plates with fettuccini. Spoon sauce over top.

Pinch of Sage

Try to find fresh cooked shrimp or purchase fresh shrimp and cook it yourself. You can use frozen cooked shrimp, but salt is added to frozen shrimp during processing.

Veggie-Lover's Crunchy Tuna Noodle Casserole

Makes 4 servings
Prep time: 25 minutes
Cook time: 15 minutes
Serving size: 1½ cups
Each serving has:
361 calories
67.1 mg sodium
20 g protein
12.1 g total fat
5.1 g saturated fat
60.1 mg cholesterol
42.8 g carbohydrate
3.7 g dietary fiber
122.6 mg calcium
363.1 mg potassium

Pinch of Sage

An easy way to crush the tortilla chips—and take out your frustration—is to close the chips in a resealable plastic bag and pound them with the flat side of a meat mallet or a rolling pin.

4 cups uncooked wide egg noodles

2 TB. unsalted butter

1 small yellow onion, diced

1 clove garlic, minced

¼ cup diced red bell pepper

¼ cup diced green bell pepper

¼ cup diced carrots

1 TB. all-purpose flour

1 cup fat-free milk

1 tsp. Salt-Shaker Substitute (recipe in Chapter 26) or other salt-free salt substitute seasoning blend

¼ tsp. freshly ground black pepper

½ cup drained no-salt-added canned peas

1 (6-oz.) can very low-sodium albacore tuna packed in water, drained and flaked

½ cup crushed unsalted tortilla chips

1. Preheat the oven to 350°F. Spray a 1½-quart glassware casserole dish with nonstick cooking spray.

2. Cook egg noodles according to package directions (omitting salt) and drain.

3. Melt 1 tablespoon butter in a large, nonstick skillet. Sauté onion, garlic, red bell pepper, green bell pepper, and carrots for 5 minutes or until softened.

4. In a small saucepan over medium heat, melt remaining 1 tablespoon butter. Whisk in flour. When smooth and bubbly, gradually whisk in milk. Bring to a simmer over medium heat. Simmer and whisk for 1 to 2 minutes or until slightly thickened. Turn off heat, and stir in Salt-Shaker Substitute and pepper. Add onion mixture. Stir in peas, tuna, and egg noodles. Stir until combined.

5. Turn mixture into the prepared casserole dish. Sprinkle tortilla chip crumbs on top, and bake for 15 to 20 minutes or until browned and heated through.

Pick of the Poultry

In This Chapter

- Taking advantage of poultry's adaptable taste
- Making healthful choices
- Using safe-handling methods
- Creating tasty and diverse meals

Poultry is a perpetual palate-pleaser with tender, juicy, meaty portions many of your family and guests alike will welcome. Plus, its ease of preparation, as well as the variations it allows—baked, broiled, grilled, roasted, sautéed, oven-fried, and so on—make it a kitchen favorite.

Poultry such as chicken, turkey, and Cornish game hens offers a mild flavor that acts as a blank slate for seasonings and other flavors and works equally well with savory or sweet. Even if you serve poultry frequently, you'll find a wide array of tastes to keep your appetite piqued. Plus poultry's a snap to prepare with as little sodium as possible.

Get ready to shake the old salt-and-pepper routine! The recipes in this chapter take you on a flavorful poultry adventure.

All Parts Are Not Created Equal

Wings, thighs, drumsticks, breasts, tenderloins, whole birds, and more. Bone-in, boneless. Skin-on, skinless. A quick scan of your supermarket's refrigerated poultry section, not to mention the freezer section, reveals just how many poultry choices you have. All parts provide complete protein with a limited amount of saturated fat.

If you're looking for a lean protein source, pick up a package of skinless breast meat. You'll save 12 milligrams sodium choosing boneless, skinless breast meat over the same serving size of dark meat from a broiler/fryer (63 milligrams vs. 75 milligrams). The difference is greater in a stewing chicken, with the dark meat containing nearly twice as much sodium as the light meat.

Pinch of Sage

A serving size of poultry is 3 ounces, which is about the size of a deck of cards. Chicken breast halves packaged in the supermarket are often heavier, though. After cooking, you might want to divide them into appropriate portions. If you do eat a larger chicken breast half, be sure to calculate the additional sodium, as well as calories, protein, fat, and so on.

No matter what your poultry-part preference, pass on the skin and deep-frying. You don't need either to prepare a well-seasoned poultry dish. Because you're flavoring without shaking on salt or other high-sodium seasonings and sauces, the skinless pieces allow those tastes to come through even better.

Skin-on birds, such as Cornish game hens and young chickens, and parts, such as thighs and drumsticks, may be your only options in your store's poultry section. So remove the skin before cooking or discard it before serving. Cooking poultry with the skin on doesn't add any fat to the meat, but it does hold in the juices for better flavor. Just peel away the skin before serving. If a recipe calls for removing the skin prior to cooking, do so before boning the poultry to make the job easier.

Better Safe Than Sorry

Thinking about all the delicious, low-sodium poultry dishes you can create may make you want to toss a few choice packages into your shopping cart. Stop! Poultry may be nearly perfect, but it does associate with some nasty bacteria. You must take care when handling it.

In the store, keep any raw juices from contaminating your hands or other groceries. Use the plastic disposable bags available at supermarkets to enclose your poultry picks. (Take a few from the produce section, if necessary.) Slip your hand into the bag wrong side out. Choose your poultry, turning the bag right side out over the package. Hit the checkout next and make a beeline for your house, storing your purchases in the refrigerator or freezer ASAP.

Thawing poultry in the refrigerator or microwave is easy. Allow 3 to 4 hours per pound for defrosting a whole bird in the refrigerator; parts require less time. Follow the manufacturer's directions for your microwave, and cook the poultry immediately. You may also thaw waterproof packages by submerging them in cold water, but you have to change the water every 30 minutes to keep it cold.

While preparing poultry, wash your hands every time before you touch something else. Using separate utensils, cutting boards, dishes, and pans for raw poultry also keeps cross-contamination at bay.

Cook your birds until the juices run clear, and check the internal temperature with a thermometer. (See the following table for suggested temperatures.)

Temperature Guidelines

Poultry Type	Recommended Temperature
All whole chickens or turkeys	180°F
Thighs, wings, or legs	180°F
Breasts or roasts	170°F
Ground chicken or turkey	165°F

Saucy Orange Chicken over Angel Hair

Makes 4 servings
Prep time: 20 minutes
Cook time: 35 minutes
Serving size: ½ cup pasta with 1 chicken breast half and ¼ sauce

Each serving has:
271 calories
99.6 mg sodium
21.8 g protein
2.8 g total fat
0.7 g saturated fat
47 mg cholesterol
39.2 g carbohydrate
2.7 g dietary fiber
45.5 mg calcium
429.1 mg potassium

4 (3-oz.) boneless, skinless chicken breast halves, trimmed, rinsed and patted dry with paper towels

1 cup unsweetened orange juice

1 tsp. *lite soy sauce*

2 TB. light brown sugar

½ tsp. ground dry mustard

¼ tsp. ground ginger

1 tsp. dried basil

1 TB. grated orange zest

½ cup sliced green onions (about 4)

½ large green bell pepper, seeds and ribs discarded, and cut into thin strips

½ large red bell pepper, seeds and ribs discarded, and cut into thin strips

1 TB. cornstarch

2 TB. fresh lemon juice

2 cups cooked angel hair pasta

1. Preheat the oven to 350°F. Lightly spray the bottom of a 13×9×2-inch glassware baking dish with nonstick cooking spray. Arrange chicken breast halves in the prepared dish.

2. Measure orange juice into a 2-cup measuring cup. Add lite soy sauce. Whisk in light brown sugar, dry mustard, ginger, basil, and orange zest until well combined. Pour over chicken.

3. Scatter green onions, green bell peppers, and red bell peppers over chicken. Cover the dish tightly with foil, and bake for 30 minutes or until chicken is cooked through, no longer pink, and the juices run clear.

4. In a small bowl, whisk together cornstarch and lemon juice, and stir into sauce around chicken. Bake for 5 minutes more or until sauce thickens slightly.

5. To serve, mound cooked pasta on a serving platter and arrange chicken on top. Scatter some onions and peppers over chicken, and spoon some sauce over all. Serve remaining sauce on the side.

Salternative: If you can afford the added sodium, this dish is also nice served over a bed of rice noodles. The sodium content varies among brands, so check the nutrition labels.

Lo-So Lingo

Lite soy sauce is lower in sodium than regular soy sauce. If you have regular soy sauce, substitute a mixture of ½ regular soy sauce and ½ water for the lite soy sauce. Depending on the brand, you may save on some sodium using this replacement.

Stovetop Cranberry Chicken

⅓ cup whole-wheat flour

¼ tsp. freshly ground black pepper

4 (3-oz.) boneless, skinless chicken breast halves, trimmed, rinsed and patted dry with paper towels

1½ TB. extra-light olive oil

1 cup water

1 cup fresh or frozen cranberries

½ cup firmly packed light brown sugar

Dash nutmeg

1 TB. red wine vinegar

2 cups cooked long-grain brown rice

Makes 4 servings
Prep time: 10 minutes
Cook time: 35 minutes
Serving size: ½ cup rice with 1 chicken breast half and ¼ sauce
Each serving has:
403 calories
57.2 mg sodium
21.4 g protein
8.1 g total fat
1.4 g saturated fat
47 mg cholesterol
60.8 g carbohydrate
4.1 g dietary fiber
42.7 mg calcium
280.5 mg potassium

1. In a shallow dish, stir together whole-wheat flour and black pepper. *Dredge* chicken in seasoned flour, coating it completely.

2. In a large, deep skillet, heat extra-light olive oil over medium heat. Brown chicken on both sides, remove from the skillet and keep warm.

3. Remove the skillet from heat. Pour in water and cranberries, and return to heat. Stir in light brown sugar, nutmeg, and red wine vinegar. Cook, stirring often, for 5 minutes or until cranberries burst. Return chicken to the skillet.

4. Reduce heat, cover, and simmer for 20 minutes or until chicken is cooked through, no longer pink, and the juices run clear. Serve each chicken breast half on a bed of rice, spooning sauce over all.

Salternative: If you're short on time or haven't cooked the rice ahead of time, substitute instant brown rice. Remember that instant rices contain some sodium, though, ranging from 5 to 20 milligrams.

Lo-So Lingo

Dredge is the motion of moving a moist or moistened food through a dry substance, such as seasoned flour, to coat the food.

Plum Delicious Chicken

Makes 4 servings
Prep time: 15 minutes
Cook time: 25 minutes
Serving size: 1 chicken breast half with about ⅓ cup sauce
Each serving has:
157 calories
43.8 mg sodium
17.8 g protein
2.1 g total fat
0.6 g saturated fat
47 mg cholesterol
17.4 g carbohydrate
2.3 g dietary fiber
22.7 mg calcium
288.7 mg potassium

4 (3-oz.) boneless, skinless chicken breast halves, trimmed, rinsed and patted dry with paper towels

½ cup heavy syrup from ready-to-serve prunes

½ tsp. ground ginger

3 cloves garlic, minced

1 TB. fresh lemon juice

¾ cup ready-to-serve prunes, pitted and quartered (about 12 to 14)

1. Preheat the oven to 350°F, and lightly spray a 2-quart glassware baking dish with nonstick cooking spray. Arrange chicken in the prepared dish.

2. Pour heavy syrup into a small bowl. Stir in ginger, add garlic and lemon juice, and then add prunes. Pour sauce over chicken, cover, and bake for 25 minutes or until cooked through, no longer pink, and the juices run clear.

 Pinch of Sage _____

If you can't get fresh lemons, use bottled lemon juice, although the flavor of fresh lemon juice is superior. Because you're depending on flavorings other than salt, you might consider keeping fresh lemons on hand.

Tropical Chicken for Two

2 (3-oz.) boneless, skinless chicken breast halves, trimmed, rinsed and patted dry with paper towels

¼ tsp. dried oregano

⅛ tsp. ground cinnamon

1 TB. extra-light olive oil

¾ cup pineapple juice

1 TB. fresh lime juice

1 tsp. cornstarch

1 tsp. dried parsley flakes

Makes 2 servings
Prep time: 10 minutes
Cook time: 15 minutes
Serving size: 1 chicken breast half with ½ sauce
Each serving has:
208 calories
45.6 mg sodium
17.3 g protein
8.8 g total fat
1.5 g saturated fat
47 mg cholesterol
13.5 g carbohydrate
0.3 g dietary fiber
16 mg calcium
275.7 mg potassium

1. Place chicken between 2 sheets of waxed paper. Pound to a ½-inch thickness using the flat side of a meat mallet or a rolling pin. Sprinkle ½ oregano and ½ cinnamon over chicken.

2. Heat extra-light olive oil in a 12-inch skillet over medium heat. Add chicken, seasoned side down. Sprinkle remaining oregano and cinnamon over chicken. Cook for 5 minutes; turn and cook other side for 5 minutes or until cooked through, no longer pink, and the juices run clear. Remove chicken to a serving platter.

3. In a small bowl, stir together pineapple juice, lime juice, and cornstarch. Pour into the skillet, and bring to a boil over medium to medium-high heat. Stir almost constantly until thickened. Stir in parsley flakes. Spoon sauce over chicken to serve.

Pinch of Sage

Fresh herbs do nicely as substitutions for salt. If a recipe calls for 1 teaspoon of a dried herb, use 1 tablespoon fresh. Drying decreases the volume of the herb, so you need more fresh herb to get the same flavor. In this recipe, substitute ¾ teaspoon chopped fresh oregano and 1 tablespoon chopped fresh parsley.

Savory Chicken with Green Beans and Mushrooms

Makes 4 servings
Prep time: 10 minutes
Cook time: 50 minutes
Serving size: 1 chicken breast half with 1 cup vegetables
Each serving has:
271 calories
174 mg sodium
21.9 g protein
12.5 g total fat
2 g saturated fat
47 mg cholesterol
17.5 g carbohydrate
5 g dietary fiber
71.1 mg calcium
356.5 mg potassium

⅓ cup whole-wheat flour

½ tsp. dried rubbed sage

½ tsp. dried thyme

4 (3-oz.) boneless, skinless chicken breast halves, trimmed, rinsed and patted dry with paper towels

3 TB. extra-light olive oil

¾ tsp. ground cloves

8 oz. sliced button mushrooms

1 (16-oz.) pkg. frozen cut green beans, thawed and drained

1. Preheat the oven to 400°F, and lightly spray the bottom of a 9×9×2-inch glassware baking dish with nonstick cooking spray.

2. In a shallow bowl, stir together whole-wheat flour, sage, and thyme. Dredge chicken in seasoned flour to coat completely.

3. In a large skillet over medium heat, heat 2 tablespoons extra-light olive oil. Brown chicken on both sides. Transfer chicken to the prepared dish. Lightly sprinkle cloves over chicken.

4. In a medium skillet, heat remaining 1 tablespoon olive oil over medium-low heat. Sauté mushrooms for 5 minutes or until colored.

5. In the same large skillet, sauté green beans, dusting with any remaining seasoned flour. Cook for 3 minutes. Stir in mushrooms. Spoon green beans and mushrooms over chicken. Cover and bake for 30 to 40 minutes or until chicken is cooked through, no longer pink, and the juices run clear and sauce is formed.

Pinch of Sage

Fresh or thawed chicken breast halves can sometimes be difficult to trim with a knife. Using your fingers to grasp and pull off the fat deposits may be easier. Just be certain to wash your hands thoroughly—before and especially after.

Family-Pleasing Oven-Fried Chicken

¼ cup whole-wheat flour

1 tsp. dried thyme

¾ tsp. Salt-Shaker Substitute (recipe in Chapter 26)

½ tsp. freshly ground black pepper

½ tsp. dried oregano

¼ tsp. garlic powder

⅛ tsp. dried crushed rosemary

⅛ tsp. paprika

2 TB. fat-free milk

4 (3-oz.) boneless, skinless chicken breast halves, trimmed, rinsed and patted dry with paper towels

Nonstick cooking spray

Makes 4 servings
Prep time: 15 minutes
Cook time: 20 minutes
Serving size: 1 chicken breast half

Each serving has:
129 calories
45.4 mg sodium
18.9 g protein
2.2 g total fat
0.6 g saturated fat
47.1 mg cholesterol
7.3 g carbohydrate
1.4 g dietary fiber
31.5 mg calcium
168.9 mg potassium

1. Adjust the oven rack to the upper-middle position, and preheat the oven to 400°F. Line a baking sheet with foil, place a wire rack on the baking sheet, and spray it with nonstick cooking spray.

2. In a shallow dish, combine whole-wheat flour, thyme, Salt-Shaker Substitute, black pepper, oregano, garlic powder, rosemary, and paprika, and stir to blend well. Pour milk into another shallow dish.

3. Dip each chicken breast half into milk, allowing excess to drip off; then dredge in seasoned flour, coating completely and gently shaking off excess. Place chicken upside down on rack. Spray undersides of chicken with nonstick cooking spray, turn, and spray tops, coating completely. Bake for 20 to 25 minutes or until cooked through, no longer pink, and the juices run clear.

Salternative: Use your favorite savory salt-free seasoning blend instead of the Salt-Shaker Substitute, if you prefer.

Pinch of Sage

When Herbert Hoover used the phrase "a chicken in every pot" during his 1928 presidential campaign, he promised prosperity and well-being. Beyond being a healthful choice, chicken, as well as turkey, is an economical option.

Grilled Asian-Spiced Chicken Thighs

Makes 6 servings

Prep time: 15 minutes

Chill time: 30 minutes

Cook time: 10 minutes

Serving size: 2 chicken thighs

Each serving has:

237 calories

91 mg sodium

26.5 g protein

11.2 g total fat

3.1 g saturated fat

96.6 mg cholesterol

6.2 g carbohydrate

0.2 g dietary fiber

15.2 mg calcium

256.7 mg potassium

3 lb. chicken thighs, skinned and boned, rinsed and patted dry with paper towels

2 TB. Asian-Inspired Spice Blend (recipe in Chapter 26)

2 TB. honey

1. Wash chicken and pat dry with paper towels.

2. In a shallow bowl, combine Asian-Inspired Spice Blend and honey, mixing thoroughly. Lightly coat chicken by "dredging" meat on both sides in honey mixture. Arrange chicken on a baking sheet or tray. Marinate in the refrigerator for at least 30 minutes.

3. Generously coat the grill rack with nonstick spray. Heat grill to high. Arrange chicken on rack, cover, and grill for 10 minutes or until cooked through, no longer pink, and the juices run clear, turning and rotating after 5 minutes.

 Pinch of Sage

Never marinate meat on the kitchen counter. Dangerous bacteria can multiply quickly at room temperature. Always marinate meat in the refrigerator.

Turkey Medallions with Sun-Dried Tomatoes and Green Onions

½ cup sun-dried tomatoes (not packed in olive oil)

Hot water

1½ lb. turkey breast tenderloins, rinsed and patted dry with paper towels

¼ tsp. ground white pepper

2 TB. extra-light olive oil

½ cup chopped green onions

Makes 6 servings
Prep time: 20 minutes
Cook time: 10 minutes
Serving size: 4 ounces turkey with ¼ cup sauce
Each serving has:
174 calories
156.8 mg sodium
27 g protein
6.2 g total fat
1.1 g saturated fat
55.6 mg cholesterol
3.2 g carbohydrate
1 g dietary fiber
5.4 mg calcium
177.6 mg potassium

1. Pack sun-dried tomatoes in a 1-cup measuring cup. Pour enough hot water over tomatoes to fill the measuring cup, and then let tomatoes stand for at least 10 minutes or until softened. Slice tomatoes, reserving liquid.

2. Slice turkey into ¾-inch-thick medallions. Season with white pepper.

3. Heat extra-light olive oil in a large skillet over medium to medium-high heat. Sauté turkey medallions for 3 minutes on each side or until cooked through, no longer pink, and the juices run clear. With a slotted spatula, remove medallions to a plate lined with paper towels and blot dry. Reduce heat to medium-low.

4. In the same skillet, sauté green onions for 1 minute. Add tomatoes and reserved liquid, and cook for 2 to 3 minutes or until heated through.

5. To serve, transfer medallions to a serving platter, and spoon sauce over top.

 Pinch of Sage

Cooking the turkey medallions on medium-high heat seals in the juices for a flavorful meal. However, sauté-ing at this temperature will create splattering. Put the skillet on a back burner, use a spatter guard if you have one, and wear an oven mitt to prevent burns while turning the turkey.

Creamy Dilled Turkey Cutlets with Vegetables

Makes 4 servings
Prep time: 5 minutes
Cook time: 15 minutes
Serving size: 4 ounces turkey with ½ cup sauce
Each serving has:
186 calories
160.4 mg sodium
32.1 g protein
2.3 g total fat
0.2 g saturated fat
46.3 mg cholesterol
9.6 g carbohydrate
1.6 g dietary fiber
98.4 mg calcium
13.2 mg potassium

Pinch of Sage

Keep in mind that frozen peas are processed with salt and are, therefore, significantly higher in sodium than other frozen vegetables.

½ TB. extra-light olive oil

1 lb. turkey cutlets, rinsed and patted dry with paper towels

1 tsp. dried dill weed

½ tsp. Salt-Shaker Substitute (recipe in Chapter 26) or other savory salt substitute

¼ tsp. freshly ground black pepper

1 cup frozen broccoli florets

½ cup frozen corn kernels

½ cup frozen cut spinach

1 cup fat-free plain yogurt

1. In a large skillet over medium heat, heat extra-light olive oil. Sauté turkey for 3 minutes. Turn and sauté on other side for 2 minutes while sprinkling on dill weed, Salt-Shaker Substitute, and black pepper.

2. Add broccoli, corn, and spinach. Cover and cook for 6 minutes or until vegetables are tender and turkey is cooked through, no longer pink, and the juices run clear.

3. Remove the skillet from heat. Stir in yogurt, blending well. Return to low heat, cover, and cook for 2 minutes or until heated through. (Do not boil.)

Salternative: You can substitute 2 cups of your favorite plain frozen veggies in this recipe.

Tasty Turkey-Stuffed Peppers

2 large green bell peppers, seeds and ribs discarded, and halved lengthwise

1 lb. ground turkey breast or ground turkey

½ cup uncooked instant brown rice

1 (8-oz.) can no-salt-added tomato sauce

½ cup finely grated carrots

¼ cup diced onions

2 cloves garlic, minced

3 TB. chopped fresh parsley

1 tsp. dried oregano

½ tsp. Salt-Shaker Substitute (recipe in Chapter 26) or other salt-free salt substitute seasoning blend

½ tsp. freshly ground black pepper

Makes 4 servings
Prep time: 15 minutes
Cook time: 55 minutes
Serving size: 1 bell pepper half
Each serving has:
249 calories
110 mg sodium
24.3 g protein
7.7 g total fat
2.1 g saturated fat
65 mg cholesterol
21 g carbohydrate
3.4 g dietary fiber
28.4 mg calcium
249.7 mg potassium

1. Preheat the oven to 350°F, and lightly spray the bottom of a 2-quart glassware baking dish with nonstick cooking spray. Place green bell pepper halves in the prepared dish.

2. In a medium bowl, combine ground turkey breast, instant brown rice, tomato sauce, carrots, onions, garlic, parsley, oregano, Salt-Shaker Substitute, and black pepper. Mix well. Spoon mixture into green bell pepper halves. Cover with nonstick foil, and bake for 55 to 60 minutes or until cooked through and no longer pink.

Pinch of Sage

If you have only regular foil, lightly spray the sheet with nonstick cooking spray and place it sprayed side down over the baking dish.

Big Beef and Prime Pork

In This Chapter

- ◆ Keeping your kitchen safe
- ◆ Making meats a healthful choice
- ◆ Cooking low-sodium red meat favorites

Many families expect to find meat on their dinner plates most nights when they come to the table. So you may have found yourself staring at a package of ground beef, wondering how to prepare it now that your doctor or nutritionist has advised against picking up the salt shaker. The good news is that the bold flavor of beef and pork can deliciously take on thick, rich, deep flavors that satisfy—without sodium.

With just a few substitutions and hints, you can put the meat back on the dinner table. Take your pick from an array of cuts to fit a variety of budgets and any number of occasions. Use the recipes in this chapter to get you started, and take the secrets back to your family-favorite recipes.

Safe at Home

You've brought home your meat selections, wrapped in plastic bags to avoid cross-contamination. You've immediately stored them on the lowest shelf of your refrigerator, below any foods to be served raw so in case the meat drips, the liquid won't affect any raw foods in your refrigerator.

When the time comes to cook your beef or pork (within 3 to 4 days), you use separate cutting boards, utensils, and dishes for the raw meat, and you wash your hands before and after handling the meat. You've done everything to make the meal safe, right?

So far, yes, you have. But you're not done. When you think you're finished cooking, how do you know if the meat is done? It's brown on the inside so you can serve it, right? Maybe.

You can't tell if meats, especially ground meats, are thoroughly cooked by sight. Although beef and pork cuts may be served medium rare or medium, ground meats must be thoroughly cooked. During the grinding process, surface bacteria such as E. coli are introduced into the meat. E. coli is not killed at refrigerator or freezer temperatures, but only through careful cooking.

The only certain test to determine if meats are safe to eat is the internal temperature. Use a meat thermometer every time. Insert the thermometer into the thickest part of the meat, being sure the thermometer doesn't rest on a bone or pass through the meat and touch the pan. Remember to wash the meat thermometer like any other utensil in hot, soapy water after every use.

Temperature Guidelines

Meat	Recommended Temperature
Ground beef, pork, and veal	160°F
Beef	
Medium rare	145°F
Medium	160°F
Well done	170°F
Pork	
Medium	160°F
Well done	170°F

Pitching the Fat

At times, beef and pork have been maligned for their fatty nature, but don't let that stop you. Just choose lean cuts of meat! Plus, trimming any visible fat keeps your intake at reasonable levels.

The recipes in this chapter call for 85-percent-lean ground beef because it is commonly available and inexpensive. Certainly, you can substitute 92-percent-lean or another leaner ground beef if you like. Although you won't want to add any fat back in with cooking oils, you may need to spray the pan with nonstick cooking spray to facilitate cooking.

Pinch Hitters

Many beef and pork recipes call for breadcrumbs or cracker crumbs as coatings and fillers. Salt-free breadcrumbs and coating mixes are available, but sometimes they're difficult to find.

Readily available sodium-free substitutions enable you to enjoy your favorite recipes again. Quick oats work well as a filler. And unsalted matzo meal makes a good coating; look for it in the ethnic aisle of your supermarket.

Fiery Steak with Southwestern Relish

Makes 4 servings
Prep time: 5 minutes
Cook time: 10 minutes
Serving size: 4 ounces steak with ⅓ cup relish

Each serving has:
312.3 calories
59.3 mg sodium
22.2 g protein
21.9 g total fat
8.3 g saturated fat
71.5 mg cholesterol
5.7 g carbohydrate
1.5 g dietary fiber
20.8 mg calcium
474.9 mg potassium

1 lb. thin-cut boneless rib-eye beef steaks

1 tsp. salt-free garlic-pepper blend

1 tsp. Firehouse Chili Powder (recipe in Chapter 26) or other salt-free chili powder blend

1⅓ cups Southwestern Relish (recipe in Chapter 25)

1. Preheat the broiler, and spray the rack of a broiler pan with nonstick cooking spray.

2. Place steaks on the broiler pan. Season both sides of steaks with garlic-pepper blend and Firehouse Chili Powder. Broil for 5 minutes. Turn and broil the other side for 5 minutes or until done. Serve with Southwestern Relish.

Salt Pitfall

Garlic-pepper blend is a mixture of garlic, black pepper, bell peppers, and onions. But different blends contain various seasonings—and sometimes salt. Read those labels carefully.

Grilled T-Bones with Charred Peppers

Grated zest and juice of
1 lime

1 clove garlic, crushed

2 tsp. dried oregano

1½ TB. extra-virgin olive oil

¼ tsp. freshly ground black
pepper

2 lb. tailless T-bone steaks

1 green bell pepper

1 red bell pepper

1 yellow bell pepper

Makes 4 servings
Prep time: 20 minutes
Chill time: 8 hours
Cook time: 25 minutes
Serving size: 4 ounces steak with ¾ cup bell peppers

Each serving has:
407.2 calories
92.3 mg sodium
33.5 g protein
26.7 g total fat
8.9 g saturated fat
80.7 mg cholesterol
7.4 g carbohydrate
2.1 g dietary fiber
29.4 mg calcium
591.5 mg potassium

1. In a large, sealable plastic bag, combine lime zest, lime juice, garlic, oregano, extra-virgin olive oil, and black pepper. Add steaks. Seal bag, turning to coat well. Marinate in the refrigerator for 8 hours or overnight.

2. Light a gas grill to low heat, and spray the rack with nonstick grilling spray.

3. Cover and grill green, red, and yellow bell peppers for 10 minutes or until blackened and charred on all sides, turning gently with tongs. Remove to a sealable plastic bag. Seal and steam for 10 minutes.

4. Grill steaks on covered grill for 10 minutes. Turn and grill for 5 minutes on other side or until done as desired. Remove to a serving platter. Let stand for a few minutes before serving.

5. Peel skins from bell peppers, and discard seeds and cap. Cut peppers into strips, and serve with steaks.

 Pinch of Sage

The bell peppers may be too hot to handle when you first remove them from the bag. Wait a minute until you can comfortably handle them. It'll be easier to peel the skins then as well.

Steak and Veggie Shish Kebabs

Makes 4 servings
Prep time: 20 minutes
Cook time: 10 minutes
Serving size: 2 skewers
Each serving has:
243.7 calories
119.2 mg sodium
29.6 g protein
8.8 g total fat
2.2 g saturated fat
78 mg cholesterol
11.8 g carbohydrate
3.3 g dietary fiber
36.1 mg calcium
1,037.5 mg potassium

1¼ lb. chuck beef steak, trimmed and cut into 2-inch cubes, 1½-inch kebab cubes, or ¾-inch boneless rib eye

8 button mushroom caps, wiped with a damp paper towel

1 medium zucchini, cut into 8 thick slices

8 (½- to 2-inch) chunks green bell peppers

8 (½- to 2-inch) chunks yellow bell peppers

8 (½- to 2-inch-thick) chunks sweet onions

8 cherry tomatoes

1 TB. extra-virgin olive oil

¼ tsp. freshly ground black pepper

1. Preheat the broiler. Spray the rack of a broiler pan with non-stick cooking spray.

2. Thread beef, mushroom caps, zucchini, green bell peppers, yellow bell peppers, sweet onions, and cherry tomatoes onto 8 wooden or metal skewers, spacing them slightly apart. Lightly brush extra-virgin olive oil over beef, mushroom caps, zucchini, and sweet onions. Season beef with black pepper.

3. Arrange skewers on rack of broiler pan. Broil 3 to 4 inches from heat for 10 minutes, turning after 5 minutes, or until beef is done as desired.

 Pinch of Sage

Serve these skewers over rice for a great meal. And when the weather's nice, prepare the shish kebabs on a hot grill—just remember to soak wooden skewers in water for at least 30 minutes first to prevent burning.

Just-Like-Mom's Meat Loaf

½ cup no-salt-added ketchup

¼ cup firmly packed light brown sugar

4 tsp. cider vinegar

2 tsp. extra-virgin olive oil

1 medium yellow onion, diced

2 cloves garlic, minced

½ tsp. dried thyme

1 tsp. Salt-Shaker Substitute (recipe in Chapter 26) or other savory salt-free salt substitute seasoning blend

½ tsp. freshly ground black pepper

¼ tsp. dry mustard

¼ tsp. ground cayenne

2 TB. dried parsley flakes

½ cup fat-free plain yogurt 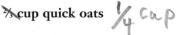 _milk_

2 large eggs

1¾ to 2 lb. meat loaf mix (ground beef, ground pork, ground veal)

⅔ cup quick oats _¼ cup_

Makes 7 to 8 servings		
Prep time: 15 minutes		
Cook time: 65 minutes		
Serving size: 4 ounces		
Each serving has:		
368.3 calories		
115.8 mg sodium		
25.5 g protein		
20.2 g total fat		
7.2 g saturated fat		
147.4 mg cholesterol		
21.4 g carbohydrate		
1.5 g dietary fiber		
72.5 mg calcium		
551.4 mg potassium		

1. Prepare a glaze by stirring together ketchup, brown sugar, and cider vinegar. Set aside.

2. In a small skillet, heat extra-virgin olive oil over medium heat. Sauté onion and garlic for 5 minutes or until tender. Set aside.

3. Preheat the oven to 350°F, and line a shallow baking pan with nonstick foil.

4. In a large bowl, combine thyme, Salt-Shaker Substitute, black pepper, dry mustard, cayenne, parsley flakes, yogurt, and eggs. Stir until evenly blended. Add meat loaf mix, oats, and onion mixture. Mix with your hands until thoroughly blended. Transfer to the prepared pan, and form into a 9×5-inch loaf. Spoon ½ glaze over top of loaf. Bake for 45 minutes. Brush remaining glaze over top of loaf, and bake for 15 minutes more or until done. Let stand for 15 to 20 minutes before cutting.

Salt Pitfall

If you prefer, serve the remaining glaze on the side instead of brushing it over the top of the loaf at the end of baking. To do this, pour the glaze into a small saucepan. Bring it to a gentle boil over medium-low heat. Cook and stir until slightly thickened, and serve with meat loaf slices.

Spaghetti and Meatballs in Marinara Sauce

Makes 8 servings
Prep time: 10 minutes
Cook time: 40 minutes
Serving size: 2 ounces spaghetti with ½ cup sauce and 3 meatballs
Each serving has:
455.6 calories
89 mg sodium
20.4 g protein
20.6 g total fat
7.1 g saturated fat
50.2 mg cholesterol
51.3 g carbohydrate
9.9 g dietary fiber
76.6 mg calcium
356.6 mg potassium

Pinch of Sage

To save on preparation and cooking time, use a commercially produced no-salt-added pasta sauce instead of preparing the marinara sauce in this recipe.

¼ cup extra-virgin olive oil

3 medium yellow onions, chopped

2 cloves garlic, chopped

6 large baby carrots, halved and sliced

2 (14.5-oz.) cans no-salt-added diced tomatoes, undrained

1 lb. 85-percent-lean ground beef

¼ tsp. freshly ground black pepper

2½ tsp. dried oregano, divided

2 tsp. dried basil

3 TB. unsalted butter

1 (16-oz.) pkg. whole-wheat spaghetti

1. In a large saucepan, heat extra-virgin olive oil over medium heat. Sauté onions, garlic, and carrots for 6 minutes or until onions are translucent. Stir in tomatoes. Transfer to a food processor, and process for 45 seconds or until smooth, scraping down sides as necessary. Return to the saucepan, and bring to a boil. Reduce heat, cover, and simmer for 15 minutes.

2. Meanwhile, mix ground beef, black pepper, 1 teaspoon oregano, and 1 teaspoon basil until evenly distributed. Shape into 1½-inch meatballs.

3. Stir butter, remaining 1½ teaspoons oregano, and remaining 1 teaspoon basil into the saucepan. Simmer, covered, for 15 minutes more.

4. Cook meatballs in a nonstick skillet over medium heat for 12 minutes or until done. Remove with a slotted spoon to a plate lined with paper towels and blot dry. Turn meatballs into marinara sauce. Continue to simmer, covered, while spaghetti cooks.

5. Cook spaghetti according to package directions (omitting salt) and drain. Serve marinara sauce and meatballs over spaghetti.

Salternative: Season the sauce with a salt-free salt substitute seasoning blend, if you prefer. You may also substitute the tomato sauce from the Individual Lasagna Casseroles recipe in Chapter 15.

After-Work Chili Mac

¾ lb. 85-percent-lean ground beef

1 small yellow onion, diced

½ green bell pepper, seeds and ribs discarded, and diced

1 tsp. Salt-Shaker Substitute (recipe in Chapter 26) or other savory salt-free salt substitute seasoning blend

½ tsp. Italian seasoning

2½ cups whole-wheat rotini pasta

1 (8-oz.) can no-salt-added tomato sauce

1 cup water

1 cup frozen whole-kernel corn

Makes 4 servings
Prep time: 5 minutes
Cook time: 12 minutes
Serving size: 1½ cups
Each serving has:
469.6 calories
71.4 mg sodium
27.3 g protein
14.2 g total fat
5.2 g saturated fat
57.8 mg cholesterol
61.1 g carbohydrate
7.4 g dietary fiber
59.7 mg calcium
604.9 mg potassium

1. In a deep, medium nonstick skillet over medium heat, cook ground beef, onion, green bell pepper, Salt-Shaker Substitute, and Italian seasoning. Cook and stir, breaking up meat, for 5 to 8 minutes or until beef is browned. Drain grease from skillet.

2. Meanwhile, cook pasta according to package directions (omitting salt) and drain.

3. Add tomato sauce, water, and corn to skillet. Bring to a boil and reduce heat. Cover and simmer for 5 minutes or until corn is cooked. Stir in pasta and heat through.

Salternative: If you can afford the additional sodium, sprinkle on a little shredded low-sodium cheddar cheese.

 Pinch of Sage

You can measure the 1 cup water by filling the empty tomato sauce can, as 8 ounces equals 1 cup. This method saves the time of scrapping the can clean.

Cincinnati-Chili-Style Dinners

Makes 7 servings	

Prep time: 10 minutes

Cook time: 1 hour 40 minutes

Serving size: 2 ounces pasta with 1 cup chili

Each serving has:

580.7 calories

218.9 mg sodium

34 g protein

14.6 g total fat

6.6 g saturated fat

49.2 mg cholesterol

83 g carbohydrate

20.9 g dietary fiber

237.5 mg calcium

1,085.2 mg potassium

Pinch of Sage

Prepare the chili the night before and heat it up the next day for a quick-fix dinner.

¾ lb. 85-percent-lean ground beef

2 medium yellow onions, chopped

1 medium green bell pepper, seeds and ribs discarded, and chopped

1 (14.5-oz.) can no-salt-added diced tomatoes, undrained

1 (15-oz.) can no-salt-added tomato sauce

1 (15-oz.) can no-salt-added small red beans, rinsed and drained

1 (15-oz.) can no-salt-added cannellini beans (white kidney beans), rinsed and drained

2½ tsp. Firehouse Chili Powder (recipe in Chapter 26) or other salt-free chili powder

1½ tsp. Salt-Shaker Substitute (recipe in Chapter 26) or other salt-free salt substitute seasoning blend

¼ tsp. paprika

¼ tsp. ground ginger

14 oz. whole-wheat capellini

1 cup shredded low-sodium cheddar cheese

1. In a large saucepan over medium heat, brown ground beef with 1 chopped onion and green bell pepper for 7 minutes or until meat is browned and onions are translucent. Drain well.

2. Add diced tomatoes, tomato sauce, red beans, and cannellini beans and stir. Add Firehouse Chili Powder, Salt-Shaker Substitute, paprika, and ginger and stir. Bring to a boil. Reduce heat, cover, and simmer for 1½ hours.

3. Meanwhile, cook capellini according to package directions (omit salt) and drain.

4. To assemble, line each of 7 plates with capellini. Ladle on chili, and scatter cheese and remaining chopped onion on top.

Rosemary-Crusted Pork Tenderloin

1 cup water

1 (1½- to 2-lb.) pkg. pork tenderloins

2 tsp. extra-light olive oil

3 cloves garlic, crushed

2 tsp. dried crushed rosemary

1 tsp. freshly ground black pepper

Makes 6 to 8 servings
Prep time: 10 minutes
Cook time: 2 hours
Serving size: 4 ounces
Each serving has:
153.8 calories
57.3 mg sodium
24 g protein
5.5 g total fat
1.6 g saturated fat
73.7 mg cholesterol
1 g carbohydrate
0.3 g dietary fiber
15 mg calcium
429.3 mg potassium

1. Preheat oven to 350°F. Spray the rack of a roasting pan with nonstick cooking spray, and pour water into the bottom of the pan.

2. Brush surface of the pork tenderloins with extra-light olive oil. Rub on garlic and then sprinkle on rosemary. Spread black pepper on a sheet of waxed paper; roll pork in pepper, keeping its rolled shape. Place pork on the rack in the pan. Cover the pan, and roast for 2 hours or until it reaches an internal temperature of 160°F.

Pinch of Sage

The garlic is very pungent while the meat roasts, but the flavor is mild in the finished tenderloin.

Onion-Smothered Pork Chops

Makes 4 servings	

Prep time: 5 minutes

Cook time: 30 minutes

Serving size: 1 pork chop with 2 tablespoons onions

Each serving has:

259.4 calories

52.9 mg sodium

24.5 g protein

15.7 g total fat

5 g saturated fat

73.1 mg cholesterol

4 g carbohydrate

1 g dietary fiber

43 mg calcium

376 mg potassium

1 TB. extra-light olive oil

4 (½-inch-thick) pork loin chops

3 tsp. Salt-Shaker Substitute (recipe in Chapter 26)

2 tsp. freshly ground black pepper

1 medium yellow onion, halved and sliced

1 cup water

1. In a large, nonstick skillet over medium heat, heat extra-light olive oil. Rub pork chops with 2 teaspoons Salt-Shaker Substitute and 1 teaspoon black pepper. Add pork chops to the skillet and brown on both sides. Add onion and water. Reduce heat, cover, and simmer for 20 minutes.

2. Turn pork chops, and season with remaining 1 teaspoon Salt-Shaker Substitute and 1 teaspoon black pepper. Uncover and cook for 5 to 10 minutes or until liquid is evaporated and onions are golden.

Salternative: Reduce the amount of black pepper if you prefer a less-spicy flavor.

 Pinch of Sage

For optimal shelf life, purchase olive oil in a tin or dark bottle and store it in a cool, dark place tightly sealed. Light and heat shortens its lifespan.

Indian Nectar Pork Chops

1 TB. extra-light olive oil

4 (½-inch-thick) pork loin chops

¾ cup apricot nectar

1 tsp. salt-free curry powder

¼ tsp. garlic powder

¼ tsp. Salt-Shaker Substitute (recipe in Chapter 26) or other salt-free salt substitute seasoning blend

Makes 4 servings
Prep time: 5 minutes
Cook time: 25 minutes
Serving size: 1 pork chop
Each serving has:
269 calories
52 mg sodium
24.1 g protein
15.5 g total fat
5 g saturated fat
73.1 mg cholesterol
7.3 g carbohydrate
0.5 g dietary fiber
28.8 mg calcium
365.1 mg potassium

1. In a large, nonstick skillet over medium-high heat, heat extra-light olive oil. Add pork chops and brown on both sides.

2. Measure apricot nectar in a measuring cup. Whisk in curry powder, garlic powder, and Salt-Shaker Substitute. Pour over pork chops. Bring to a simmer, reduce heat, and simmer, uncovered, for 10 minutes. Turn pork chops and simmer for 10 minutes more or until done.

Pinch of Sage

Serve these easily made pork chops with whole-wheat couscous or brown rice for an enjoyable meal.

Maple-Barbecue Country-Style Pork Ribs

Makes 6 servings
Prep time: 20 minutes
Cook time: 1 hour, 40 minutes
Serving size: 4 ounces meat
Each serving has:
520.9 calories
89 mg sodium
25.2 g protein
26 g total fat
9.5 g saturated fat
102.9 mg cholesterol
47.5 g carbohydrate
0.9 g dietary fiber
84.2 mg calcium
532.6 mg potassium

1½ lb. boneless country-style pork spareribs

1 cup unsweetened apple-sauce

1 cup pure maple syrup

½ cup no-salt-added ketchup

6 TB. fresh lemon juice

¼ tsp. ground cinnamon

¼ tsp. paprika

¼ tsp. garlic powder

¼ tsp. Salt-Shaker Substitute (recipe in Chapter 26) or other salt-free salt substitute seasoning blend

¼ tsp. freshly ground black pepper

1. Preheat the oven to 325°F. Spray an 8×8-inch baking pan with nonstick cooking spray.

2. Place spareribs in a large pan. Cover with water, and bring to a boil. Reduce heat to low, and simmer for 10 minutes.

3. Meanwhile, combine applesauce, maple syrup, ketchup, lemon juice, cinnamon, paprika, garlic powder, Salt-Shaker Substitute, and black pepper in a medium bowl. Stir to blend.

4. Arrange spareribs in the prepared baking pan, spacing them slightly apart. Spoon ½ sauce over spareribs. Bake, uncovered, for 1½ hours or until done, basting with remaining sauce about every 20 minutes.

 Pinch of Sage

This recipe makes plenty of barbecue sauce so you can reserve a portion to serve as a dipping sauce with the spareribs. To avoid contamination, be sure to bring the barbecue sauce to a boil before serving as you would a marinade that has been in contact with raw meat.

Chapter 15

Meatless Meals

In This Chapter

♦ Piling up your plate with vegetables and grains
♦ Stretching your budget with meatless entrées
♦ Filling up on fiber
♦ Serving cholesterol-free dishes

When you want something hearty, fresh, and delicious for dinner, consider a meatless meal. Just because you aren't serving meat doesn't mean you're giving up flavor; vegetables provide plenty of great tastes. Plus, flavorful vegetables and whole grains supply fiber, which slows digestion and helps you feel full and satisfied.

If your dietary needs include low-cholesterol meals, meatless meals make it easy. Many of the recipes included in this chapter are cholesterol-free, and you can omit the cheese in the others.

What's more, most vegetables, pastas, grains, herbs, and spices are reasonably priced. Great taste, low cost, high fiber, low cholesterol—it's win-win again and again!

Fresh Food for Less

You will see one of the benefits of preparing a meatless main dish every now and then on your grocery receipt. Fresh vegetables and grains are comfortably affordable. And if you're a gardener, you may have a bumper crop of any of these ingredients you'll want to use at their peak of freshness.

Even if you don't have a garden full of veggies to pick from, the dishes in this chapter give you a great excuse for combing local farmers' markets and roadside stands for the freshest produce at the best price. Nothing beats the taste of freshly picked veggies! So you may just have your family asking especially for these dishes!

Here's to Your Health!

Vegetables and whole grains naturally provide plenty of fiber. A main dish made of these ingredients helps you reach the 25 or more grams you should eat each day. If you need to boost your fiber intake, try substituting a whole-wheat pasta or grain in any recipe.

> **Lo-So Lingo**
>
> **Low-density lipoprotein** carries cholesterol through your arteries contributing to arterial plaque—hard deposits that may block the arteries. Reduce your risk of heart attack or stroke by keeping your LDL below 160 mg/dL (below 100, if you have heart disease). **High-density lipoprotein** moves cholesterol to your liver to be passed from your body. HDL may even take cholesterol out of plaques, slowing development. You want an HDL number of 40 mg/dL or above.

Additionally, eating a meatless meal often enables you to choose a cholesterol-free dinner. Cholesterol—it's bad, it's good, it's confusing. Cholesterol is a waxy-type substance transported through your blood by lipoproteins. *Low-density lipoprotein* (LDL) can contribute to plaque buildup in your arteries—this is "bad" cholesterol. *High-density lipoprotein* (HDL) moves cholesterol from the arteries to the liver to be passed out of your body—this is the "good" cholesterol.

Your body produces cholesterol, and you also ingest cholesterol from animal sources such as meats, poultry, fish and seafood, whole dairy products, and eggs. By choosing a meatless meal (hold the cheese), you can keep your cholesterol intake to a minimum. For optimal heart and artery health, select dishes that are low in saturated fats and cholesterol. We provide this information in the nutritional analysis for each recipe. So take a look, and you'll find several heart-healthy meals in this chapter to get you started.

Fresh Tomato and Mozzarella Ziti

¼ cup extra-virgin olive oil

¼ cup chopped fresh basil

1 TB. chopped fresh oregano

¼ tsp. crushed red pepper flakes

2 cloves garlic, minced

¼ tsp. freshly ground black pepper

4 oz. fresh mozzarella cheese

2 large tomatoes, cored and diced

8 oz. ziti pasta

Makes 4 servings
Prep time: 10 minutes
Cook time: 10 minutes
Serving size: 1½cups
Each serving has:
419.1 calories
50.6 mg sodium
12.7 g protein
20.9 g total fat
6.1 g saturated fat
22.3 mg cholesterol
45.3 g carbohydrate
3 g dietary fiber
188.4 mg calcium
272 mg potassium

1. In a large serving bowl, combine extra-virgin olive oil, basil, oregano, crushed red pepper flakes, garlic, black pepper, mozzarella cheese, and tomatoes. Set aside to allow flavors to mingle and mixture to reach room temperature.

2. Cook pasta according to package directions (omit salt). Drain well and turn into a serving bowl. Stir to combine, and serve immediately.

Salternative: Serve this no-cook sauce with other pasta shapes, such as penne, bow ties, or linguini.

Salt Pitfall _____

Be sure to choose fresh mozzarella cheese, which is naturally lower in sodium. The lowest-sodium fresh mozzarella is sold packed in water.

Herbed Red Bell Pepper Sauce over Vermicelli

Makes 4 servings
Prep time: 10 minutes
Cook time: 10 minutes
Serving size: 2 ounces pasta with ½ cup sauce
Each serving has:
291.3 calories
11.6 mg sodium
7.7 g protein
8.1 g total fat
1.1 g saturated fat
0 mg cholesterol
47.3 g carbohydrate
3.9 g dietary fiber
50.1 mg calcium
228.7 mg potassium

8 oz. vermicelli pasta

2 red bell peppers, seeds and ribs discarded, and chopped

¼ cup balsamic vinegar

2 TB. extra-virgin olive oil

3 cloves garlic, minced

2 TB. chopped fresh rosemary leaves

1 TB. chopped fresh oregano leaves

½ tsp. crushed red pepper flakes

½ cup chopped fresh parsley

1. Cook pasta according to package directions (omit salt) and drain.

2. In a food processor, process red bell peppers with balsamic vinegar until very finely chopped.

3. In a small saucepan, heat extra-virgin olive oil over medium-low heat. Sauté garlic for 1 to 2 minutes or until golden. Stir in rosemary, oregano, and crushed red pepper flakes. Turn in red bell pepper mixture, and stir to combine. Heat over medium heat until simmering. Remove from heat; stir in parsley; and spoon sauce over pasta to serve.

Salternative: Serve this sauce over other pasta shapes, such as rotini, bow ties, or pipette.

Pinch of Sage _____

Kitchen shears make quick work of chopping fresh herbs. You can keep the blades sharp by cutting through a piece of steel wool.

Bell Pepper Pasta Sauce over Capellini

3 TB. extra-virgin olive oil

1 cup thinly sliced green, red, and yellow bell peppers

1 medium yellow onion, halved and thinly sliced

2 large cloves garlic, minced

1½ lb. plum tomatoes, cored and diced

8 oz. whole-wheat capellini pasta or thin spaghetti

½ tsp. crushed red pepper flakes

Pinch freshly ground black pepper

1 TB. finely chopped fresh basil or more to taste

Makes 4 servings
Prep time: 10 minutes
Cook time: 20 minutes
Serving size: 2 ounces pasta with ½ cup sauce
Each serving has:
333.8 calories
20.2 mg sodium
10.2 g protein
11.6 g total fat
1.6 g saturated fat
0 mg cholesterol
52.8 g carbohydrate
9.7 g dietary fiber
42.7 mg calcium
509.6 mg potassium

1. Heat 1 tablespoon extra-virgin olive oil in a large, heavy skillet over medium heat. Sauté bell peppers and onion for 5 to 6 minutes or until tender (without browning), stirring frequently. Add garlic and tomatoes and stir. Cook over medium-high heat for 13 to 15 minutes or until thickened.

2. Meanwhile, cook pasta according to package directions (omit salt) and drain.

3. Remove the skillet from heat. Stir in crushed red pepper flakes, black pepper, and basil. Stir in remaining 2 tablespoons olive oil. Serve sauce over pasta.

Salternatives: Add a dash of salt-free salt substitute seasoning blend when you add the black pepper, if you prefer. You may substitute dried basil for fresh by using 1 teaspoon dried basil or more to taste.

Pinch of Sage

Dried herbs have less volume than fresh herbs, so you need less of a dried herb than a fresh one. The ratio is about 1 to 3, or 1 teaspoon to 1 tablespoon (3 teaspoons). Always adjust the amounts to taste if you substitute fresh for dry or vise versa.

Winter Vegetable Spaghetti

Makes 6 servings
Prep time: 10 minutes
Cook time: 15 minutes
Serving size: 2 cups
Each serving has:
389.7 calories
36.9 mg sodium
12.2 g protein
17 g total fat
2.4 g saturated fat
0 mg cholesterol
53.1 g carbohydrate
11.1 g dietary fiber
72.3 mg calcium
441.2 mg potassium

1 (13.25-oz.) pkg. whole-wheat thin spaghetti

½ head cauliflower, broken into small florets

2 stalks broccoli, broken into small florets

7 TB. extra-virgin olive oil

1 medium yellow onion, diced

2 cloves garlic, minced

3 TB. chopped fresh parsley, or 1 tsp. dried parsley flakes

¼ tsp. garlic powder

¼ tsp. freshly ground black pepper

1. Cook spaghetti according to package directions (omit salt) and drain.

2. Steam cauliflower and broccoli for 5 to 7 minutes or until fork-tender.

3. In a large skillet over medium-low to medium heat, heat extra-virgin olive oil. Add onion and garlic, and sauté for 5 minutes or until tender and lightly golden. Stir in parsley, garlic powder, and black pepper. Sauté for 1 minute and then stir in cauliflower and broccoli.

4. In a large serving bowl, toss spaghetti with cauliflower mixture and serve.

Salt Pitfall

When cooking spaghetti, remember to omit the optional salt from the cooking water. Omit any optional oil, as well, to keep from adding unnecessary fat to your dish. Just remember to stir the spaghetti occasionally to keep it from clumping or sticking.

Garden-Fresh Balsamic Tomato Sauce over Angel Hair

5 cups diced tomatoes

1 cup diced yellow onions

3 cloves garlic, minced

½ cup chopped fresh basil, or 2½ TB. dried basil

¼ cup balsamic vinegar

2 TB. extra-virgin olive oil

1 tsp. granulated sugar

12 oz. whole-wheat angel hair pasta

¾ cup shredded fresh mozzarella cheese

Makes 6 servings
Prep time: 10 minutes
Cook time: 5 minutes
Serving size: 2 ounces pasta with 1 cup sauce
Each serving has:
321.6 calories
87.7 mg sodium
13.5 g protein
8.2 g total fat
2.3 g saturated fat
8.2 mg cholesterol
53.6 g carbohydrate
9.3 g dietary fiber
138.5 mg calcium
485.2 mg potassium

1. In a large, *nonreactive* bowl, combine tomatoes, onions, garlic, basil, balsamic vinegar, extra-virgin olive oil, and sugar. Stir well and cover with plastic wrap. Let stand at room temperature for at least 3 to 4 hours.

2. Cook pasta according to package directions (omit salt) and drain.

3. To serve, line plates with pasta, top with sauce, and sprinkle 2 tablespoons cheese on each serving.

Salternative: This dish is just as good without the mozzarella cheese. If you're trying to save on your sodium count and enjoy the taste, chuck the cheese.

Lo-So Lingo

When a recipe calls for a **nonreactive** dish, use glass, stainless-steel, enameled ceramic, or other material. These won't react with the acid in the tomatoes and vinegar as an aluminum or copper bowl would.

Individual Lasagna Casseroles

Makes 4 servings
Prep time: 20 minutes
Cook time: 40 minutes
Serving size: 1 casserole
Each serving has:
529.5 calories
386 mg sodium
25.7 g protein
25.5 g total fat
12.1 g saturated fat
122.1 mg cholesterol
50.8 g carbohydrate
4.9 g dietary fiber
440.4 mg calcium
269.2 mg potassium

6 lasagna noodles

2 TB. extra-virgin olive oil

2 cloves garlic, minced

1 (15-oz.) can no-salt-added tomato sauce

1 (14.5-oz.) can no-salt-added diced tomatoes, undrained

1 tsp. dried basil

½ tsp. dried oregano

1 tsp. Salt-Shaker Substitute (recipe in Chapter 26)

1 tsp. freshly ground black pepper

1¾ cups shredded fresh mozzarella cheese, divided

1 cup lite ricotta cheese

1 large egg

8 (⅛- to ¼-inch-thick) lengthwise slices medium zucchini

1. Omitting salt, cook lasagna noodles according to package directions. Drain and then cut in half.

2. In a medium saucepan over medium heat, heat extra-virgin olive oil. Add garlic and sauté for 30 seconds or until garlic sizzles. Add tomato sauce, diced tomatoes, basil, oregano, Salt-Shaker Substitute, and ½ teaspoon black pepper. Bring to a simmer. Reduce heat, and simmer for 10 minutes or until slightly thickened.

3. Preheat the oven to 400°F. Place a baking sheet on the bottom oven rack in case of drips.

4. In a medium bowl, combine 1½ cups mozzarella cheese, ricotta cheese, egg, and remaining ½ teaspoon black pepper. Stir until blended.

5. In 4 individual casserole serving dishes, spoon a smooth portion of sauce to cover the bottom of the casserole dishes. Layer lasagna noodle half over sauce. Layer sauce, ½ zucchini slices, and ½ cheese mixture over top. Repeat layering. Top with noodle halves. Spoon sauce over top to cover, and sprinkle on remaining mozzarella cheese.

6. Place casserole dishes in the oven on the top rack over baking sheet. Bake for 20 to 25 minutes or until bubbly and tender. (Tent the dishes with foil if lasagna browns too quickly.) Let stand for 5 minutes before serving.

Salternative: To save the time of preparing the sauce, substitute a commercially prepared no-salt-added pasta sauce.

Pinch of Sage

You can prepare this tomato sauce to use with other pasta dishes, such as the Spaghetti and Meatballs recipe in Chapter 14. Or use leftover sauce as a dip for the Pan-Fried Zucchini Rounds in Chapter 5.

Grilled Veggie Pasta Toss

12 oz. bow-tie pasta

6 cups Hearty Grilled Veggie
Salad (recipe in Chapter 9)
warmed

¾ cup shredded fresh
mozzarella cheese

Makes 6 servings
Prep time: 5 minutes
Cook time: 10 minutes
Serving size: 2 ounces pasta with 1 cup veggies
Each serving has:
262.9 calories
57.1 mg sodium
10.9 g protein
4.7 g total fat
2.2 g saturated fat
10.9 mg cholesterol
45 g carbohydrate
2.6 g dietary fiber
87.4 mg calcium
181.9 mg potassium

1. Cook pasta according to package directions (omit salt). Drain.

2. To serve, line 6 plates with pasta. Spoon warm Hearty Grilled Veggie Salad over pasta. Sprinkle 2 tablespoons mozzarella cheese over each serving.

Pinch of Sage

Should you have any leftover Hearty Grilled Veggie Salad, this recipe is a great way to enjoy those leftovers. Cook enough pasta and shred enough cheese for the amount of vegetables you have remaining.

Tofu and Veggie Stir-Fry

Makes 4 servings
Prep time: 10 minutes
Cook time: 6 minutes
Serving size: 1 cup stir-fry with ½ cup rice
Each serving has:
276 calories
51.8 mg sodium
12.4 g protein
11.3 g total fat
1.7 g saturated fat
0 mg cholesterol
32.9 g carbohydrate
3.8 g dietary fiber
66.6 mg calcium
590.6 mg potassium

 Pinch of Sage

The secret to stir-frying is to have all your ingredients ready. Once you start cooking, you have to keep stirring. But in the end, you'll have a nutrition-packed meal on the table in no time.

2 TB. sesame oil

2 cloves garlic, minced

½ tsp. ground ginger

1 cup julienne-cut zucchini

1 cup julienne-cut yellow squash

1 cup sliced button mushrooms

½ red bell pepper, seeds and ribs discarded, and cut into thin strips

½ cup Chinese snow peas, trimmed

1 (16-oz.) pkg. firm tofu, drained and squeezed, and cut into cubes

½ tsp. ground cayenne

½ tsp. onion powder

½ tsp. cornstarch

¼ cup unsweetened orange juice

2 cups cooked long-grain brown rice

1. In a wok over medium-high heat, heat sesame oil, garlic, and ginger. When sizzling, add zucchini, yellow squash, mushrooms, bell pepper, and snow peas. Cook and stir for 2 minutes. Add tofu, cayenne, and onion powder. Cook and stir for 2 to 3 minutes.

2. In a small bowl, stir cornstarch into orange juice. Pour into wok, and cook and stir for 1 minute. Remove the wok from heat, and serve tofu and veggies over rice.

Salternative: If you don't have a wok, you can stir-fry in a large nonstick skillet.

Moroccan Couscous-Stuffed Peppers

3 TB. unsalted pine nuts

½ tsp. extra-virgin olive oil

1 small yellow onion, diced

1 clove garlic, minced

¾ cup cooked whole-wheat couscous or regular couscous

4 sun-dried tomatoes, re-hydrated and chopped

3 TB. golden raisins

⅛ tsp. freshly ground black pepper

Large pinch ground cinnamon

1 large red, yellow, or orange bell pepper, seeds and ribs discarded, and halved

Makes 2 servings
Prep time: 10 minutes
Cook time: 30 minutes
Serving size: 1 bell pepper half
Each serving has:
243.3 calories
1 mg sodium
7.6 g protein
8.1 g total fat
1.2 g saturated fat
0 mg cholesterol
39 g carbohydrate
4.9 g dietary fiber
39.2 mg calcium
571.1 mg potassium

1. Preheat the oven to 375°F. Spray a small baking dish with nonstick cooking spray.

2. In a small skillet over medium heat, toast pine nuts, shaking occasionally to keep from burning. Remove pine nuts to a small bowl.

3. In the same skillet over medium heat, add extra-virgin olive oil. Sauté onion for 2 minutes or until softened and lightly golden. Add garlic and sauté for 30 seconds. Turn garlic into the bowl with pine nuts. Stir in couscous, sun-dried tomatoes, golden raisins, black pepper, and cinnamon. Blend well.

4. Spoon mixture into bell pepper halves, and place peppers in the prepared dish. Bake for 20 minutes or until golden brown on top and bell peppers are tender-crisp.

Salt Pitfall

Purchase sun-dried tomatoes found in plastic packaging. The jarred type packed in olive oil are processed with sodium.

Veggie-Topped Polenta Pizza Squares

Makes 4 servings
Prep time: 15 minutes
Cook time: 20 minutes
Serving size: 2 slices
Each serving has:
374.3 calories
189.6 mg sodium
14.1 g protein
5.1 g total fat
2.9 g saturated fat
16.4 mg cholesterol
67.5 g carbohydrate
8 g dietary fiber
193.2 mg calcium
126.2 mg potassium

5 cups hot, cooked *polenta* **(cook polenta according to package directions, omitting salt)**

1 (8-oz.) can no-salt-added tomato sauce

¼ tsp. dried basil

⅛ tsp. dried oregano

⅛ tsp. garlic powder

⅛ tsp. onion powder

⅛ tsp. freshly ground black pepper

1 cup shredded or finely chopped fresh mozzarella cheese

1 small tomato, thinly sliced

½ small yellow onion, sliced

¼ medium green bell pepper, seeds and ribs discarded, and thinly sliced

2 button mushrooms, wiped with a damp paper towel and sliced

2 TB. sliced black olives or no-salt-added sliced black olives

1. Preheat the oven to 350°F. Spray a 13×9×2-inch baking dish with nonstick cooking spray.

2. Spoon polenta into the prepared dish, forming a crust with a rim around the edges.

3. In a small bowl, stir together tomato sauce, basil, oregano, garlic powder, onion powder, and black pepper. Spoon tomato sauce mixture over crust. Sprinkle on cheese. Top with tomato slices, onion slices, green bell pepper slices, mushroom slices, and olive slices. Bake for 20 minutes or until hot and cheese is bubbly. Let stand for 5 minutes before cutting and serving. Eat with a fork.

Salternative: If you prefer a thinner crust, use a little less polenta.

Lo-So Lingo

Polenta is corn-meal mush. Prepare polenta according to the package directions, omitting the salt as you would when preparing pasta, noodles, rice, and hot cooked cereals.

Part 5

Side by Side

At most meals, we tend to focus on the entrée. But without the wonderful foods served on the side, eating just wouldn't be as pleasurable.

You can prepare breads, salads, and side dishes—all the flavorful foods that round out our meals—with your sodium requirements in mind. Plus, you'll benefit from their contribution of fiber, vitamins, minerals, and antioxidants to your diet. With all the great recipes in the following chapters, you're sure to find just the right accompaniments to your best main dishes.

Chapter 16

The Bread Basket

In This Chapter

- ◆ Substituting for high-sodium leavening agents
- ◆ Working with active dry yeast
- ◆ Kneading a smooth, elastic dough
- ◆ Whipping up a quick-bread batter

Bread—it's the staff of life, traditionally made with the salt of the earth. But take heart: you can bake the comforting, homey breads you love without all the salt.

Whether you yearn for a delicious, yeasty-smelling bread or a quick-made bread, you can bake bread without salt or the salty leavening agents they often require. So warm up your oven and get ready to delight in the tempting aromas of freshly baked breads.

Sodium Switcheroo

Most bread baking requires leavening. Yeast breads use, of course, yeast to get their rise. All other breads that need a lift use baking powder and/or baking soda. Because you're reducing the sodium in your cooking, these ingredients won't fit your needs.

To make these breads, you need to do a sodium switcheroo. Do you know that you can purchase sodium-free baking powder and sodium-free baking soda that will allow you to bake without all the added sodium? Yes, indeed you can!

Salt Pitfall _____

If you start craving fresh baked goods and think a recipe is okay because it calls for just a little baking soda or baking powder, keep in mind that these leavening agents are very high in sodium. Just 1 teaspoon baking soda has 1,231 milligrams sodium. A single teaspoon of your standard double-acting aluminum sulfate baking powder contains nearly 480 milligrams sodium.

When baking with sodium-free baking substitutions, read the package directions carefully, as you may be required to use more (about double) the amount called for in the ingredient lists. (For more detailed information about sodium-free leavening agents, see Chapter 2.)

The Yeast You Knead to Know

The recipes in this chapter call for active dry yeast. You can purchase .25-ounce packages, which contain 2¼ teaspoons yeast. Always check the expiration date on each package, as old yeast won't facilitate rising.

If a recipe requires you to dissolve the yeast in warm water or other liquid, heat the water to 100°F to 110°F. When a recipe indicates that you should combine the yeast with the flour or other dry ingredients, the added liquids should reach temperatures between 120°F to 130°F first. The best way to gauge the temperature of liquids added to yeast is to use a thermometer. If you're an old pro, you may be able to judge it by feel, but a thermometer is a bit more precise. If you get the liquids too hot, you'll kill the yeast and the bread won't rise.

When you've mixed the dough and it's time to let it rise, cover the dough in the mixing bowl or in another greased bowl with a clean dishcloth. Then, set the covered dough in a warm place to rise; the temperature should be about 80°F to 85°F. If there isn't anyplace in your home that's at least 80°F, place the covered dough on a wire rack over a pan of very hot water. You may also try placing the covered dough inside your oven with the oven light on. (Leave enough space between racks or to the broiler element for the dough to rise.) If the recipe requires a second rising, use the same methods.

Some yeast bread recipes require you to knead the dough. To do this, turn out the dough onto a lightly floured work surface. With the heels of your hands, push the dough down and forward and then fold the dough over on itself, pushing it down and forward again. Give it a quarter turn and repeat the process until the dough is smooth and elastic.

When a recipe calls for letting the dough rest, don't feel tempted to skip this step. The gluten needs to relax to achieve a desirable texture.

The Quick and the Bread

If you're not using yeast in your bread, then you're making a quick bread. Contrary to the name, most quick breads take about an hour to bake. These types of breads use the term "quick" because the batter mixes up so much more quickly than the process of kneading and twice rising a dough for the typical yeast bread.

Quick breads can be both sweet and savory. And you can almost always use the batters for baking muffins, as well—just adjust the baking time, as muffins will bake up much more quickly.

 Pinch of Sage

To test if a quick bread is done, insert a cake tester or a wooden pick into the center of the loaf. If the tester comes out clean, the bread is done. If the bread is still moist inside, the tester will come out tacky with wet crumbs. If you don't have a cake tester, a strand of dry spaghetti makes a good substitute.

Classic Cornmeal Biscuits

Makes 1 dozen
Prep time: 15 minutes
Cook time: 11 minutes
Serving size: 1 biscuit
Each serving has:
130.9 calories
7.8 mg sodium
2.5 g protein
6.1 g total fat
1.8 g saturated fat
0.3 mg cholesterol
17.1 g carbohydrate
1 g dietary fiber
52.8 mg calcium
123.4 mg potassium

1½ cups all-purpose flour

½ cup yellow cornmeal

2 tsp. sodium-free baking powder

⅓ cup trans-fat-free vegetable shortening

⅔ cup fat-free milk

1. Preheat the oven to 450°F. Spray a baking sheet with nonstick cooking spray.

2. In a large bowl, stir together flour, cornmeal, and baking powder. Using a pastry blender, 2 knives, or your fingertips, cut in shortening until coarse crumbs form. Stir in milk with a fork until moistened and dough cleans the side of the bowl.

3. Lightly sprinkle additional cornmeal onto a work surface, and pat dough to ½-inch thickness. Cut biscuits with a 2-inch cutter and place on the prepared baking sheet. Bake for 11 to 14 minutes or until lightly browned and raised.

 Pinch of Sage _____

If you don't have a 2-inch biscuit cutter or a round cookie cutter, you can use the top of a glass in a pinch.

Basic Yeast Rolls

1 (.25-oz.) pkg. active dry yeast

1 cup lukewarm water (100°F to 110°F)

¼ cup granulated sugar

1½ TB. trans-fat-free vegetable shortening

3 cups all-purpose flour

1 large egg, slightly beaten

Makes 14 rolls
Prep time: 30 minutes
Rise time: 2 hours
Cook time: 10 minutes
Serving size: 1 roll
Each serving has:
126.9 calories
5.4 mg sodium
3.2 g protein
2.1 g total fat
0.4 g saturated fat
15.2 mg cholesterol
23.6 g carbohydrate
1 g dietary fiber
2.1 mg calcium
12 mg potassium

1. In a large bowl, dissolve yeast in lukewarm water. Stir in sugar and shortening. Alternately add flour and egg with a wooden spoon until dough forms and starts to clean the side of the bowl.

2. Cover dough with a clean dishcloth. Set in a warm place, and let rise for 30 minutes. Punch down dough. Cover with plastic wrap and chill. Punch down dough 2 or 3 times every 30 to 60 minutes.

3. When ready to bake, turn out dough onto a lightly floured work surface, incorporating just enough flour to keep it from being too tacky. Roll out dough to about a ½-inch thickness. Cut out rolls with a 2½-inch cutter, and place on large nonstick baking sheets at least 1 inch apart. Cover with clean dishcloths, and let rest for 10 minutes.

4. Meanwhile, preheat the oven to 350°F. Bake rolls for 10 to 11 minutes or until lightly browned.

Pinch of Sage

You can hold this dough in the refrigerator for several hours until you're ready to bake the rolls. Time when you'll punch down the chilled dough to meet your intended baking time.

Fresh Tortillas

Makes 6
Prep time: 40 minutes
Cook time: 15 minutes
Serving size: 1 tortilla
Each serving has:
266.2 calories
0.4 mg sodium
5.5 g protein
12.8 g total fat
3 g saturated fat
0 mg cholesterol
31.7 g carbohydrate
3.4 g dietary fiber
4.5 mg calcium
8.6 mg potassium

1 cup all-purpose flour

1 cup whole-wheat flour

2 tsp. Salt-Shaker Substitute
(recipe in Chapter 26)

6 TB. trans-fat-free
vegetable shortening

1 cup cool water or as
needed to clean the sides
of the bowl

1. In a medium bowl, stir together all-purpose flour, whole-wheat flour, and Salt-Shaker Substitute. Cut in shortening with a pastry blender until mixture resembles coarse crumbs and no large lumps remain. Using a fork, stir in a little water at a time until dough forms a ball and cleans the bowl.

2. Turn dough out on a well-floured work surface. Divide dough into 6 equal portions, and roll each into a ball. Cover dough with a clean dishcloth, and let rest for 15 minutes.

3. Flour a work surface, rolling pin, and your hands. Flatten each ball of dough into a circle with the heel of your hand. Roll out dough to a thin, 9- to 10-inch circle.

4. Heat a large, nonstick skillet over medium-high to medium heat. Carefully transfer dough to the skillet. Cook for 1 to 2 minutes or until done on underside. (Flatten out air bubbles a bit to even cooking.) Turn and cook on the other side for 30 to 60 seconds or until browned.

 Pinch of Sage _____

This recipe makes large, burrito-style tortillas. If you'd like smaller tortillas, divide the dough into 8 or 10 balls. Flatten each ball of dough with the heel of your hand and then roll out the dough to a thin circle about 8 inches or 6 inches in diameter.

Pita Pockets

1 tsp. active dry yeast

1 cup lukewarm water
(100°F to 110°F)

1 tsp. granulated sugar

1 TB. extra-light olive oil

3 cups unbleached all-
purpose flour

Makes 8 pita pockets
Prep time: 1 hour, 10 minutes
Rise time: 1 hour
Cook time: 5 minutes
Serving size: 1 pita pocket
Each serving has:
183.4 calories
0.6 mg sodium
4.7 g protein
2.5 g total fat
0.2 g saturated fat
0 mg cholesterol
35.2 g carbohydrate
1.6 g dietary fiber
0.6 mg calcium
10 mg potassium

1. In a medium bowl, dissolve yeast in lukewarm water. Stir in sugar and olive oil. Work in flour with a wooden spoon until incorporated.

2. Turn out dough onto a lightly floured work surface. Knead for 8 to 10 minutes or until perfectly smooth and elastic. Transfer dough to a large bowl sprayed with nonstick cooking spray, turning dough over to coat. Cover with a clean dishcloth, and set in a warm place to rise for 1 hour.

3. Turn out dough onto a lightly floured work surface, and gently punch down. Divide dough into 8 equal pieces, forming into balls. Cover with plastic wrap coated with nonstick cooking spray, and let rest for 10 minutes.

4. Preheat the oven to 450°F, placing 2 large baking sheets in the preheating oven.

5. Flatten each dough ball, and roll out to 6-inch circles about ¼ inch thick. Lightly sprinkle a little flour over tops, if needed. Cover with plastic wrap coated with nonstick cooking spray, and let rest for 10 minutes.

6. Transfer dough to hot baking sheets, and bake for 5 to 7 minutes or until puffed up and golden. Cool at least slightly on baking sheets on wire racks before serving.

Pinch of Sage

These pita pockets are easiest to use if you cut them in half with a sharp knife. If any didn't puff well, use the knife to slice the pocket fully open.

Sweet Wheat Buns

Makes 1½ dozen
Prep time: 25 minutes
Rise time: 1 hour
Cook time: 15 minutes
Serving size: 1 bun
Each serving has:
181.9 calories
21.7 mg sodium
5.1 g protein
6.5 g total fat
3.5 g saturated fat
60.8 mg cholesterol
25.2 g carbohydrate
1.7 g dietary fiber
22.4 mg calcium
42.7 mg potassium

Pinch of Sage

For even baking, rotate your baking pans from front to back and top rack to bottom rack halfway through the baking time.

3 cups unbleached all-purpose flour

1 cup whole-wheat flour

1 (.25-oz.) pkg. active dry yeast

1 cup fat-free milk

½ cup unsalted butter

4 large eggs at room temperature

2 tsp. lemon extract

5 TB. granulated sugar

1. In a large bowl, stir together all-purpose flour and whole-wheat flour. Add yeast and stir to combine. Make a well in the center.

2. In a small saucepan, heat milk and butter to 120°F, stirring to melt butter.

3. Add eggs to well in dry ingredients. Pour in milk mixture. Add lemon extract. Beat with a wooden spoon until well combined and elastic. Cover bowl with a clean dishcloth, and set in a warm place to rise for 1 hour.

4. Spray 2 large baking sheets with nonstick cooking spray. Turn out dough onto a lightly floured work surface, and using your fingers, gently and gradually work in sugar. Pinch off dough in pieces about the size of hockey pucks and place on the prepared baking sheets. Cover with clean dishcloths, and let rest for 10 minutes.

5. Meanwhile, preheat the oven to 400°F. Bake buns for 15 to 20 minutes or until browned and done.

Easy Spoon Bread

2 cups water

1 cup yellow cornmeal

2 TB. unsalted butter

4 large eggs

½ cup fat-free milk

Makes 6 servings
Prep time: 20 minutes
Cook time: 45 minutes
Serving size: 1 wedge
Each serving has:
170.2 calories
53.4 mg sodium
6.9 g protein
7.7 g total fat
3.4 g saturated fat
152.1 mg cholesterol
19.4 g carbohydrate
2 g dietary fiber
42.2 mg calcium
140.9 mg potassium

1. Preheat the oven to 400°F. Grease an 8-inch-round casserole dish with nonstick cooking spray with flour.

2. In a medium saucepan, bring water to a boil. Slowly stir in cornmeal. Reduce heat to low, and cook and stir for 5 minutes. Remove from heat and let stand for 5 to 10 minutes to cool slightly.

3. Add butter to the saucepan. Beat eggs with milk and add to the saucepan. Stir cornmeal mixture until blended and turn into the prepared dish.

4. Bake for 40 to 45 minutes or until top is browned and bread is done. Serve hot, cutting into wedges.

 Pinch of Sage _____

You may want to serve this custard-style bread with the gravy or meat juices from your meal. It's also good served with butter and/or syrup.

Tangy Glazed Lemon Bread

Makes 12 servings
Prep time: 20 minutes
Cook time: 50 minutes
Serving size: 1 slice
Each serving has:
226 calories
16.5 mg sodium
4 g protein
9.9 g total fat
4.1 g saturated fat
50.6 mg cholesterol
31.3 g carbohydrate
1.4 g dietary fiber
40.6 mg calcium
95.5 mg potassium

Pinch of Sage

A medium lemon yields about 1 tablespoon zest and 2 tablespoons juice, perfect for this recipe. If you need both the zest and the juice from a lemon, grate the zest before squeezing the juice.

6 TB. unsalted butter, melted

1 cup granulated sugar

2 large eggs at room temperature

½ cup fat-free milk

1 tsp. sodium-free baking powder

1 TB. grated lemon zest

½ cup unsalted chopped walnuts

1 cup all-purpose flour

½ cup whole-wheat flour

2 TB. fresh lemon juice

2 TB. confectioners' sugar

1. Preheat the oven to 350°F. Grease a 9×5×3-inch nonstick loaf pan with nonstick cooking spray with flour.

2. In a large mixing bowl, blend butter and granulated sugar. Add eggs and beat until thoroughly blended. Add milk, baking powder, lemon zest, and walnuts, and mix well. Add all-purpose flour and whole-wheat flour, mixing just until moistened.

3. Turn batter into the prepared pan, and spread evenly into the corners. Bake for 50 to 55 minutes or until a cake tester inserted in the center comes out clean.

4. Meanwhile, stir together lemon juice and confectioners' sugar. Remove the loaf pan to a wire rack. With the tines of a large fork, poke holes all over the top of loaf. Stir lemon juice mixture, and pour over top of loaf. Cool in the pan for 15 minutes. Remove loaf from the pan, and cool completely on a wire rack.

Sweet Strawberry Bread

1 (16-oz.) pkg. unsweetened frozen strawberries, thawed

½ cup unsalted butter, softened

1 cup granulated sugar

½ tsp. pure almond extract

2 large eggs, separated

2 cups all-purpose flour

1 tsp. sodium-free baking powder

1 tsp. sodium-free baking soda

Makes 12 servings
Prep time: 30 minutes
Cook time: 55 minutes
Serving size: 1 slice
Each serving has:
231.1 calories
116.7 mg sodium
3.2 g protein
8.6 g total fat
4.9 g saturated fat
55.4 mg cholesterol
35.8 g carbohydrate
1.5 g dietary fiber
28.4 mg calcium
108.7 mg potassium

1. Preheat the oven to 350°F. Grease a 9×5×3-inch nonstick loaf pan with nonstick cooking spray with flour.

2. Drain strawberries well, reserving ¼ cup juice. Chop strawberries and set aside.

3. In a large mixing bowl, mix butter, sugar, and almond extract for 2 to 3 minutes or until well blended. Add egg yolks and beat until well blended. On low speed, mix in flour, baking powder, and baking soda until fine crumbs form. By hand, stir in reserved strawberry juice until evenly distributed. Fold in strawberries until blended.

4. In a small mixing bowl, beat egg whites on medium speed with an electric mixer until frothy. Increase speed to high and beat until stiff peaks form. Fold egg whites into strawberry mixture until blended.

5. Turn batter into the prepared pan, pushing into the corners. *Tamp* pan lightly. Bake for 55 to 60 minutes or until a cake tester inserted in the center comes out clean. Cool in the pan for 15 minutes on a wire rack. Remove from pan, and cool completely on wire rack.

Lo-So Lingo

Tamp means to tap the baking pan on the counter a few times to release any air bubbles from the batter.

Apple Raisin Bread

Makes 12 servings
Prep time: 20 minutes
Cook time: 1 hour
Serving size: 1 slice
Each serving has:
270.1 calories
74.2 mg sodium
5.3 g protein
8.1 g total fat
1.3 g saturated fat
35.5 mg cholesterol
46 g carbohydrate
2.8 g dietary fiber
65.5 mg calcium
289.3 mg potassium

¾ cup dark raisins

¼ cup natural apple juice

1½ cups all-purpose flour

1 cup quick oats

¾ cup light brown sugar

1½ tsp. sodium-free baking powder

½ tsp. sodium-free baking soda

1½ tsp. ground cinnamon

1¼ cups unsweetened applesauce

⅓ cup extra-light olive oil

2 large eggs, beaten

¼ cup fat-free milk

1. Preheat the oven to 350°F. Grease the bottom of an 8½×4½-inch nonstick loaf pan with nonstick cooking spray with flour.

2. In a small bowl, soak raisins in apple juice. Set aside.

3. In a large bowl, stir together flour, oats, brown sugar, baking powder, baking soda, and cinnamon. Add applesauce, olive oil, eggs, and milk. Stir just until dry ingredients are moistened; then stir in raisin mixture.

4. Pour batter into the prepared pan. Bake for 60 to 65 minutes or until top is browned and a cake tester inserted in the center comes out clean. Remove to a wire rack to cool for 10 minutes. Remove loaf from the pan, and cool completely on a wire rack.

Pinch of Sage

You'll find nonstick cooking spray with flour in your grocer's baking aisle next to the regular nonstick cooking spray. It's great for easy, one-step coating. If you can't find nonstick cooking spray with flour, you can spray the pan with regular nonstick cooking spray and then lightly dust the pan with flour, shaking out any excess.

Chapter 17

The Salad Bar

In This Chapter

- ◆ Reaping the rewards of nutritious salads
- ◆ Filling your diet with plenty of veggies and fruits
- ◆ Topping with low-sodium dressings
- ◆ Enjoying easy-to-prepare recipes

Many meals begin with a salad even if it's as simple as a small tossed green salad with a couple vegetables. This custom is well founded, as easily prepared salads supply plenty of vitamins, minerals, antioxidants, and fiber.

What makes an ordinary salad perfect is a great-tasting dressing. With a salad dressing as equally healthful as the salad it enhances, you can confidently relish in its goodness. Many salad dressings are high in sodium, so keep an eye on that. The recipes that follow keep your sodium intake in check while allowing you an ample assortment of side salads.

Easy to prepare, packed with nutrients, readily made low in sodium—no wonder salads open meals so often.

Greens and Beans

A great green salad or bean salad allows a healthful foundation to a satisfying meal. And beginning your meal with a filling salad can keep you from overindulging in less-nutritious offerings.

The green salads shared here call for spring mix greens, baby spinach, butter lettuce, and radicchio. But you don't have to stick to these greens. You can substitute a wide variety of greens, from what you have in the crisper that needs used up to specially selected lettuces. Give Bibb lettuce, romaine, Belgian endive, peppery arugula, escarole, red leaf lettuce, or even standard iceberg lettuce a try.

> **Pinch of Sage**
>
> Dress green salads just before serving to prevent the salad greens from wilting. If you have to hold a salad, keep the dressing separate until serving time.

The same goes for bean salads. You can substitute any number of no-salt-added canned beans or cooked dried beans. Maybe you love limas, great northern beans, pinto beans, aduki beans, navy beans, or others. Mix them up to keep your taste buds tingling.

Pasta-bilities

Pasta salads are comforting foods, often dressed in rich, creamy salad dressings. As long as you keep the portion size in check, you can easily indulge in their homey feeling.

Any pasta salad can be made with a variety of shapes. If you have a different pasta shape in your pantry or simply prefer to use something other than the shape called for, you can—just keep a few guidelines in mind.

A substitute should be the same size as the shape called for. Popular small cuts are orzo, acini de pepe, and small shells. Favorite medium shapes are rotini, bow ties (or farfalle), elbow macaroni, and wagon wheels. Various large pastas such as manicotti and jumbo shells can be stuffed with salad mixtures. Strands vary in thickness or width, ranging from very dainty angel hair to spaghetti, as well as from linguini to fettuccini.

Heavy or chunky salads and sauces need substantial carriers. Try radiatore, penne, rigatoni, and fusilli. Lighter salads and thinner sauces complement smooth, delicate pasta varieties, such as ditalini and vermicelli.

Whole-wheat pastas are growing in popularity and are becoming available in a wider array of shapes. Choose whole-wheat varieties to increase your whole grain consumption.

With a low-sodium dressing to coat and the addition of healthful fruits and veggies, pasta salads can be an appetizing way to add a nutritious side dish to any meal.

Fruit-astic

If you're not partial to eating raw fruit out of hand, a prepared fruit salad is a tasty means to reach the recommended 2 cups of fruit a day for a 2,000-calorie diet. You can serve a fruit salad as an appetizing first course or a scrumptious side dish. Many fruit salads make mouth-watering desserts, as well, for a nutritious, naturally sweet ending to an everyday meal.

Fruit salads are also perfect for any number of gatherings. Luncheon, shower, and reunion guests happily welcome the fresh taste. The good news for you is that the fruit-astic recipes in this chapter are easy to prepare.

Crimson-Jeweled Baby Spinach Salad

Makes 6 servings
Prep time: 30 minutes
Serving size: 1 cup
Each serving has:
208.7 calories
50.4 mg sodium
3 g protein
13.4 g total fat
1.6 g saturated fat
0 mg cholesterol
22.9 g carbohydrate
2.5 g dietary fiber
42.5 mg calcium
192.5 mg potassium

2 TB. white wine vinegar

3 TB. extra-virgin olive oil

2 (11-oz.) cans mandarin orange sections, drained (reserve 3 TB. liquid)

¼ tsp. ground nutmeg

½ cup dried cranberries

1 (6-oz.) pkg. baby spinach leaves (3 cups)

½ cup unsalted walnut pieces

1. In a large salad bowl, combine vinegar, olive oil, reserved mandarin orange liquid, and nutmeg. Whisk until blended. Stir in dried cranberries, and toss to coat. Let stand for at least 20 minutes.

2. Stir in mandarin oranges. Add spinach and toss to coat completely. Toss in walnut pieces. Serve immediately, or hold in refrigerator until serving time.

Salt Pitfall

Spinach, as well as other dark leafy greens such as kale and turnip greens, is a bit higher in sodium than many other vegetables. However, these greens are packed with nutrients, so include them, as you're able, in a healthful diet because of their power-packed nutritional punch. Still other dark leafy greens, such as beet greens and chicory greens, are much higher in sodium. Ask your doctor or nutritionist if these greens can be a part of your sodium-restricted diet.

Grape and Walnut Spinach Salad

1 (6-oz.) pkg. baby spinach

1½ cups halved seedless green grapes

1 cup unsalted walnut halves and pieces

6 TB. Creamy Herb Dressing (recipe in Chapter 24)

Makes 8 servings
Prep time: 10 minutes
Serving size: ½ cup
Each serving has:
122.1 calories
40.1 mg sodium
2.9 g protein
8.9 g total fat
0.9 g saturated fat
0.2 mg cholesterol
10.2 g carbohydrate
2.2 g dietary fiber
46.1 mg calcium
126.4 mg potassium

1. Combine spinach, grapes, and walnuts in a large salad bowl.
2. Drizzle Creamy Herb Dressing over salad. Toss until evenly coated.

Pinch of Sage

Serve additional salad dressing on the side if any of your diners enjoy more lavishly coated greens.

Creamy Avocado and Pink Grapefruit Toss

Makes 4 servings
Prep time: 10 minutes
Serving size: 1½ cups
Each serving has:
145.5 calories
20.1 mg sodium
3.2 g protein
10.9 g total fat
2.7 g saturated fat
5.3 mg cholesterol
12.1 g carbohydrate
6.8 g dietary fiber
44.8 mg calcium
601.8 mg potassium

4 cups mixed butter lettuce and radicchio salad greens

1 pink grapefruit, peeled and sectioned

1 ripe medium avocado, peeled, pitted, and sliced

½ cup Creamy Avocado Dressing (recipe in Chapter 24)

1. Line each of 4 plates with 1 cup salad greens. Scatter ¼ grapefruit sections and ¼ avocado slices on top.

2. Serve each salad with 2 tablespoons Creamy Avocado Dressing. Serve immediately.

 Pinch of Sage _____

To prevent the avocado slices from discoloring, rub them all over with a little fresh lemon juice.

Spring Mix with Sun-Dried Tomatoes and Fresh Mozzarella

2 cups spring mix greens

8 sun-dried tomatoes, rehydrated

4 oz. fresh mozzarella cheese, sliced

¼ cup Balsamic Vinaigrette (recipe in Chapter 24)

Makes 4 servings
Prep time: 10 minutes
Serving size: ⅔ cup
Each serving has:
193.5 calories
292.9 mg sodium
7.2 g protein
16.4 g total fat
5.7 g saturated fat
20 mg cholesterol
5.7 g carbohydrate
1.1 g dietary fiber
173.5 mg calcium
231.3 mg potassium

1. On each of 4 salad plates, arrange ½ cup greens, 2 sun-dried tomatoes, and 1 ounce mozzarella cheese.

2. Drizzle 1 tablespoon Balsamic Vinaigrette over each salad.

Pinch of Sage _____

To rehydrate the sun-dried tomatoes, cover them with boiling hot water. Let stand for 5 minutes or until plumped, and drain.

Crunchy Cucumber Salad

½ cup fat-free plain yogurt

¼ cup unsalted chopped almonds

2 TB. chopped fresh chives or 2 tsp. dried

½ tsp. fresh lemon juice

1½ medium cucumbers, peeled and very thinly sliced

Makes 4 servings
Prep time: 15 minutes
Serving size: ½ cup
Each serving has:
83.3 calories
16.9 mg sodium
4.3 g protein
4.5 g total fat
0.3 g saturated fat
0.6 mg cholesterol
7.7 g carbohydrate
2.3 g dietary fiber
61.7 mg calcium
198.4 mg potassium

1. In a medium bowl, combine yogurt, almonds, chives, and lemon juice. Stir until well blended.

2. Add cucumbers to yogurt mixture, and gently stir until evenly coated. Serve immediately or cover and chill until serving time.

Salternative: Season the cucumbers with Salt-Shaker Substitute (recipe in Chapter 26) or another salt-free salt substitute seasoning blend if you like.

Cowboy Rice and Black Bean Salad

Makes 10 servings
Prep time: 20 minutes
Chill time: 8 hours
Serving size: ⅔ cup
Each serving has:
97.3 calories
90.7 mg sodium
3.6 g protein
0.8 g total fat
0.1 g saturated fat
0 mg cholesterol
20.9 g carbohydrate
3.9 g dietary fiber
23.5 mg calcium
238.1 mg potassium

2 cups cooked long-grain brown rice

1 (15-oz.) can no-salt-added black beans, rinsed and drained

2 cups frozen whole-kernel corn

1 medium red bell pepper, seeds and ribs discarded, and chopped

1 small yellow onion, peeled and diced

1 jalapeño pepper, seeds and ribs discarded, and minced

¼ cup cider vinegar

1½ TB. fresh lime juice

¼ cup chopped fresh cilantro

1 tsp. Firehouse Chili Powder (recipe in Chapter 26) or other salt-free chili powder

1. In a large bowl, combine rice, beans, corn, red bell pepper, onion, jalapeño pepper, cider vinegar, lime juice, cilantro, and Firehouse Chili Powder. Stir to mix thoroughly.

2. Cover and chill overnight. Stir again before serving.

 Pinch of Sage

Store limes in the refrigerator, but return them to room temperature before juicing to extract more juice. If you're rushed, pop the lime into the microwave for 3 to 10 seconds or just until the chill is taken off.

Basic Three-Bean Salad

½ cup cider vinegar

¼ cup extra-virgin olive oil

1 TB. honey

½ tsp. dry mustard

¼ tsp. garlic powder

¼ tsp. onion powder

¼ tsp. ground black pepper

¼ tsp. ground cayenne

1 (15-oz.) can no-salt-added green beans, drained and rinsed

1 (15-oz.) can no-salt-added cannellini beans, drained and rinsed

1 (15-oz.) can low-sodium garbanzo beans, drained and rinsed

4 green onions, trimmed and thinly sliced

1 rib celery, finely diced

Makes 10 servings
Prep time: 20 minutes
Chill time: 2 hours
Serving size: ½ cup
Each serving has:
139.2 calories
98.1 mg sodium
4.5 g protein
6.1 g total fat
0.7 g saturated fat
0 mg cholesterol
16.8 g carbohydrate
4.3 g dietary fiber
47.8 mg calcium
131.7 mg potassium

1. In a large bowl, combine cider vinegar, olive oil, honey, dry mustard, garlic powder, onion powder, black pepper, and cayenne. Whisk until well blended.

2. Add green beans, cannellini beans, garbanzo beans, green onions, and celery. Gently stir to coat. Cover and chill for at least 2 hours before serving. Stir again before serving.

 Pinch of Sage _____

You can use any three-bean combination you prefer for this salad—just keep them of the no-salt-added or low-sodium variety.

Pearly Fruit Salad

Makes 4 servings
Prep time: 5 minutes
Cook time: 10 minutes
Chill time: 4 hours
Serving size: ½ cup
Each serving has:
58.1 calories
5.5 mg sodium
1.5 g protein
0.2 g total fat
0 g saturated fat
0.2 mg cholesterol
13.1 g carbohydrate
1 g dietary fiber
14.1 mg calcium
51.2 mg potassium

⅓ cup *acini de pepe* pasta

2 TB. fat-free plain yogurt

½ apple, unpeeled, cored and finely chopped

⅓ cup drained mandarin orange sections

10 seedless green grapes, halved

1. In a small saucepan, cook pasta according to package directions (omitting salt). Drain and rinse under cold water.

2. In a small bowl, stir yogurt into apples to coat. Stir in mandarin orange sections and grapes. Stir pasta (about 1 cup cooked) into fruit mixture. Chill for at least 4 hours before serving.

Lo-So Lingo

Italian for "peppercorns," **acini de pepe** is a small pasta, sometimes grouped with pastinas (see note in Chapter 10). The tiny, beadlike pasta is commonly used in soups and cold salads.

Tropical White Tie Salad

2 cups bow tie pasta

2 kiwifruit, peeled, halved, and sliced

2 cups chopped fresh pineapple

1 cup seedless red or green grapes

2 medium Braeburn apples, unpeeled, cored, and chopped

1 (6-oz.) container fat-free, sugar-free strawberry-banana yogurt

¼ cup unsweetened orange juice

Makes 12 servings
Prep time: 20 minutes
Cook time: 10 minutes
Chill time: 4 hours
Serving size: ⅔ cup
Each serving has:
113.3 calories
10.9 mg sodium
2.9 g protein
0.5 g total fat
0.1 g saturated fat
0.3 mg cholesterol
25.2 g carbohydrate
2.3 g dietary fiber
31.4 mg calcium
142.9 mg potassium

1. Cook pasta according to package directions (omit salt). Rinse under cold water, and drain thoroughly.

2. In a large bowl, combine kiwifruit, pineapple, grapes, and apples. In a small bowl, stir together yogurt and orange juice until blended. Pour over fruit mixture, and stir to coat. Add pasta and stir until evenly coated.

3. Cover and chill for at least 4 hours before serving. Stir again before serving.

Pinch of Sage

If you find this salad too tart, stir a little honey into the yogurt mixture.

Homey Macaroni Salad

Makes 18 servings
Prep time: 10 minutes
Chill time: 4 hours
Serving size: ½ cup
Each serving has:
146.6 calories
18.7 mg sodium
4.8 g protein
1.8 g total fat
0.5 g saturated fat
47.9 mg cholesterol
27.7 g carbohydrate
1 g dietary fiber
19.8 mg calcium
43 mg potassium

4 cups elbow macaroni pasta (8 cups cooked)

2 large hard-cooked eggs, finely chopped

½ green bell pepper, seeds and ribs discarded, and finely diced

¼ cup minced yellow onions

1¾ cups Classic Potato Salad Dressing (recipe in Chapter 24)

¼ tsp. celery seed

¼ tsp. freshly ground black pepper

1. Cook pasta according to package directions (omit salt). Rinse under cold water, and drain thoroughly.

2. Combine pasta, hard-cooked eggs, green bell pepper, and onions. Stir in Classic Potato Salad Dressing, celery seed, and black pepper. Mix well.

3. Cover and chill for at least 4 hours or until thoroughly chilled before serving.

Salternative: While this salad makes a great picnic dish for a crowd, you may halve the recipe for a smaller yield.

 Pinch of Sage

To hard-cook the eggs, place raw eggs in a saucepan full of cold water. Cover and bring to a boil over high heat. When boiling, remove saucepan from heat and let stand, covered, for 20 minutes. Immediately rinse with cold water until cooled.

Crunchy Apple Coleslaw

½ cup fat-free, sugar-free vanilla yogurt

½ cup fat-free sour cream

1 Golden Delicious apple, unpeeled, cored, and diced

2 cups shredded red cabbage

¼ cup unsalted slivered almonds

Makes 7 servings
Prep time: 10 minutes
Chill time: 1 hour
Serving size: ½ cup
Each serving has:
65.7 calories
25.8 mg sodium
2.6 g protein
1.8 g total fat
0.1 g saturated fat
3.2 mg cholesterol
9.9 g carbohydrate
1.5 g dietary fiber
67.2 mg calcium
127.5 mg potassium

1. In a medium bowl, blend together yogurt and sour cream. Stir in apple to coat. Stir in red cabbage and almonds until evenly coated.

2. Cover and chill for at least 1 hour before serving. Stir again before serving.

Pinch of Sage

Coarsely shred the red cabbage in a food processor using a medium shredding disc to make quick work of it, as well as to limit the staining of your hands, countertops, and cutting board.

Tangy Lemon Waldorf Salad

Makes 10 servings
Prep time: 20 minutes
Chill time: 1 hour
Serving size: ½ cup
Each serving has:
60 calories
11.8 mg sodium
1.3 g protein
2.1 g total fat
0.2 g saturated fat
0.4 mg cholesterol
10.2 g carbohydrate
1.3 g dietary fiber
34.1 mg calcium
112.6 mg potassium

3 small McIntosh apples, cored and finely chopped

1 (6-oz.) container fat-free, sugar-free lemon yogurt

1 small rib celery, diced

¼ cup dark raisins

¼ cup unsalted chopped walnuts

1. In a medium bowl, stir apples into yogurt. Stir in celery, raisins, and walnuts until evenly coated.

2. Chill for at least 1 hour before serving. Stir again before serving. Serve on plates lined with lettuce leaves, if desired.

 Pinch of Sage

It's best to prepare this salad the same day as you serve it. The apples will weep and discolor if held for a day or two.

Layered Sweet Banana Salad

1 cup firmly packed light brown sugar

1 large egg, beaten

1½ TB. white vinegar

3½ TB. water

1 TB. unsalted butter

5 bananas

⅓ cup unsalted chopped peanuts

Makes 8 servings
Prep time: 10 minutes
Cook time: 8 minutes
Serving size: ½ cup
Each serving has:
229.6 calories
19 mg sodium
2.9 g protein
5 g total fat
1.5 g saturated fat
30.3 mg cholesterol
46.3 g carbohydrate
3 g dietary fiber
29.8 mg calcium
142.7 mg potassium

1. In a medium saucepan, combine brown sugar, egg, vinegar, and water. Bring to a boil over high heat, stirring constantly. Reduce heat to medium. Cook and stir for 5 to 7 minutes or until thickened. Remove from heat, and stir in butter.

2. In a serving dish, alternately layer bananas, brown sugar mixture, and peanuts as your serving dish allows. Serve warm or at room temperature.

Salt Pitfall

Stir steadily while bringing the brown sugar mixture to a boil or you'll risk cooking the egg instead of blending it into the mixture.

Frosty Apricot Salad

Makes 9 servings
Prep time: 15 minutes
Freeze time: 4 hours
Serving size: 2½×2½-inch square
Each serving has:
97.7 calories
33.4 mg sodium
4.7 g protein
3.8 g total fat
0.5 g saturated fat
1.3 mg cholesterol
12.4 g carbohydrate
1.8 g dietary fiber
102.1 mg calcium
290.9 mg potassium

3 (6-oz.) containers fat-free, sugar-free orange crème yogurt

1 TB. grated orange zest

1 lb. unpeeled fresh apricots, halved and pitted

½ cup unsalted chopped peanuts

1. In a medium bowl, stir together yogurt and orange zest until combined.

2. Cut each apricot half into 4 slices. Stir apricot slices and peanuts into yogurt mixture. Turn into an 8×8×2-inch casserole dish that's been sprayed with nonstick cooking spray.

3. Freeze for 4 hours or until firm. Cut into squares to serve, arranging on lettuce-lined salad plates as desired.

 Pinch of Sage _____

For easier cutting, remove this frozen salad from the freezer about 10 minutes before serving time.

Busy-Day Ambrosia

2 (11-oz.) cans mandarin orange sections, drained (½ cup liquid reserved in a 2-quart measuring cup)

¼ cup honey

2 TB. fresh lemon juice

2 bananas, sliced

¼ cup sweetened flaked coconut

Makes 6 servings
Prep time: 10 minutes
Serving size: ½ cup
Each serving has:
134.6 calories
13.5 mg sodium
1.3 g protein
1 g total fat
0.9 g saturated fat
0 mg cholesterol
32.7 g carbohydrate
1.5 g dietary fiber
13.9 mg calcium
164.4 mg potassium

1. To the measuring cup with the reserved liquid add honey and lemon juice. Stir until blended.

2. Combine mandarin orange sections and bananas in a medium bowl. Pour honey mixture over top and stir. Sprinkle coconut over top. Serve immediately, or chill briefly until serving time.

Melon Berry Cups

2 TB. fresh lime juice

¼ cup honey

6 cups bite-size honeydew chunks

1 cup fresh blueberries

Makes 14 servings
Prep time: 10 minutes
Serving size: ½ cup
Each serving has:
50.1 calories
8.1 mg sodium
0.5 g protein
0.1 g total fat
0 g saturated fat
0 mg cholesterol
13.2 g carbohydrate
0.7 g dietary fiber
5.5 mg calcium
212.1 mg potassium

1. In a large bowl, stir together lime juice and honey until well blended. Stir in honeydew until well coated. Gently stir in blueberries until thoroughly combined.

2. Serve immediately or refrigerate until serving time, serving in individual serving cups as desired.

Salternative: If you're not using this salad as a carry-in dish, decrease the recipe as needed.

Salt Pitfall _____
Don't feed honey to children younger than 1 year old. The digestive systems of infants may be too immature to digest possibly present bacterial spores, which can make the babies sick.

Chapter 18

À la Carte Items

In This Chapter

- ◆ Preparing vegetables without the salt shaker
- ◆ Serving side dishes from simple to spectacular
- ◆ Reaching the recommended daily servings of vegetables
- ◆ Keeping your entire meal low in sodium

After deciding on what to cook for dinner, do you know what you'll serve beyond the entrée? Are you in such a rut that when you tell your family you're having fish, they expect to see rice pilaf, green beans, and carrots on the table as well? If you usually give little thought to side dishes, let your need for low-sodium foods be the impetus to planning a full, harmonized meal.

Side dishes can be satisfying and delicious. More important to you, all your side dishes can fit into your sodium-restricted diet. Veggies, noodles, and grains are good vehicles for spices, herbs, and other flavorings. You may enjoy some of these side dishes so much that you'll decide on dinner in relation to what entrée complements them best.

Veggie Venue

If you've grown accustomed to steaming a couple vegetables and shaking on salt and pepper, you'll be relieved to learn that you can prepare tasty veggies just as easily without adding salt. The simple addition of lemon juice, herbs, or unsalted nuts can easily liven up your veggies. You can choose more involved sides, as well, when you have the time or occasion.

Pinch of Sage

If you're a die-hard salt-and-pepper vegetable seasoner, veggies are a great way to try out the various tastes of salt-free salt-substitute seasoning blends, including the Salt-Shaker Substitute recipe in Chapter 26.

Because vegetables are so easy to prepare, make several—of various colors—to complete each meal. This is an easy way to reach the 2½ cups vegetables recommended for a 2,000-calorie daily diet.

Noodles and Grains

Noodles and pastas are comfort foods that make a homemade meal feel homey. Of course, remember to prepare all your noodles and pastas without the optional salt called for in the package directions. You won't lose a bit of flavor either, as noodles are perfect blank canvases for seasonings.

Serving side dishes made with grains is a tasty way to add more whole grains to your diet. Once again, always cook any grain without the optional salt (or optional fat) suggested on packages.

You're probably familiar with rice, but other grains may be more foreign for you. Check out millet and buckwheat groats or kasha (roasted buckwheat groats; find these in your grocer's grain and dried bean section). These, along with other grains you may find such as quinoa, barley, and bulgur, offer variety and great taste for your family.

Splash of Lemon Asparagus

24 spears asparagus   1 TB. fresh lemon juice

1. Steam asparagus spears for 3 to 5 minutes or until tender-crisp.

2. Remove asparagus to a serving platter. Drizzle lemon juice over all.

Makes 6 servings
Prep time: 5 minutes
Cook time: 3 minutes
Serving size: 4 spears
Each serving has:
15.4 calories
1.3 mg sodium
1.5 g protein
0.1 g total fat
0 g saturated fat
0 mg cholesterol
3.1 g carbohydrate
1.4 g dietary fiber
13.6 mg calcium
177.9 mg potassium

 Pinch of Sage

Forego the tedious task of peeling the skin off the bottom of each asparagus spear. Simply snap off the bottom of each spear and discard.

Basil-Tarragon Sautéed Mushrooms

1 TB. Herb-Flecked Butter   1 (8-oz.) pkg. sliced button
(recipe in Chapter 26)   mushrooms

1. Melt Herb-Flecked Butter in a medium, nonstick skillet over medium heat.

2. Turn mushrooms into a skillet. Sauté for 4 to 5 minutes or until tender.

Salternative: You may substitute sliced baby portobello mushrooms if you prefer their meatier taste.

Makes 4 servings
Prep time: 2 minutes
Cook time: 5 minutes
Serving size: ⅓ cup
Each serving has:
39.3 calories
2.5 mg sodium
1.7 g protein
2.9 g total fat
1.8 g saturated fat
7.5 mg cholesterol
2.3 g carbohydrate
0.7 g dietary fiber
3.6 mg calcium
212.4 mg potassium

 Pinch of Sage

Crimini? Baby portobellos? It's simply a marketing game. Portobello mushrooms are the mature form of crimini mushrooms. As portobello mushrooms grew in popularity, manufacturers began marketing crimini mushrooms as baby portobello mushrooms, sometimes with a higher price tag.

Tomato-Studded Sugar Snap Peas

Makes 4 servings
Prep time: 15 minutes
Cook time: 5 minutes
Serving size: ½ cup
Each serving has:
73.5 calories
10.7 mg sodium
2.7 g protein
2.6 g total fat
0.4 g saturated fat
0 mg cholesterol
10.3 g carbohydrate
2.9 g dietary fiber
60.3 mg calcium
227.5 mg potassium

2 tsp. extra-virgin olive oil

½ tsp. garlic powder

2 cups fresh sugar snap peas, rinsed and trimmed

½ cup diced tomatoes (about 1 medium)

¼ cup diced yellow onions

1. In a small skillet over medium heat, heat olive oil. Stir in garlic powder. Cook for 30 seconds or just until golden.

2. Add sugar snap peas to the skillet. Sauté for 2 to 4 minutes or until nearing desired tenderness.

3. Add tomatoes and onions to the skillet. Sauté for 2 minutes or until onions are translucent.

Salternative: If fresh sugar snap peas are unavailable, you can substitute frozen sugar snap peas that have been thawed and drained. Cook in the skillet until heated through.

Indian-Curried Cauliflower

Makes 8 servings
Prep time: 10 minutes
Cook time: 8 minutes
Serving size: 1 cup
Each serving has:
22.8 calories
26 mg sodium
1.8 g protein
0.2 g total fat
0 g saturated fat
0.2 mg cholesterol
4.7 g carbohydrate
1.9 g dietary fiber
27.2 mg calcium
225.7 mg potassium

1 medium head cauliflower, cut into medium florets

¼ cup fat-free plain yogurt

1 TB. fresh lime juice

1½ to 2 tsp. salt-free curry powder or more to taste

1. Steam cauliflower florets for 8 minutes or until crisp-tender. Remove cauliflower to a serving dish.

2. In a small bowl, stir together yogurt, lime juice, and curry powder until well blended. Pour over cauliflower, and stir until evenly coated.

 Pinch of Sage

When seasoning with curry powder, add a small amount at first and then add more to your taste. Curry powder can have a strong flavor if you're not used to it. You can always add more as needed—but you can't take it out if you added too much!

Dilly Carrots Almondine

½ lb. baby carrots

½ cup water

1 TB. unsalted butter

2 TB. unsalted sliced almonds

½ tsp. dried dill weed

Scant ½ tsp. ground nutmeg

Makes 3 servings
Prep time: 5 minutes
Cook time: 15 minutes
Serving size: ½ cup
Each serving has:
94.9 calories
40.8 mg sodium
1.8 g protein
5.8 g total fat
2.6 g saturated fat
10 mg cholesterol
9 g carbohydrate
2.3 g dietary fiber
32.5 mg calcium
30.8 mg potassium

1. In a small saucepan, boil carrots in water for 10 minutes or until tender-crisp. Drain and set aside.

2. In the same saucepan over low heat, melt butter. Stir in almonds, dill weed, and nutmeg. Cook for 1 to 2 minutes. Return carrots to the saucepan, stir until evenly coated, and serve immediately.

Salternative: You can substitute fresh dill for the dried variety, but remember you need to use more fresh to equal the same flavor of using dry. In this recipe, use ½ tablespoon chopped fresh dill, adjusting to taste.

Green Beans Almondine

1 (16-oz.) pkg. frozen French-style green beans

1 TB. unsalted butter

¼ cup unsalted sliced almonds, toasted

Makes 6 servings
Prep time: 10 minutes
Cook time: 10 minutes
Serving size: ½ cup
Each serving has:
63.1 calories
3 mg sodium
2 g protein
4 g total fat
1.4 g saturated fat
5 mg cholesterol
6 g carbohydrate
2.1 g dietary fiber
44.9 mg calcium
152.5 mg potassium

1. Prepare green beans according to package directions; drain.

2. Stir butter into green beans until melted. Stir in almonds until evenly distributed. Serve immediately.

Pinch of Sage

To toast almonds, put them in a dry skillet over medium heat for 2 to 5 minutes. Watch the almonds carefully and shake often as they are quick to burn.

Roasted Potatoes with Basil

Makes 4 servings
Prep time: 10 minutes
Cook time: 30 minutes
Serving size: 3 potatoes
Each serving has:
123.3 calories
3.5 mg sodium
2.9 g protein
5.6 g total fat
3.5 g saturated fat
15 mg cholesterol
14.7 g carbohydrate
2.2 g dietary fiber
7.2 mg calcium
495.4 mg potassium

1 lb. tiny new potatoes (*B size*)

2 TB. unsalted butter

¼ tsp. freshly ground black pepper

2 TB. chopped fresh basil

1. Preheat the oven to 450°F. Scrub new potatoes and place in a small casserole dish.

2. Melt butter and stir in black pepper and basil. Drizzle seasoned butter over new potatoes. Cover and bake for 30 minutes or until fork-tender.

Salternative: Feel free to substitute your favorite herb for basil.

Lo-So Lingo

B size potatoes are 1½ to 2¼ inches in diameter. You'll likely find them in a loose bin in the produce section.

Oven-Crisped Fries

2 medium all-purpose
potatoes

Nonstick cooking spray

¼ tsp. onion powder

⅛ tsp. garlic powder

Pinch ground white pepper

Makes 2 servings		
Prep time: 5 minutes		
Cook time: 20 minutes		
Serving size: ⅔ cup		
Each serving has:		
101.7 calories		
0.2 mg sodium		
4.1 g protein		
0 g total fat		
0 g saturated fat		
0 mg cholesterol		
26.4 g carbohydrate		
3.1 g dietary fiber		
21.2 mg calcium		
724.5 mg potassium		

1. Place the oven rack in the highest position, and preheat the oven to 400°F. Generously spray a nonstick baking sheet with nonstick cooking spray.

2. Cut potatoes into ¼-inch matchsticks. Arrange in a single layer on the prepared sheet. Spray with nonstick cooking spray to coat. Bake for 10 minutes. Turn potatoes, and bake for 10 minutes more or until crisp.

3. In a small dish, combine onion powder, garlic powder, and white pepper. Stir to combine. Sprinkle over fries, tossing to coat. Serve with no-salt-added ketchup.

Salternative: Some people like to leave the skin on their potatoes when making fries. However, if you prefer skinless, feel free to peel the potatoes.

Quick Cowboy Corn Fritters

Makes 1½ dozen
Prep time: 10 minutes
Cook time: 12 minutes
Serving size: 2 fritters
Each serving has:
114.9 calories
79.4 mg sodium
2.6 g protein
6.6 g total fat
1 g saturated fat
23.6 mg cholesterol
12.1 g carbohydrate
1.3 g dietary fiber
5.7 mg calcium
27.6 mg potassium

1 (15.25-oz.) can unsalted whole-kernel corn, drained

1 large egg, beaten

2 green onions, tops sliced and white parts diced

½ red bell pepper, seeds and ribs discarded, and diced

¼ cup whole-wheat flour

¼ cup extra-light olive oil

1. In a medium bowl, combine corn, egg, green onions, red bell pepper, and whole-wheat flour. Stir until well mixed.

2. In a medium skillet over medium heat, heat olive oil. When hot, spoon in corn mixture to make 2-inch fritters, frying in batches. Fry for 2 minutes or until golden brown. Turn and fry for 2 minutes more or until golden brown on underside. Remove with a slotted spoon to a paper-towel-lined plate to drain.

Salternative: A 15.25-ounce can of whole-kernel corn equals 1¾ cups when drained. You can use the equivalent of thawed and drained frozen corn for this recipe if you like.

Simple Caraway Noodles

Makes 4 servings
Prep time: 5 minutes
Cook time: 10 minutes
Serving size: 1 cup
Each serving has:
144.2 calories
5 mg sodium
3.4 g protein
6.6 g total fat
3.7 g saturated fat
38 mg cholesterol
17.5 g carbohydrate
1 g dietary fiber
12 mg calcium
26.6 mg potassium

3 cups uncooked wide egg noodles

2 TB. unsalted butter

1 tsp. caraway seeds

1. Cook egg noodles according to package directions (omit salt). Drain and return to the pan.

2. Stir butter into noodles until melted. Stir in caraway seeds until evenly distributed.

Salternative: Add more caraway seeds if you like their distinctive sweet, tangy flavor.

Fettuccini with Basil-Almond Pesto

8 oz. fettuccini pasta

1 cup packed fresh basil leaves

1 TB. packed fresh parsley leaves

1 clove garlic, minced

2 TB. unsalted sliced almonds, toasted

¼ cup extra-virgin olive oil

1 TB. finely grated Parmesan cheese

Makes 8 servings
Prep time: 20 minutes
Cook time: 10 minutes
Serving size: 1 ounce pasta with 1 tablespoon pesto
Each serving has:
169.8 calories
6.5 mg sodium
3.9 g protein
8.1 g total fat
1.1 g saturated fat
0.3 mg cholesterol
20.3 g carbohydrate
1.3 g dietary fiber
22.1 mg calcium
59.7 mg potassium

1. Cook pasta according to package directions (omit salt). Lightly drain.

2. Place basil and parsley in a food processor, and pulse until chopped. Add garlic and almonds, and pulse until finely chopped. Pour in olive oil. Process for 20 seconds or until smooth, scraping down sides as necessary. Spoon mixture into a small bowl, and stir in Parmesan cheese.

3. Add pesto to pasta, and toss to coat. Serve warm or at room temperature.

Pinch of Sage

To refrigerate the pesto sauce, directly press plastic wrap onto the surface to prevent discoloration. You'll need to use the pesto within a few days.

Classic Spaghetti with Garlic and Olive Oil

Makes 4 servings
Prep time: 5 minutes
Cook time: 10 minutes
Serving size: ½ cup
Each serving has:
143.5 calories
0.8 mg sodium
3.4 g protein
5.5 g total fat
0.8 g saturated fat
0 mg cholesterol
19.9 g carbohydrate
1.2 g dietary fiber
6.3 mg calcium
24.9 mg potassium

4 oz. thin spaghetti or regular spaghetti

1 large clove garlic

1½ TB. extra-virgin olive oil

Pinch freshly ground black pepper

Snipped fresh parsley (optional)

1. Cook spaghetti according to package directions (omit salt). Drain, reserving 1 to 2 tablespoons cooking water. Return spaghetti to the cooking pot.

2. Meanwhile, press garlic through a garlic press into a small skillet. Pour in olive oil. Heat over medium-low heat for 3 to 4 minutes or until garlic is a deep, golden color, stirring frequently to prevent burning.

3. Pour garlic mixture and reserved cooking liquid over spaghetti. Toss to coat. Season with pepper. Garnish with snipped fresh parsley, if desired.

 Pinch of Sage

Watch the garlic carefully as it cooks because it's quick to burn. If you manage to burn the garlic every time, stir ¼ teaspoon water into the garlic before adding the olive oil to the skillet.

Lo Mein Noodles with Stir-Fried Vegetables

6 oz. lo mein noodles

2½ TB. sesame oil

⅔ cup trimmed Chinese snow peas

4 green onions, trimmed and sliced

1 medium red Serrano chili pepper, seeds and ribs discarded, and thinly sliced

½ cup julienne-cut carrots

1 (8-oz.) can sliced water chestnuts, drained and rinsed

2 TB. chopped fresh cilantro

Makes 6 servings
Prep time: 15 minutes
Cook time: 6 minutes
Serving size: 1 ounce noodles with ⅓ cup vegetables
Each serving has:
177.7 calories
11.5 mg sodium
4.1 g protein
6.5 g total fat
0.9 g saturated fat
0 mg cholesterol
26.6 g carbohydrate
3.9 g dietary fiber
20.7 mg calcium
105.4 mg potassium

1. Cook lo mein noodles according to package directions (omit salt). Rinse and drain well. Toss noodles with 1½ tablespoons sesame oil.

2. Heat remaining 1 tablespoon sesame oil in a wok over high heat. Add snow peas, onions, chili pepper, carrots, and water chestnuts. Stir-fry for 3 minutes or until vegetables are crisp-tender. Remove from heat, and stir in cilantro.

3. Serve stir-fried vegetables over noodles.

Salternative: You can substitute a less fiery chili pepper for the Serrano pepper if you prefer.

Pinch of Sage

To remove some of the chili pepper's heat, thoroughly cut away the chili pepper's ribs and discard all the seeds. This will make the dish more enjoyable.

Tex-Mex Rice

Makes 6 servings
Prep time: 5 minutes
Cook time: 7 minutes
Serving size: ½ cup
Each serving has:
82.3 calories
4.6 mg sodium
2 g protein
0.7 g total fat
0.1 g saturated fat
0 mg cholesterol
17 g carbohydrate
1.5 g dietary fiber
12.2 mg calcium
119.7 mg potassium

2 cups cooked long-grain brown rice

1 cup Fresh-Taste Tomato Salsa (recipe in Chapter 25) or other low-sodium tomato salsa

1. In a saucepan over medium heat, combine rice and Fresh-Taste Tomato Salsa.

2. Cook, stirring occasionally, for 7 to 10 minutes or until heated through.

 Pinch of Sage

Regular long-grain brown rice has a long cooking time, but you can find sodium-free packages. Cook a large batch when you have the time to save on the bit of sodium in quick-cooking instant rices (5 to 20 milligrams per serving).

Mediterranean Millet

4 sun-dried tomatoes

½ cup hot water

2 TB. extra-virgin olive oil

1 medium yellow onion, peeled and finely diced

½ small eggplant, diced

2 cloves garlic, crushed

1 (14.5-oz.) can no-salt-added diced tomatoes, undrained

1½ cups cooked whole millet

½ tsp. dried basil

⅛ tsp. freshly ground black pepper

1 (15-oz.) can no-salt-added cannellini beans, rinsed and drained

Makes 10 servings
Prep time: 10 minutes
Cook time: 25 minutes
Serving size: ½ cup
Each serving has:
107.8 calories
219 mg sodium
3.4 g protein
3.2 g total fat
0.4 g saturated fat
0 mg cholesterol
16.8 g carbohydrate
2.9 g dietary fiber
41.7 mg calcium
115.7 mg potassium

1. Soak sun-dried tomatoes in hot water until softened, and then chop tomatoes.

2. In a large, deep skillet, heat olive oil over medium-low heat. Sauté onion and eggplant for 10 minutes or until tender. Add garlic, and stir in diced tomatoes. Simmer for 10 to 15 minutes.

3. Add millet, basil, sun-dried tomatoes, soaking water, black pepper, and cannellini beans to the skillet. Stir to combine and heat through.

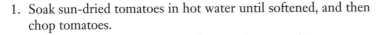

 Pinch of Sage

Prepare the millet without the optional oil or butter to save on the fat. Try toasting the millet in a dry skillet for extra flavor.

Fruited Couscous

Makes 6 servings
Prep time: 10 minutes
Cook time: 8 minutes
Serving size: ½ cup
Each serving has:
155.50 calories
3.8 mg sodium
5.1 g protein
2.5 g total fat
0.2 g saturated fat
0 mg cholesterol
30.2 g carbohydrate
4.3 g dietary fiber
32.2 mg calcium
233.4 mg potassium

1 cup sliced baby portobello (or crimini) mushrooms

½ medium yellow onion, peeled and diced

¾ cup uncooked whole-wheat couscous

¼ cup chopped dried apricots

¼ cup dark raisins

¼ cup chopped fresh parsley

1½ cups water

¼ cup unsalted chopped almonds

1. In a medium saucepan, combine mushrooms, onion, couscous, apricots, raisins, parsley, and water. Stir and bring to a boil. Reduce heat to low, cover, and simmer for 6 to 8 minutes or until fruit is tender and liquid is absorbed.

2. Stir in almonds until evenly distributed.

Salternative: Change the taste of this side dish by substituting dried cranberries for the apricots or pine nuts for the almonds.

Pinch of Sage

Although couscous is a coarsely ground pasta, it's often sold alongside grains and used as you would a grain. Couscous has long been a staple in North African cooking, where it's used much like rice. If you can't find whole-wheat couscous, simply substitute regular couscous in this recipe.

Walnut-Apricot Dressing

1½ cups dried apricots

5 TB. unsalted butter

1⅓ cups diced yellow onions

2 ribs celery, diced

5 cups cooked long-grain brown rice

⅔ cup unsalted chopped walnuts

⅓ cup toasted sesame seeds

1 heaping tsp. ground cinnamon

¼ tsp. freshly ground black pepper

Makes 16 servings
Prep time: 45 minutes
Cook time: 30 minutes
Serving size: ½ cup
Each serving has:
195.5 calories
16 mg sodium
3.8 g protein
8.7 g total fat
2.6 g saturated fat
9.4 mg cholesterol
26.1 g carbohydrate
3 g dietary fiber
35.1 mg calcium
287.2 mg potassium

1. Cut apricots in half. Soak in enough cool water to cover for 30 minutes.

2. Meanwhile, preheat the oven to 350°F, and spray a 13×9×2-inch baking dish with nonstick cooking spray.

3. Melt butter in a large skillet. Sauté onions and celery over medium heat for 5 to 7 minutes or until softened.

4. Drain apricots well. Combine rice, onion mixture, and apricots in the prepared dish. Add walnuts, sesame seeds, cinnamon, and black pepper, and stir to thoroughly combine. Bake for 30 to 35 minutes or until top is golden.

Pinch of Sage

Remember to cook the rice without the optional salt and butter often called for on the package directions.

Part 6

The Sweet Spot

Finding sodium-appropriate desserts and other sweets can be a challenge, as salt and other high-sodium products are perennial ingredients in baked goods. But with a few helpful substitutions and low-sodium ingredients, you can delight in yummy cookies, scrumptious brownies and fudges, creamy sauces and puddings, luscious cakes, rich cheesecakes, tasty pies and tarts, and mouth-watering crisps and cobblers.

We have used unsalted butter in preparing the following treats because it's widely available and always sodium-free. If you need to watch your saturated fat and cholesterol intake, you can choose to substitute a sodium-sensible margarine. Just keep in mind that any baked good should be prepared with a margarine that contains at least 60 percent fat. Spreads lower in fat cannot be used for baking purposes.

Chapter 19

The Cookie Jar

In This Chapter

- Bypassing salty, store-bought cookies
- Baking mouth-watering cookies low in sodium
- Using sodium-free baking powder and baking soda
- Controlling your urge to devour the whole batch

If you're missing a favorite treat of milk and cookies because you're following a new low-sodium diet, cheer up. Cookies, in moderation, can be incorporated into a restricted diet. You just need a low-sodium recipe, or you can prepare a much-loved recipe using sodium-wise leavening agents.

Even low-sodium cookies are treats, though. You'll still need to control your urge to eat until they're gone. The upside is that you'll keep your cookie jar full longer.

Aisle Have to Pass

A trip down your supermarket's cookie aisle may surprise you. Most of those yummy cookies in the pretty packages with pictures that make your mouth water are packed with sodium.

If you find it hard to believe that a cookie is salty, try a taste test. After you've weaned yourself off a heavily salted diet and are eating at your personal sodium-responsible point, get one of those cookies that you crave. You may want to have a glass of water nearby because trust us—packaged cookies will taste salty to you now.

A Batch of Solutions

Of course, if you like to bake, you can whip up a low-sodium cookie recipe anytime you're feeling like a certain furry, blue monster (who happens to be improving his diet now, too—a lot like you). And if you don't enjoy baking cookies from scratch, you can purchase a low-sodium cookie mix. Really though, mixing up the dough for a simple cookie may be easier than getting your hands on a special low-sodium packaged mix.

The recipes in this chapter give you a collection of cookies to bake that don't require special sodium-free leavening agents. If you have a recipe collection of favorite cookies you just don't want to give up, you can give sodium-free baking powder, sodium-free baking soda, and low-sodium cream of tartar products a try. Having a stash of suitable baking products to use in place of traditional high-sodium baking ingredients allows you to bake many of your favorite recipes. Just remember that even cutting out much of the sodium doesn't give you free reign to devour the whole batch. Cookies are still hefty deliverers of saturated fat and calories. Be aware of the serving size of 1 or 2 cookies. (For more information on special leavening agents, see Chapter 2.)

One reason you'll need to watch your portions is the amount of unsalted butter called for in these recipes. The butter keeps these unleavened treats soft and palatable. If your doctor or nutritionist has suggested a sodium-sensible margarine, please follow that recommendation.

Salt Pitfall

Low-fat margarine spreads can't be used for baking. If you substitute margarine for unsalted butter in these cookie recipes, you'll need one with at least 60 percent fat.

Shortbread Jam Thumbprints

⅔ cup granulated sugar

1 cup (2 sticks) unsalted butter, softened

1¼ tsp. pure almond extract

2 cups all-purpose flour

¼ cup seedless red raspberry spreadable fruit or other favorite spreadable fruit

½ cup confectioners' sugar

1½ tsp. water

Makes 4 dozen	
Prep time: 35 minutes	
Cook time: 24 minutes	
Serving size: 2 cookies	
Each serving has:	
142.1 calories	
0.7 mg sodium	
1 g protein	
7.5 g total fat	
4.7 g saturated fat	
20 mg cholesterol	
17.4 g carbohydrate	
0.3 g dietary fiber	
0.1 mg calcium	
0.5 mg potassium	

1. Preheat the oven to 350°F. In a large mixing bowl, combine sugar, butter, and ½ teaspoon almond extract. Beat with an electric mixer on medium speed for 2 to 3 minutes or until light and fluffy, scraping down side of the bowl as needed. Add flour on low speed, and beat for 2 to 3 minutes or until well mixed and dough forms.

2. Shape dough into 1-inch balls, and place on ungreased cookie sheets 2 inches apart. Using your thumb, make an indentation in the center of each cookie. (Small cracks may form; gently push any large cracks back together.) Fill each indentation with ¼ teaspoon red raspberry spreadable fruit.

3. Bake for 12 to 14 minutes or until edges of cookies are golden. Let stand for 1 minute on the cookie sheets. Remove cookies to a wire rack set over a sheet of waxed paper to cool.

4. In a small bowl, combine confectioners' sugar, remaining ¾ teaspoon almond extract, and water. Whisk together until smooth. Drizzle in a thin stream over tops of cookies. Allow glaze to set. Store in an airtight container, separating layers with waxed paper.

 Pinch of Sage

If you have a rounded ½-teaspoon measuring spoon, you can use it to make the indentations in the cookies for more uniform pockets that'll help keep the spreadable fruit from oozing onto your cookie sheets.

Russian Tea Cakes

Makes 3 dozen
Prep time: 20 minutes
Chill time: 2 hours
Cook time: 24 minutes
Serving size: 1 cookie
Each serving has:
86.7 calories
0 mg sodium
0.8 g protein
6.2 g total fat
3.2 g saturated fat
13.3 mg cholesterol
6.8 g carbohydrate
0.3 g dietary fiber
0 mg calcium
0.2 mg potassium

1 cup (2 sticks) unsalted butter, softened

¼ cup plus 3 TB. confectioners' sugar

1 tsp. pure vanilla extract

2 cups all-purpose flour

½ cup unsalted chopped pecans, toasted

1. In a large mixing bowl, combine butter, ¼ cup confectioners' sugar, and vanilla extract. Mix with an electric mixer on medium speed for 3 minutes or until well blended, scraping down side of the bowl as needed. Mix in flour and pecans for 2 to 3 minutes or until dough forms. Cover and chill dough for 2 hours.

2. Preheat the oven to 375°F, and grease cookie sheets with non-stick cooking spray.

3. Roll dough into 1-inch balls, and place on the prepared cookie sheets 2 inches apart. Bake for 8 to 10 minutes or until just lightly browned. Let stand on the cookie sheet for 1 minute before removing to a wire rack to cool.

4. Measure 3 tablespoons confectioners' sugar on a sheet of waxed paper. Roll tops of cookies in confectioners' sugar, shaking off excess. Store cookies in an airtight container, separating layers with waxed paper.

 Pinch of Sage _____

To toast pecans, place the nuts in a dry skillet over medium heat for 2 to 5 minutes, shaking occasionally to prevent burning.

Sweet Maple Cookies

2⅓ cups firmly packed light brown sugar

1 cup (2 sticks) unsalted butter, softened

2 large eggs at room temperature

1 tsp. pure vanilla extract

½ tsp. pure maple extract

2 cups all-purpose flour

Makes 6 dozen
Prep time: 15 minutes
Cook time: 36 minutes
Serving size: 1 cookie
Each serving has:
63.6 calories
4.5 mg sodium
0.5 g protein
2.6 g total fat
1.6 g saturated fat
12.6 mg cholesterol
9.5 g carbohydrate
0.1 g dietary fiber
6.8 mg calcium
26.5 mg potassium

1. Preheat the oven to 375°F. In a large mixing bowl, combine brown sugar, butter, eggs, vanilla extract, and maple extract. Mix with an electric mixer on medium speed for 2 to 3 minutes or until well blended, scraping down side of the bowl as needed. By hand, stir in flour until incorporated and dough cleans the side of the bowl.

2. Using a small cookie scoop or tablespoon, drop dough onto nonstick cookie sheets 2 inches apart. Bake for 6 to 8 minutes or until just golden around the edges. Let stand on the cookie sheets for 1 to 2 minutes before removing to wire racks to cool completely. Store in an airtight container.

Pinch of Sage

If you can't find pure maple extract for these super-sweet cookies, you can substitute imitation maple extract.

Golden Lemon Ribbons

Makes 4 dozen
Prep time: 30 minutes
Chill time: 3 hours
Cook time: 10 minutes
Serving size: 2 ribbons
Each serving has:
84.8 calories
5.9 mg sodium
1.8 g protein
4 g total fat
1.5 g saturated fat
40.4 mg cholesterol
10.3 g carbohydrate
0.4 g dietary fiber
4.2 mg calcium
7.5 mg potassium

½ cup confectioners' sugar

4 TB. unsalted butter, softened

2 large eggs at room temperature

2 large egg yolks at room temperature

1 TB. fresh lemon juice

2 tsp. grated lemon zest

2 cups all-purpose flour

Canola oil

1. In a small mixing bowl, combine confectioners' sugar, butter, eggs, and egg yolks. Beat with an electric mixer on medium speed for 2 to 3 minutes until blended, scraping down side of the bowl as needed. Stir in lemon juice and lemon zest.

2. Measure flour into a medium bowl. Stir in lemon mixture until blended and dough forms. Cover and chill for 3 hours.

3. On a lightly floured work surface, roll out dough to a ¼-inch thickness. Using a sharp knife, cut dough into ¾×2½-inch strips. Cut a slash down the center of each strip, and pull one end through the opening. (Strips should resemble a knotless bow tie.)

4. Heat 1 inch canola oil in an electric skillet to 375°F. Fry ribbons in batches until they float and are golden. Remove with a slotted spoon to a paper-towel-lined plate, and drain well. Serve warm or at room temperature. Store in an airtight container.

Pinch of Sage

If you need to chill the dough for more than 3 hours, let the dough stand at room temperature for a few minutes to make it more workable before rolling it out.

Peppermint Candy–Sprinkled Cookies

1¼ cups confectioners' sugar

1 cup (2 sticks) plus 1 TB. unsalted butter, softened

1½ tsp. pure vanilla extract

¼ tsp. pure peppermint extract

1¼ cups all-purpose flour

½ cup cornstarch

2 TB. fat-free milk

10 hard peppermint candies, finely crushed

Makes 39 cookies
Prep time: 30 minutes
Chill time: 30 minutes
Cook time: 36 minutes
Serving size: 2 cookies
Each serving has:
84.8 calories
1.1 mg sodium
0.4 g protein
4.9 g total fat
3.1 g saturated fat
13.1 mg cholesterol
9.6 g carbohydrate
0.1 g dietary fiber
1.1 mg calcium
1.7 mg potassium

1. In a large mixing bowl, combine ½ cup confectioners' sugar, 1 cup butter, vanilla extract, and peppermint extract. Beat with an electric mixer on medium speed for 2 to 3 minutes or until well mixed. Reduce speed to low, and add flour and cornstarch. Beat for 3 to 4 minutes or until thoroughly blended. Cover and chill dough for 30 minutes.

2. Preheat the oven to 350°F. Form dough into 1-inch balls, and place 2 inches apart on nonstick cookie sheets. Bake for 12 to 13 minutes or just until edges are lightly browned. Let cookies stand on cookie sheets for 2 minutes before gently removing to a wire rack placed over waxed paper to cool.

3. To make a glaze, combine remaining ¾ cup confectioners' sugar, remaining 1 tablespoon butter, and milk in a small bowl. Whisk until smooth, and spread over tops of cookies. Sprinkle candies over top. Let set before storing in an airtight container, separating layers with waxed paper.

Pinch of Sage

These delicate cookies need to be topped with finely crushed candies. To crush the hard peppermint candies, unwrap and place them in a sealable plastic bag. Pound them into fine pieces using a rolling pin or the flat side of a meat mallet.

Classic No-Bake Cookies

Makes 3½ dozen
Prep time: 20 minutes
Cook time: 5 minutes
Serving size: 2 cookies
Each serving has:
212.6 calories
3.8 mg sodium
4.5 g protein
6.8 g total fat
1.9 g saturated fat
5.8 mg cholesterol
35 g carbohydrate
2.9 g dietary fiber
23.1 mg calcium
131.2 mg potassium

2 cups granulated sugar

½ cup fat-free milk

4 TB. unsalted butter

2 TB. cocoa powder

3 cups quick oats

¾ cup unsalted chopped pecans

1 tsp. pure vanilla extract

1. In a large, heavy saucepan, combine sugar, milk, butter, and cocoa powder. Bring to a boil over high heat, stirring constantly. Boil and stir for 2 minutes. Remove from heat.

2. Stir in oats, pecans, and vanilla extract. Stir until thoroughly combined. Working quickly and carefully, drop mixture from a tablespoon onto the waxed paper. Cool until set.

 Pinch of Sage

> Precisely measuring the dry ingredients (not overmeasuring) and working quickly while the mixture is hot lends to the success of this recipe. If the mixture cools too much before you finish forming the cookies, you can reheat the mixture over low heat—but you may lose some cookies to the pan.

Pistachio-Studded Lime Cookies

1 cup (2 sticks) unsalted butter, softened

¾ cup granulated sugar

2 large egg yolks

1 TB. plus 5 tsp. fresh lime juice

3 tsp. grated lime zest

1½ cups all-purpose flour

1 cup yellow cornmeal

½ tsp. ground cardamom

1½ cups confectioners' sugar

1 TB. water

2 drops green food coloring

⅓ cup unsalted chopped pistachios

Makes 3 dozen	
Prep time: 40 minutes	
Freeze time: 1 hour	
Cook time: 27 minutes	
Serving size: 1 cookie	
Each serving has:	
122.1 calories	
0.6 mg sodium	
1.3 g protein	
5.9 g total fat	
3.3 g saturated fat	
25.2 mg cholesterol	
16.4 g carbohydrate	
0.6 g dietary fiber	
2.8 mg calcium	
25.8 mg potassium	

1. In a large mixing bowl, beat butter and sugar with an electric mixer on medium speed for 2 minutes or until light and fluffy, scraping down side of bowl as needed. Add egg yolks, 1 tablespoon lime juice, and 2 teaspoons lime zest, and beat for 1 minute or until well blended, scraping down side of bowl as needed.

2. In a medium bowl, stir together flour, cornmeal, and cardamom until blended. Add to the mixing bowl, beating on low speed until dough forms.

3. Divide dough in half onto sheets of waxed paper. Form each half into a 10-inch log, wrapping in waxed paper. Freeze dough for 1 hour or until firm.

4. Preheat the oven to 350°F. Unwrap logs and cut dough into slices. Arrange slices 1 inch apart on nonstick cookie sheets. Bake for 9 to 11 minutes or until edges are golden. Let stand on cookie sheet for 1 minute before removing to a wire rack to cool completely.

5. In a medium bowl, combine confectioners' sugar, remaining 5 teaspoons lime juice, remaining 1 teaspoon lime zest, water, and green food coloring. Stir until smooth. Spread over tops of cookies, sprinkling pistachios over wet icing. Let stand until set. Store in an airtight container, separating layers with waxed paper.

 Pinch of Sage

You can make-ahead the cookie dough and store it well wrapped in the freezer for up to 1 month. When you're ready to serve the cookies, allow the frozen logs to stand at room temperature for about 10 minutes before slicing.

Almond Macaroons

Makes 32 cookies
Prep time: 25 minutes
Cook time: 30 minutes
Serving size: 1 cookie
Each serving has:
63.7 calories
4.1 mg sodium
0.9 g protein
2 g total fat
0.2 g saturated fat
0 mg cholesterol
11.2 g carbohydrate
0.3 g dietary fiber
12.4 mg calcium
25.4 mg potassium

1 (8-oz.) can almond paste

1¼ cups granulated sugar

2 large egg whites

1. Preheat the oven to 325°F. Line cookie sheets with parchment paper.

2. Cut almond paste into small pieces in a large mixing bowl. Add sugar. Beat with an electric mixer on low speed for 15 minutes or until fine crumbs form. Add egg whites, and mix until dough forms.

3. Using a small cookie scoop or tablespoon, drop dough onto the prepared cookie sheets 1 inch apart. Bake for 15 to 17 minutes or until golden. Cool completely on cookie sheets on wire racks. Peel cookies off the parchment paper, and store in an airtight container.

 Pinch of Sage _____

You can store unused egg yolks in the refrigerator in a covered container with a little added water for a day or two.

Sugared Cinnamon Sticks

1 cup (2 sticks) unsalted butter, softened

1 tsp. pure almond extract

1 TB. ground cinnamon

3 TB. granulated sugar

2 cups all-purpose flour

Makes 3½ dozen	
Prep time: 25 minutes	
Cook time: 22 minutes	
Serving size: 2 cookies	
Each serving has:	
126.5 calories	
0.1 mg sodium	
1.2 g protein	
8.6 g total fat	
5.3 g saturated fat	
22.9 mg cholesterol	
10.8 g carbohydrate	
0.6 g dietary fiber	
4.1 mg calcium	
2 mg potassium	

1. Preheat the oven to 300°F. Lightly grease cookie sheets with nonstick cooking spray with flour.

2. In a medium bowl, combine butter, almond extract, cinnamon, 2 tablespoons sugar, and flour. Using a pastry blender, cut in butter until dough forms and cleans side of the bowl.

3. Roll dough into ropes ½ inch in diameter. Cut into 2-inch sections, and arrange sections on the prepared cookie sheets, spacing slightly. Bake for 22 to 25 minutes or just until cookies are colored.

4. Remove cookies to a wire rack to cool slightly. Sprinkle remaining 1 tablespoon sugar over tops of cookies. Cool completely before storing in an airtight container.

Pinch of Sage _____

For less mess, place a sheet of waxed paper under the wire rack. After sprinkling the cookies with sugar, fold up the waxed paper and toss it.

20

Brownies, Bars, and Fudges

In This Chapter

- ◆ Preparing sodium-responsible treats easily from scratch
- ◆ Avoiding the sodium in prepackaged mixes
- ◆ Spotting high-sodium ingredients
- ◆ Indulging in sweet treats without overindulging

Sweet bites are sometimes the perfect ending to a meal or a wonderful afternoon pleasure. You've perhaps discovered they can be too high in sodium. What to do? Make your own!

Brownies, bars, and fudges are simple enough to whip up. By doing so, you can indulge a craving without ruining your resolve to stick to your low-sodium diet.

Thinking Outside the Box

Boxed brownie and dessert mixes boast homemade taste with the convenience of a single dry ingredient. One of the dry ingredients in that mix, though, is salt; another is baking soda; perhaps another is baking powder. Then, you'll add a couple eggs, and the sodium count is too excessive for your needs. If you're a confirmed boxed-mix baker, you can find some low-sodium mixes to whip up.

But we'll let you in on a secret: baking from scratch can be just as easy. If you keep a few basic ingredients on hand—flour, cocoa powder, pure vanilla extract—you can stir up a brownie batter in just a few more measurements over a prepackaged mix.

Plus, making brownies and bars from your own scratch recipes allows you to substitute low-sodium ingredients:

- If your doctor or nutritionist has approved your use of a potassium chloride salt substitute, switch one intended for baking with the salt called for in a recipe.

- Sodium-free baking soda and baking powder can greatly reduce the sodium in a sweet treat.

- Also try replacing any mayonnaise with fat-free plain yogurt.

- Trade regular peanut butter for natural peanut butter.

- If the milk chocolate called for in a recipe takes the sodium count too high, replace some or all of it with semi-sweet or another type of chocolate.

- Use the unsalted variety for all nuts.

Substitute, substitute, substitute!

Pinch of Sage

A 6-ounce package (1 cup) milk chocolate chips contains 80 to 133 milligrams sodium. The same package of semi-sweet chocolate chips has only 18 milligrams sodium, and you can find sodium-free semi-sweet chocolate chips.

Itty, Bitty Bites

We all crave a little something sweet now and then. Just be careful that reducing the sodium count of your favorite treats doesn't lull you into believing you can wolf down the whole pan. Fat, cholesterol, and calories still count, so it's best to stick to the suggested serving size.

Chocolate-Chocolate-Chip Brownies

1 cup all-purpose flour

¼ cup cocoa powder

1 cup granulated sugar

½ cup (1 stick) unsalted butter, softened

2 large eggs at room temperature

1 tsp. pure vanilla extract

¼ cup miniature semisweet chocolate chips

Makes 1 dozen
Prep time: 15 minutes
Cook time: 25 minutes
Serving size: 1 bar
Each serving has:
208.7 calories
11.1 mg sodium
2.4 g protein
9.9 g total fat
5.9 g saturated fat
55.4 mg cholesterol
28.4 g carbohydrate
1.2 g dietary fiber
6.6 mg calcium
53.3 mg potassium

1. Preheat the oven to 350°F. Grease an 8×8×2-inch baking pan with nonstick cooking spray with flour.

2. In a large mixing bowl, combine flour, cocoa powder, sugar, butter, eggs, and vanilla extract. Beat with an electric mixer on medium speed for 3 minutes or until well blended. Fold in chocolate chips.

3. Spread batter in the prepared pan. Bake for 25 minutes or until brownies test done. Cool in the pan on a wire rack. Cut into bars to serve.

Salternative: Substitute unsalted chopped walnuts for the chocolate chips, if you prefer.

Pinch of Sage

Cocoa powder is a good way to satisfy your chocolate cravings. It has only 1 milligram sodium in a tablespoon. Plus, it has no saturated fat, no cholesterol, and only 12 calories per tablespoon.

Bleached Blondies

Makes 1 dozen
Prep time: 10 minutes
Cook time: 25 minutes
Serving size: 1 bar
Each serving has:
181.3 calories
10.7 mg sodium
2 g protein
8.3 g total fat
4.9 g saturated fat
55.4 mg cholesterol
24.5 g carbohydrate
0.3 g dietary fiber
4.3 mg calcium
11 mg potassium

1 cup all-purpose flour

1 cup granulated sugar

½ cup (1 stick) unsalted butter, softened

2 large eggs at room temperature

1 tsp. pure vanilla extract

1. Preheat the oven to 350°F. Grease an 8×8×2-inch baking pan with nonstick cooking spray with flour.

2. In a large mixing bowl, combine flour, sugar, butter, eggs, and vanilla extract. Beat with an electric mixture on medium speed for 3 minutes or until well blended.

3. Spread batter evenly in the prepared pan. Bake for 25 to 30 minutes or until golden and tests done. Cool in the pan on a wire rack. Cut into bars to serve.

Salternative: You can fold ¼ cup unsalted chopped walnuts or pecans into the batter.

 Pinch of Sage

Blondies are good snacks for people who can't have chocolate. They're really just brownies without the chocolate flavoring.

Walnut-Studded Chocolate Sponge Bars

¾ cup all-purpose flour

¼ cup cocoa powder

½ cup granulated sugar

¼ cup miniature semisweet chocolate chips

¼ cup unsalted chopped walnuts

1 large egg at room temperature

½ cup fat-free sour cream

¼ cup water

1 tsp. pure vanilla extract

12 unsalted walnut halves

Makes 1 dozen
Prep time: 15 minutes
Cook time: 22 minutes
Serving size: 1 bar
Each serving has:
133.5 calories
13.6 mg sodium
3.1 g protein
5.1 g total fat
1.4 g saturated fat
18.7 mg cholesterol
20.3 g carbohydrate
1.4 g dietary fiber
23.1 mg calcium
94 mg potassium

1. Preheat the oven to 325°F. Grease an 8×8×2-inch baking dish with nonstick cooking spray with flour.

2. In a large bowl, combine flour, cocoa powder, and sugar, and stir until blended. Stir in chocolate chips and walnuts. Make a well in the center of dry ingredients.

3. In a small bowl, beat egg. Whisk in sour cream, water, and vanilla extract until blended. Pour wet ingredients into the well of dry ingredients. Fold in dry ingredients just until moistened.

4. Gently spread batter into the prepared dish. Evenly space walnut halves across top of batter. Bake for 22 minutes or until edges are firm and center is just set. Remove to a wire rack to cool. Cut into bars.

Pinch of Sage

Use a light hand when you fold together the ingredients. You don't want to overmix this batter. The bars will go from spongy to rubbery.

Chocolate-Crusted Pecan Bars

Makes 2 dozen
Prep time: 30 minutes
Cook time: 35 minutes
Serving size: 1 bar
Each serving has:
214.7 calories
20.4 mg sodium
3.4 g protein
13.3 g total fat
5.3 g saturated fat
29.9 mg cholesterol
21.8 g carbohydrate
1.5 g dietary fiber
55 mg calcium
122 mg potassium

Pinch of Sage

If you're looking to reduce the cholesterol in recipes, replace the called-for egg with an egg substitute.

1¼ cups all-purpose flour

1 cup confectioners' sugar

½ cup cocoa powder

1 cup (2 sticks) unsalted butter, softened

1 (14-oz.) can fat-free sweetened condensed milk

1 large egg, at room temperature

2 tsp. pure vanilla extract

1½ cups unsalted chopped pecans

1. Preheat the oven to 350°F. Coat a 13×9×2-inch baking pan with nonstick cooking spray with flour.

2. In a large bowl, stir together flour, confectioners' sugar, and cocoa powder. Using a pastry blender, two knives, or your fingertips, cut in butter until mixture is crumbly. Using your fingers, press evenly into the bottom of the prepared pan. Bake for 15 minutes.

3. Meanwhile, combine sweetened condensed milk, egg, and vanilla extract in a medium mixing bowl. Beat with an electric mixer on medium speed for 2 minutes or until blended. Stir in pecans. Spread evenly over crust. Bake for 20 to 25 minutes or until topping is set. Cool on a wire rack. Cut into bars to serve.

Golden Sunshine Bars

½ cup plus 2 tsp.
confectioners' sugar

2¼ cups all-purpose flour

1 cup (2 sticks) unsalted
butter, softened

4 large eggs, beaten

1 cup granulated sugar

6 TB. fresh orange juice

Makes 20 servings
Prep time: 10 minutes
Cook time: 55 minutes
Serving size: 1 bar
Each serving has:
197.9 calories
13.2 mg sodium
2.6 g protein
10 g total fat
5.9 g saturated fat
66.5 mg cholesterol
24.2 g carbohydrate
0.5 g dietary fiber
5 mg calcium
21.4 mg potassium

1. Preheat the oven to 300°F. To make crust, combine ½ cup confectioners' sugar and 2 cups flour in a large bowl. Using a pastry blender, two knives, or your fingertips, cut in butter until coarse crumbs form. Using your fingers, press crust mixture into a 13×9×2-inch baking pan. Bake for 30 minutes or until edges are just golden.

2. In a large mixing bowl, combine eggs, granulated sugar, orange juice, and remaining ¼ cup flour. Beat for 2 to 3 minutes or until well blended. Pour egg mixture over hot crust, and bake for 25 to 30 minutes or until set.

3. Sprinkle remaining 2 teaspoons confectioners' sugar over top. Cut into bars while still warm.

Pinch of Sage

The orange filling for these bars will not appear done, but still wet and glossy. You need to test the dryness with your fingertip.

Lemony Cloud Bars

Makes 16 servings
Prep time: 35 minutes
Chill time: 47 minutes
Serving size: 1 bar
Each serving has:
164.2 calories
16 mg sodium
2.3 g protein
7.2 g total fat
4.3 g saturated fat
44.4 mg cholesterol
22.8 g carbohydrate
0.4 g dietary fiber
22.8 mg calcium
38.6 mg potassium

⅓ cup plus ¼ cup unsalted butter

¼ cup confectioners' sugar

1¼ cups all-purpose flour

1 cup granulated sugar

2 large eggs, separated

1 TB. grated lemon zest

¼ cup fresh lemon juice

1 cup fat-free milk

1. Preheat the oven to 350°F. To prepare crust, blend ⅓ cup butter with confectioners' sugar in a large mixing bowl. Mix in 1 cup flour until fine crumbs form. Using your fingers, press mixture into the bottom of an ungreased 9×9×2-inch nonstick baking pan. Set aside.

2. To prepare topping, combine remaining ¼ cup butter, granulated sugar, and remaining ¼ cup flour in the same large mixing bowl. Mix with an electric mixer on medium speed for 10 minutes or until well combined and packing firm around edge of bowl if not scraped. Beat in egg yolks, lemon zest, and lemon juice. Blend in milk. Set aside.

3. Bake crust for 12 minutes or until golden around edges.

4. Meanwhile, with clean, dry beaters, beat egg whites in a small mixing bowl until soft peaks form. Fold egg whites into lemon mixture until well combined. (Do not blend or stir.) Pour topping over hot crust, and bake for 35 to 40 minutes or until top is a deep golden brown. Cool in the pan on a wire rack. Cut into bars, and refrigerate any leftovers.

Salt Pitfall

Take care when separating your eggs. The whites won't peak if you've gotten even a drop of yolk in them.

Toasted Fruity Granola Bars

3½ cups rolled oats

½ cup sesame seeds

½ cup chopped almonds

¾ cup unsalted butter

½ cup firmly packed light brown sugar

½ cup honey

½ tsp. ground nutmeg

½ cup chopped dried apricots

½ cup golden raisins

½ cup sweetened flaked coconut

Makes 2 dozen
Prep time: 15 minutes
Cook time: 35 minutes
Serving size: 1 bar
Each serving has:
230.2 calories
12.7 mg sodium
5.2 g protein
4.3 g total fat
1.2 g saturated fat
15 mg cholesterol
31.2 g carbohydrate
3.3 g dietary fiber
35.1 mg calcium
191.1 mg potassium

1. Preheat the oven to 350°F. In a 10×15-inch nonstick baking pan, combine oats, sesame seeds, and almonds. Bake for 15 minutes or until almonds are lightly browned, stirring every 5 minutes.

2. Meanwhile, in a large saucepan over low heat, melt butter. Remove from heat. Stir in brown sugar, honey, and nutmeg. Add oat mixture, apricots, raisins, and coconut. Stir until evenly coated.

3. Grease the 10×15-inch baking pan with nonstick cooking spray with flour. Turn mixture into the prepared pan, and press in evenly. Bake for 20 minutes or until browned and bubbling in the center. Cool on a wire rack for 20 minutes before cutting into bars. Cool completely before storing in an airtight container.

Salternative: You can grease and flour the baking pan by hand if you don't have nonstick cooking spray with flour. The pan will be hot from the oven, though! For safety, prepare another 10×15-inch baking pan for baking the bars.

Pinch of Sage

If you buy your sesame seeds already toasted, just add them to the oat mixture after removing the baking pan from the oven following step 1.

Micro-Quick Chocolate Fudge

Makes 64 pieces
Prep time: 15 minutes
Cook time: 3 minutes
Chill time: 3 hours
Serving size: 2 pieces
Each serving has:
170 calories
11.4 mg sodium
2.5 g protein
9.7 g total fat
4.1 g saturated fat
0 mg cholesterol
21.4 g carbohydrate
1.5 g dietary fiber
13.2 mg calcium
104.5 mg potassium

½ cup dark corn syrup

⅓ cup fat-free evaporated milk

3 cups semisweet chocolate chips

¾ cup confectioners' sugar

2 tsp. pure vanilla extract

1½ cups unsalted chopped walnuts

1. Line an 8×8×2-inch pan with plastic wrap. In a 3-quart microwave-safe dish, combine dark corn syrup and evaporated milk, stirring with a wooden spoon to blend well. Cook on high for 3 minutes or until boiling well. Remove from the microwave.

2. Quickly stir in chocolate chips until melted and mixture is blended. Quickly add confectioners' sugar, vanilla extract, and walnuts, stirring until blended. Beat mixture with the wooden spoon for 1 to 2 minutes or until thick and glossy.

3. Turn mixture into the prepared pan, spreading evenly. Chill for 3 hours or until firm. Cut into squares to serve. Store leftovers in the refrigerator.

 Pinch of Sage

Having the ingredients premeasured helps you add them quickly and confidently to the heated mixture.

Super-Easy Peanut Butter Marble Fudge

2½ cups confectioners' sugar

2 TB. plus 2 tsp. cocoa powder

1 cup unsalted natural peanut butter at room temperature

⅓ cup unsalted butter, melted

1½ tsp. pure vanilla extract

Makes 45 squares	
Prep time: 15 minutes	
Chill time: 1 hour	
Serving size: 2 squares	
Each serving has:	
149 calories	
0.3 mg sodium	
2.6 g protein	
8.4 g total fat	
2.4 g saturated fat	
7.1 mg cholesterol	
16.1 g carbohydrate	
0.9 g dietary fiber	
1 mg calcium	
10.4 mg potassium	

1. In a large bowl, combine confectioners' sugar, cocoa powder, peanut butter, butter, and vanilla extract. Stir until thoroughly blended. (Mixture will be stiff.)

2. Press mixture into a 9×5-inch nonstick loaf pan that's been sprayed with nonstick cooking spray. Chill for 1 hour or until firm. Cut into squares.

Pinch of Sage

This sweet treat makes a great gift for fudge lovers, as it's quick and easy to make. You can double the recipe, pressing the fudge into a 9×9-inch nonstick baking pan sprayed with nonstick cooking spray.

Chapter 21

Ooey-Gooey Sauces and Puddings

In This Chapter

- Avoiding ready-made high-sodium sauces and puddings
- Limiting ingredients with troublesome sodium amounts
- Lowering sodium in sauces and puddings
- Keeping an eye on the serving size

When you're craving something sweet, creamy, and ooey-gooey, you need to be mindful of the sodium content. Dessert sauces, syrups, and puddings vary in their nature. Many commercially available, fudge-type ice-cream toppings are too high in sodium for a restricted diet, and most prepared puddings include salt and other sodium-rich foods as ingredients. You need to avoid regular pudding mixes, as well, whether preparing the pudding or adding the pudding mix to a recipe.

Hold on to your spoon, though! You can easily prepare decadent, scrumptious sauces and puddings to savor while not wrecking your sodium resolve. You'll be blissfully licking up every last drop of the recipes in this chapter.

Ingredient Safeguards

Many creamy sauces and puddings use milk and other dairy products, as well as eggs, to achieve their rich, silky texture. As long as your recipes are well balanced in their use of these ingredients, the sodium per serving should fit your needs. Watch those recipes heavy in these ingredients.

Chocolate is a favorite flavor when it comes to ooey-gooey sauces and smooth puddings. Semisweet chocolate and unsweetened chocolate are good choices for recipes. Double-check the amount of milk chocolate called for, as this form of chocolate does have some sodium.

Nuts are another favorite addition to sweet sauces. Be sure yours are unsalted.

Watching the Big Dipper

Sauces and puddings are creamy, rich, and delicious—and very easy to overindulge in. Many times, our eyes are just bigger than our stomachs. To keep your portions in check, you may need to measure out individual servings to be certain you're not getting more than you even realize.

If you want a second serving, that's fine, as long as you do it knowingly and tally up the nutrition analysis numbers.

Nutty Chocolate Velvet Sauce

4 TB. unsalted butter

1 cup unsalted chopped pecans

½ tsp. pure vanilla extract

1 cup semisweet chocolate chips

Makes 1¼ cups
Prep time: 5 minutes
Cook time: 10 minutes
Serving size: 2 tablespoons
Each serving has:
234.9 calories
0 mg sodium
2.7 g protein
19.4 g total fat
7.5 g saturated fat
12 mg cholesterol
16.1 g carbohydrate
2.3 g dietary fiber
8.4 mg calcium
121.5 mg potassium

1. In a heavy skillet over medium heat, melt butter. Reduce heat to low, and stir in pecans. Cook for 6 to 8 minutes or until butter is lightly browned and pecans are lightly toasted, stirring very frequently. Remove from heat.

2. Stir in vanilla extract and chocolate chips until chocolate is melted. Serve warm over frozen yogurt, ice cream, angel food cake, plain pound cake, or white cake, as desired.

Salternative: If you like, substitute unsalted chopped walnuts for the pecans.

Maple-Walnut Topping

1¼ cups unsalted chopped walnuts

1 cup pure maple syrup

¼ cup water

Makes 1¾ cups
Prep time: 5 minutes
Cook time: 30 minutes
Serving size: 2 tablespoons
Each serving has:
130 calories
2.3 mg sodium
1.6 g protein
7 g total fat
0.7 g saturated fat
0 mg cholesterol
16.8 g carbohydrate
0.7 g dietary fiber
25.9 mg calcium
93.9 mg potassium

1. In a small saucepan, combine walnuts, maple syrup, and water. Heat over high heat until mixture bubbles around the edge of the pan. Reduce heat to low.

2. Cover and cook for 25 minutes or until thickened. Serve hot or cold over ice cream or cake, as desired. Refrigerate leftovers.

Fudge Crackle Coating

Makes 2 cups
Prep time: 10 minutes
Cook time: 10 minutes
Serving size: 2 tablespoons
Each serving has:
195.5 calories
3.9 mg sodium
1.6 g protein
15.2 g total fat
9.4 g saturated fat
25.2 mg cholesterol
16.5 g carbohydrate
1.7 g dietary fiber
10.2 mg calcium
99.3 mg potassium

1 cup confectioners' sugar

½ cup heavy cream

8 TB. (1 stick) unsalted butter

¾ cup semisweet chocolate chips

4 (1-oz.) squares unsweetened chocolate

1½ tsp. pure vanilla extract

1. In a medium saucepan, combine confectioners' sugar, heavy cream, and butter. Cook over medium heat until smooth, stirring constantly. (Do not boil.) Remove from heat.

2. Stir in chocolate chips, unsweetened chocolate, and vanilla extract. Stir until chocolate is melted and mixture is smooth. Let cool slightly before serving. Refrigerate any leftovers.

 Pinch of Sage

Pour this rich sauce over frozen yogurt or ice cream and let it stand until it hardens for a fudgy, cracked coating. You can sprinkle unsalted chopped nuts over the sauce before it sets if you like.

Sweet Caramel Sauce

1½ TB. firmly packed light brown sugar

1 TB. unsalted butter

1 cup plus 1½ TB. water

1 TB. cornstarch

Makes 1 cup
Prep time: 5 minutes
Cook time: 8 minutes
Serving size: 2 tablespoons
Each serving has:
26 calories
1.4 mg sodium
0 g protein
1.4 g total fat
0.9 g saturated fat
3.8 mg cholesterol
3.4 g carbohydrate
0 g dietary fiber
2.5 mg calcium
9 mg potassium

1. In a small saucepan, combine brown sugar, butter, and 1 cup water. Bring to a boil over high heat. Remove the saucepan from heat, and reduce heat to medium.

2. In a small cup, measure 1½ tablespoons water. Whisk in cornstarch until blended. Stir into saucepan, and return to heat. Cook over medium heat for 5 minutes, stirring occasionally. Remove from heat, and serve hot over ice cream or bread pudding, as desired.

Creamy Breakfast Syrup

½ cup granulated sugar

½ cup light corn syrup

½ cup light cream

½ tsp. pure vanilla extract

Makes 1 cup
Prep time: 5 minutes
Cook time: 10 minutes
Serving size: 2 tablespoons
Each serving has:
150.6 calories
30 mg sodium
0.3 g protein
4.6 g total fat
2.9 g saturated fat
16.6 mg cholesterol
28.7 g carbohydrate
0 g dietary fiber
11.1 mg calcium
16 mg potassium

1. In a medium saucepan, combine sugar, corn syrup, and light cream. Stir to blend. Bring to a boil over medium heat. Boil for 5 minutes or until slightly thickened, stirring occasionally.

2. Remove the saucepan from heat. Stir in vanilla extract. Serve warm over pancakes, waffles, or french toast, as desired.

Simply Vanilla Pudding

Makes 2 servings
Prep time: 5 minutes
Cook time: 15 minutes
Serving size: ½ cup
Each serving has:
321.7 calories
92.9 mg sodium
6.1 g protein
3.5 g total fat
2.2 g saturated fat
14.6 mg cholesterol
66.3 g carbohydrate
0.1 g dietary fiber
224.2 mg calcium
286.3 mg potassium

½ cup granulated sugar

2 TB. cornstarch

1½ cups 2 percent milk

1 tsp. pure vanilla extract

1. In a medium saucepan, combine sugar and cornstarch. Gradually whisk in milk.

2. Cook and stir over medium heat for 15 minutes or until boiling and very thick. Remove from heat, and stir in vanilla extract.

3. Pour pudding into a small bowl. Cool slightly, and then chill for at least 2 hours before serving or until cold.

 Pinch of Sage _____

To prevent a thick skin from forming on the top of the pudding, press plastic wrap directly onto the surface of the pudding before chilling.

Smooth Chocolate Pudding

1 cup semisweet chocolate
chips

2 TB. water

1 (16-oz.) pkg. firm tofu,
well drained and chopped

¼ cup fat-free milk

1 TB. pure vanilla extract

Makes 5 servings
Prep time: 10 minutes
Chill time: 1 hour
Serving size: ½ cup
Each serving has:
325.7 calories
16.7 mg sodium
13.6 g protein
18.8 g total fat
9 g saturated fat
0.3 mg cholesterol
30.7 g carbohydrate
3.4 g dietary fiber
115.3 mg calcium
168.9 mg potassium

1. In a heavy, small saucepan over low heat, melt chocolate chips with water, stirring to blend.

2. In a food processor, combine tofu, chocolate mixture, milk, and vanilla extract. Process for 1 to 2 minutes or until blended and smooth, scraping down sides as necessary. Cover and chill for 1 hour before serving.

 Pinch of Sage _____

Don't rush melting the chocolate chips. Keep the saucepan over low heat and melt the chocolate just until you can stir the chips smooth.

Creamy Raisin Rice Pudding

Makes 7 servings
Prep time: 20 minutes
Cook time: 5 minutes
Serving size: ½ cup
Each serving has:
224.9 calories
65.8 mg sodium
5.4 g protein
0.2 g total fat
0.1 g saturated fat
0 mg cholesterol
50.2 g carbohydrate
1.1 g dietary fiber
137.9 mg calcium
262.5 mg potassium

2 cups uncooked instant white rice

1 (12-oz.) can fat-free evaporated milk

1 cup water

½ cup granulated sugar

½ cup dark raisins

½ tsp. ground cinnamon

1½ tsp. pure vanilla extract

1. In a medium saucepan, combine rice, evaporated milk, water, sugar, and raisins. Bring to a boil over high heat while stirring constantly.

2. Remove the saucepan from heat. Quickly stir in cinnamon and vanilla extract. Cover and let stand for 15 minutes, quickly stirring every 5 minutes. Serve warm or chill to serve cold.

Salternative: If you prefer golden raisins, substitute them in this recipe, or try any dried fruit you like—cherries, cranberries, blueberries—for a different taste.

 Pinch of Sage

When regular homogenized milk has had 60 percent of its water removed, it's called evaporated milk. Evaporated milk and sweetened condensed milk are not interchangeable in recipes, as sweetened condensed milk contains a large amount of added sugar. You can add an equal amount of water to evaporated milk and substitute the mixture for fresh milk in a recipe, which can be more budget friendly.

Cake-Crusted Lemon Pudding

2 large eggs, separated

1 TB. unsalted butter, softened

2 TB. all-purpose flour

¾ cup granulated sugar

¼ cup fresh lemon juice

1 cup fat-free milk

Makes 4 servings
Prep time: 25 minutes
Cook time: 35 minutes
Serving size: ½ cup
Each serving has:
246.4 calories
63.9 mg sodium
5.6 g protein
5.4 g total fat
2.6 g saturated fat
115 mg cholesterol
44.9 g carbohydrate
0.2 g dietary fiber
89 mg calcium
151.6 mg potassium

1. Preheat the oven to 350°F. In a small mixing bowl, beat egg whites until stiff peaks form. Set aside.

2. In a large mixing bowl, beat butter and flour until fine crumbs form. Add sugar, egg yolks, lemon juice, and milk. Beat until well blended, and fold in egg whites.

3. Pour mixture into a pudding dish or a 1-quart baking dish. Bake for 35 minutes or until top is browned. Remove to a wire rack. Serve warm or cold.

Pinch of Sage

Make easy work of separating eggs by using an egg separator. Or if you prefer, you can use the time-tried method of passing the yolk back and forth from one egg shell half to the other. Either way, take care to keep the yolk intact, as just a speck of egg yolk in your egg whites will keep them from whipping up.

Chapter 22

Sweet Endings

In This Chapter

- Preparing low-sodium desserts
- Substituting sodium-sensible ingredients
- Keeping your additions from piling on the sodium
- Maintaining portion control

What's dinner without dessert? Maybe you know the answer to this question because your doctor or nutritionist has warned you away from your favorite baked dessert dishes, and now your sweet tooth feels neglected.

The recipes in this chapter can cheer up both you and your sweet tooth. As long as you make helpful substitutions and maintain an appropriate portion, you can happily dig in to desserts again. Go grab your fork!

A Piece of Cake

Whether the occasion is a birthday, a wedding, a baby shower, a graduation, or some other special milestone, we celebrate with cake. Made with traditional baking ingredients, a cake is a bit high in sodium. However, you can bake your own low-sodium cakes using sodium-free baking substitutes. (For more information on sodium-free baking products, see Chapter 2.)

Not a from-scratch baker? You can choose from several low-sodium cake mixes, as well as frosting mixes, to whip up a "homemade" cake from a box. But you may find the cake recipes that follow are especially delicious if you give them a try.

Say "Cheesecake!"

Cream cheese—the creamy, cheesy ingredient that gives a cheesecake the taste and texture that melts on your tongue—contains at least 80-some milligrams sodium per 1-ounce serving. (The number jumps up dramatically when the cream cheese is fat-free.) Each block of cream cheese is 8 ounces; some cheesecake recipes call for as many as 4 blocks! You don't have to be an ace at math to know that number is perilous. And that's not adding in any sodium from the graham cracker crust, sour cream, or eggs. What's a cheesecake connoisseur to do?

Give the two cheesecake variations in this chapter a try. You may find a low-sodium alternative you like. Otherwise, you'll just have to save up all your sodium budget to blow on a teensy, tiny sliver of your favorite.

My Sweetie Pie (or Sweet Tart)

When it comes to pies and tarts, they're not all created equal. In regard to sodium, fruit pies and tarts are likely to be more reasonable than mile-high cream pies. Plus, preparing the dessert yourself allows you to cut any salt from the crust recipe.

> **Pinch of Sage**
>
> You'll benefit—sodium-wise, calorie-wise, and fat-wise—if you get into the habit of cutting your 9-inch pies and tarts into 8 slices instead of just 6.

If you like your pie with a slice of cheddar cheese or a scoop of ice cream, choose low-sodium products. You don't want to bake a special low-sodium pie only to top it with high-sodium additions.

Crisps and Cobblers

Crisps are good dessert choices for those on a sodium-restricted diet. Typical ingredients are reasonable in sodium, if not sodium-free. Cobblers may require some rising agent, so be certain to substitute a sodium-free baking product as needed.

An important pitfall to avoid when choosing crisps and cobblers for dessert is piling them high with sodium-dense additions. If you like your crisps and cobblers served with frozen yogurt, ice cream, or whipped cream, keep an eye on the serving size of both the crisp or cobbler and the topping. The topping's going to provide some additional sodium, so be sure to tally up the total for the entire dessert.

Golden Lemon Pound Cake

1½ cups (3 sticks) unsalted butter, softened

3 cups granulated sugar

5 large eggs at room temperature

3 cups all-purpose flour

2 TB. pure lemon extract

¾ cup lemon-lime soda pop

Makes 12 servings
Prep time: 35 minutes
Cook time: 1¼ hours
Serving size: 1 slice
Each serving has:
546.8 calories
28.4 mg sodium
5.6 g protein
24.6 g total fat
14.7 g saturated fat
148.5 mg cholesterol
75.1 g carbohydrate
1 g dietary fiber
11.3 mg calcium
29.4 mg potassium

1. Preheat the oven to 325°F. Spray a 12-cup fluted tube pan with nonstick cooking spray with flour.

2. In a large mixing bowl, blend butter and sugar in an electric mixer on medium speed for 20 minutes or until thoroughly combined and very creamy. Add eggs, 1 at a time, beating well after each addition. Add flour and lemon extract. Beat until incorporated. Gently fold in soda pop until blended.

3. Pour batter into the prepared pan. Bake for 1¼ hours or until a cake tester inserted in the center comes out clean. Cool in the pan on a wire rack for 20 minutes. Turn out cake onto the wire rack to cool completely.

Pinch of Sage

To test for doneness, insert a cake tester into the center of the cake. If the tester comes out clean, the cake is done. The cake needs more baking time if the tester comes out moist and coated with crumbs. If you don't have a cake tester, a wooden pick or a strand of spaghetti makes a good substitute.

Decadent Chocolate-Orange Cake

Makes 12 servings
Prep time: 55 minutes
Cook time: 50 minutes
Chill time: 8 hours
Serving size: 1 slice
Each serving has:
503 calories
56.2 mg sodium
7.7 g protein
34.5 g total fat
20.4 g saturated fat
238.1 mg cholesterol
44 g carbohydrate
1.8 g dietary fiber
29.3 mg calcium
166.2 mg potassium

1⅔ cups semisweet chocolate chips

1 tsp. instant coffee granules

10 large eggs, separated

1¼ cups unsalted butter, softened

1¼ cups plus 2 TB. granulated sugar

½ cup light whipping cream

2 TB. grated orange zest

¼ tsp. fresh orange juice

¼ tsp. pure vanilla extract

1. Preheat the oven to 350°F. Grease a 9-inch springform pan with nonstick cooking spray with flour.

2. In a small saucepan over lowest heat, melt chocolate chips with coffee granules, stirring until smooth. Cool.

3. In a large mixing bowl, beat egg whites on medium speed with an electric mixer until frothy. Increase speed to high and beat until stiff peaks form. Set aside.

4. In another large mixing bowl, blend butter and 1¼ cups sugar with an electric mixture on medium speed for 2 minutes or until light and fluffy. Add chocolate mixture, beating until blended. Add egg yolks, 1 at a time, beating well after each addition. Beat for 15 minutes. Fold in egg whites until blended.

5. Pour batter into the prepared pan. Bake for 50 minutes or until a cake tester inserted in the center comes out clean. Cool completely in the pan on a wire rack. Cover and chill for at least 8 hours.

6. In a small, chilled mixing bowl, combine whipping cream, orange zest, remaining 2 tablespoons sugar, orange juice, and vanilla extract. With chilled beaters, beat on medium speed for 3 to 4 minutes or until soft peaks form. Remove cake from the pan and frost on the top and side, or chill frosting until time to frost cake. Cover and chill cake if not serving immediately.

Pinch of Sage

Chill the beaters and small mixing bowl by placing them in the refrigerator before mixing the frosting. When your ingredients, bowl, and beaters are cold, your whipped cream will remain stable for several hours after beating.

Lightweight Carrot Cake

3 large eggs, separated

½ cup granulated sugar

⅔ cup fat-free milk

1 tsp. fresh lemon juice

1 cup cake flour

1 cup whole-wheat flour

1 cup firmly packed light brown sugar

1 tsp. sodium-free baking powder

1 tsp. sodium-free baking soda

1½ tsp. ground cinnamon

⅓ cup light olive oil

1½ cups grated carrots

1 TB. confectioners' sugar

Makes 16 servings
Prep time: 25 minutes
Cook time: 30 minutes
Serving size: 1 piece
Each serving has:
195.4 calories
105.2 mg sodium
3.4 g protein
5.7 g total fat
0.9 g saturated fat
40.1 mg cholesterol
33.8 g carbohydrate
1.6 g dietary fiber
47.9 mg calcium
142.3 mg potassium

1. Preheat the oven to 350°F. Grease a 13×9×2-inch baking pan with nonstick cooking spray with flour.

2. In a small mixing bowl, beat egg whites with an electric mixer on medium speed until frothy. Gradually add granulated sugar, increase speed to high, and beat until stiff.

3. Measure milk into a measuring cup. Stir in lemon juice and then let stand.

4. In a large mixing bowl, combine cake flour, whole-wheat flour, brown sugar, baking powder, baking soda, and cinnamon. Stir to blend. Add olive oil and milk mixture; mix well. Add egg yolks and mix well. Fold in egg whites, and then fold in carrots.

5. Turn batter into the prepared pan. Bake for 30 minutes or until a cake tester inserted in the center comes out clean. Cool on a wire rack. Sprinkle confectioners' sugar over top of cake just before serving.

Pinch of Sage

You can frost this carrot cake with a traditional cream cheese frosting if you need to, but remember that cream cheese is high in sodium, especially if you opt for the fat-free version to avoid the saturated fat and cholesterol of regular cream cheese.

Yogurt-Baked Cheesecake

Makes 8 servings
Prep time: 15 minutes
Cook time: 22 minutes
Chill time: 2 hours
Serving size: 1 slice
Each serving has:
91.3 calories
65.4 mg sodium
4 g protein
0 g total fat
0 g saturated fat
1.3 mg cholesterol
19.7 g carbohydrate
0.3 g dietary fiber
78.6 mg calcium
37.9 mg potassium

3 egg whites at room temperature

2 cups fat-free plain yogurt

3 TB. granulated sugar

1 tsp. pure vanilla extract

1 TB. fresh lemon juice

1 TB. cornstarch

1 cup cherry pie filling

1. Preheat the oven to 325°F. In a small mixing bowl, beat egg whites with an electric mixture on medium speed until frothy. Increase speed to high and beat until soft peaks form.

2. In a large mixing bowl, combine yogurt, sugar, vanilla extract, lemon juice, and cornstarch. Mix until blended. Fold in egg whites.

3. Turn mixture into a 9-inch nonstick pie pan. Bake for 22 to 25 minutes or until top is golden. Cool on a wire rack and then chill for at least 2 hours before serving. Spoon 2 tablespoons cherry pie filling over each slice.

Salternative: Use the fruit topping of your choice for a prettier presentation with good taste. Try blueberry, strawberry, peach, or your favorite.

 Pinch of Sage _____

Like a traditional cheesecake, this yogurt cheesecake will crack on the top. Covering it up with a fruit topping is a simple solution.

Silky Tofu Cheesecake

1½ cups graham cracker crumbs

1 cup plus 2 tsp. granulated sugar

2 TB. water

1 TB. extra-light olive oil

1 (14-oz.) pkg. soft tofu, well drained and coarsely chopped

⅓ cup fat-free milk

1 large egg at room temperature

1 TB. grated lemon zest

¼ cup fresh lemon juice

3 TB. all-purpose flour

Makes 12 servings
Prep time: 25 minutes
Cook time: 45 minutes
Serving size: 1 slice
Each serving has:
171.3 calories
76.2 mg sodium
5.3 g protein
4.8 g total fat
0.8 g saturated fat
17.8 mg cholesterol
28.1 g carbohydrate
0.8 g dietary fiber
50.6 mg calcium
38 mg potassium

1. Preheat the oven to 350°F. Grease a 9-inch springform pan with nonstick cooking spray with flour.

2. To make crust, combine graham cracker crumbs, 2 teaspoons sugar, water, and olive oil in a medium bowl. Stir with a fork until evenly moistened. Pat onto bottom and about ½ inch up side of the prepared pan.

3. To prepare filling, combine tofu, milk, egg, remaining 1 cup sugar, lemon zest, lemon juice, and flour in a food processor. Purée for 30 seconds or until smooth. Pour filling into crust.

4. Place a pan of hot water on the bottom oven rack and cheesecake on the middle oven rack. Bake for 45 minutes or until just set in center. Remove the pan to a wire rack, and run a knife around the edge of the pan to loosen cheesecake. Cool completely, and then cover and chill for at least 2 hours before serving. Top with cherry, blueberry, or strawberry pie filling as desired.

 Pinch of Sage

When you're baking in a springform pan, set the pan on a baking sheet until you're sure it's not going to leak. If it starts to leak, bake with the sheet under the pan.

Perfect Pie Crust

Makes 1 (9-inch) pie crust
Prep time: 15 minutes
Serving size: ⅛ of crust
Each serving has:
137.5 calories
0.1 mg sodium
1.5 g protein
9.3 g total fat
2.3 g saturated fat
0 mg cholesterol
11.5 g carbohydrate
0.5 g dietary fiber
0.1 mg calcium
0 mg potassium

6 TB. trans-fat-free shortening

1 cup all-purpose flour

5 TB. cold water

1. In a medium bowl, cut shortening into flour with a pastry blender, two knives or your fingertips until crumbly. Add water, 1 tablespoon at a time, stirring with a fork until dough forms and cleans the side of the bowl.

2. Turn out dough onto a lightly floured work surface, and roll out to an 11-inch circle. Fold circle into quarters, and transfer to a 9-inch nonstick pie pan. Place point of dough in the center of the pan, unfolding and pressing dough into the pan. With a sharp knife, trim edge of dough as needed. Flute or crimp edge as desired. Follow desired pie recipe to fill and bake.

Salt Pitfall _____

Use only the amount of water needed to form a dough, which may be more or less than the amount called for.

Crunchy Oat Crust

1 cup quick oats

⅓ cup unsalted chopped pecans

¼ cup light brown sugar

4 TB. unsalted butter, melted

Makes 1 (9-inch) pie crust
Prep time: 10 minutes
Cook time: 10 minutes
Serving size: ⅛ of crust
Each serving has:
186 calories
3.1 mg sodium
3.8 g protein
10.4 g total fat
4 g saturated fat
15 mg cholesterol
20.3 g carbohydrate
2.5 g dietary fiber
19.8 mg calcium
127.8 mg potassium

1. Preheat the oven to 350°F. In a medium bowl, stir together oats, pecans, and brown sugar. Drizzle in butter. Stir with a fork until evenly moistened.

2. Turn mixture into a nonstick 9-inch pie pan. Press evenly onto the bottom and up the side of the pan to form a crust. Bake for 10 minutes or until lightly browned and set. Cool on a wire rack before filling as desired.

Salternative: You can use your favorite unsalted chopped nuts for this pie crust, such as walnuts, peanuts, or almonds.

Pinch of Sage

Brown sugar is sold in light and dark varieties. The designations refer to the color produced by the amount of added molasses. If you only have dark brown sugar available, you can substitute ⅔ cup dark brown sugar plus ⅓ cup granulated sugar for 1 cup light brown sugar.

No-Bake Cherry Vanilla Pie

Makes 8 servings
Prep time: 10 minutes
Chill time: 2 hours
Serving size: 1 slice
Each serving has:
267.6 calories
20.3 mg sodium
5.1 g protein
12 g total fat
5.6 g saturated fat
15.6 mg cholesterol
35.8 g carbohydrate
2.5 g dietary fiber
56.4 mg calcium
206.4 mg potassium

1 (6-oz.) container fat-free, sugar-free cherry-vanilla yogurt

1 cup French vanilla frozen whipped topping, thawed

1 (15-oz.) can pitted cherries, well drained

1 Crunchy Oat Crust (recipe earlier in this chapter)

1. In a medium bowl, stir together yogurt and whipped topping. Stir in cherries.

2. Turn mixture into Crunchy Oat Crust. Chill for at least 2 hours before serving.

Salternative: Substitute plain whipped topping if the French vanilla version isn't available.

 Pinch of Sage

Experiment and create your own favorite version of this easy-to-make pie by using different whipped topping flavors, yogurt flavors, and fruit.

Cake-Crusted Lemon Custard Pie

1 Perfect Pie Crust (recipe earlier in this chapter)

2 large eggs at room temperature, separated

1 TB. unsalted butter, softened

2 TB. all-purpose flour

¾ cup granulated sugar

¼ cup fresh lemon juice

1 cup fat-free milk

Makes 8 servings
Prep time: 25 minutes
Cook time: 40 minutes
Serving size: 1 slice
Each serving has:
260.7 calories
32 mg sodium
4.3 g protein
12 g total fat
3.6 g saturated fat
57.5 mg cholesterol
34 g carbohydrate
0.6 g dietary fiber
44.6 mg calcium
75.8 mg potassium

1. Preheat the oven to 350°F. With the tines of a fork, prick the bottom and sides of Perfect Pie Crust. Bake for 5 minutes.

2. Meanwhile, in a small mixing bowl, beat egg whites with an electric mixture on medium speed until frothy. Increase speed to high and beat until stiff peaks form. Set aside.

3. In a large mixing bowl, beat butter and flour until fine crumbs form. Add sugar, egg yolks, lemon juice, and milk. Beat until well blended. Fold in egg whites.

4. Pour mixture into partially baked pie crust. Bake for 35 minutes or until top is browned and filling is set. Remove to a wire rack to cool. Serve at room temperature or cold.

Pinch of Sage

If you would enjoy this lemony pudding without the pie crust, see the recipe for Cake-Crusted Lemon Pudding in Chapter 21.

Harvest Pumpkin Pie

Makes 8 servings
Prep time: 10 minutes
Cook time: 1 hour
Serving size: 1 slice
Each serving has:
322 calories
34.4 mg sodium
4 g protein
15.3 g total fat
5.6 g saturated fat
69.7 mg cholesterol
43.3 g carbohydrate
2.1 g dietary fiber
55.2 mg calcium
235.7 mg potassium

2 large eggs at room temperature

1 cup light brown sugar

½ cup light whipping cream

1 (15-oz.) can solid-pack pumpkin, not pumpkin pie filling

1 tsp. pumpkin pie spice

1 Perfect Pie Crust (recipe earlier in this chapter)

1. Preheat the oven to 425°F. In a large mixing bowl, beat eggs on medium speed for 3 minutes or until thick and lemon-colored. Add brown sugar, whipping cream, pumpkin, and pumpkin pie spice. Beat for 1 to 2 minutes or until well blended.

2. Pour pumpkin mixture into Perfect Pie Crust. Bake for 10 minutes. Reduce the oven temperature to 350°F. Bake for 50 minutes or until a knife inserted in the center comes out clean. Cool completely on a wire rack before cutting.

 **Pinch of Sage**

If the edge of your pie crust is browning too quickly while the pie cooks, you can use a pie shield to protect it from over-browning. Covering the edge of the crust with aluminum foil works, too.

Rainbow Fruit Tart

⅓ cup unsalted butter, softened

1¼ cups all-purpose flour

5 TB. ice water

1 cup egg substitute

⅓ cup granulated sugar

1 tsp. pure almond extract or pure vanilla extract

¼ cup fat-free milk

1 cup mixed fruit (sliced peaches, peeled, halved and sliced kiwifruit, sliced bananas, mandarin orange segments, crushed pineapple, or other fruits)

Makes 8 servings
Prep time: 30 minutes
Cook time: 45 minutes
Serving size: 1 slice
Each serving has:
207.4 calories
59.7 mg sodium
6.1 g protein
8.7 g total fat
4.9 g saturated fat
20.5 mg cholesterol
25.7 g carbohydrate
1.1 g dietary fiber
27.3 mg calcium
159.1 mg potassium

1. Preheat the oven to 350°F. In a medium bowl, cut butter into flour using a pastry blender, two knives or your fingertips until mixture is crumbly. Add ice water, 1 tablespoon at a time, stirring mixture with a fork until dough forms and cleans the side of the bowl.

2. Turn out dough onto a lightly floured work surface, and roll out to an 11-inch circle. Fold circle into quarters, and transfer to a 9-inch nonstick pie pan, placing point of dough in the center of the pan and unfolding and pressing dough into the pan. Make a ½-inch decorative flute around the edge.

3. In a medium bowl, combine egg substitute, sugar, and almond extract. Whisk to blend.

4. In a small saucepan over high heat, heat milk until bubbles form around edge of the pan. Gradually whisk milk into egg substitute mixture. Pour into crust. Bake for 45 minutes or until set. Cool completely on a wire rack, and then cover and chill for 2 hours.

5. To serve, arrange mixed fruit decoratively on top of filling.

 Pinch of Sage

If you choose fruits that will quickly discolor, such as apples or bananas, rub the cut surfaces with a little lemon juice to prevent browning.

Merry Berry Tart

Makes 8 servings
Prep time: 30 minutes
Cook time: 45 minutes
Serving size: 1 slice
Each serving has:
207.6 calories
60.2 mg sodium
6.3 g protein
9 g total fat
5 g saturated fat
20.5 mg cholesterol
25.5 g carbohydrate
1.6 g dietary fiber
30.9 mg calcium
172.1 mg potassium

1¼ cups all-purpose flour

2 TB. cocoa powder

⅓ cup unsalted butter, softened

5 TB. ice water

1 cup egg substitute

⅓ cup granulated sugar

1 tsp. pure vanilla extract

¼ cup fat-free milk

1 cup mixed berries (sliced strawberries, blueberries, red raspberries, and/or blackberries)

1. Preheat the oven to 350°F. In a medium bowl, stir together flour and cocoa powder. Cut in butter with a pastry blender or two knives until mixture is crumbly. Add ice water, 1 tablespoon at a time, stirring mixture with a fork until dough forms and cleans side of bowl.

2. Turn out dough onto a work surface lightly dusted with cocoa powder and roll out to an 11-inch circle. Fold circle into quarters, and transfer to a 9-inch nonstick pie pan, placing dough point in the center of the pan and unfolding and pressing dough into the pan. Make a ½-inch decorative flute around the edge.

3. In a medium bowl, combine egg substitute, sugar, and vanilla extract. Whisk to blend.

4. In a small saucepan over high heat, heat milk until bubbles form around edge of the pan. Gradually whisk milk into egg substitute mixture. Pour into crust. Bake for 45 minutes or until set. Cool completely on a wire rack, and then cover and chill for 2 hours.

5. To serve, arrange mixed berries decoratively on top of filling.

Pinch of Sage

To easily flute the edge of the crust, trim any excess dough with a sharp knife, leaving about a 1 inch overhand around the rim. Fold the dough under itself, making it even with the edge of the pie pan. Place each thumb on either side of the crust edge. Crimp by pushing one thumb forward and the other thumb backward. Work your way around the edge, inserting one thumb into a previously made indentation and shaping a new notch with the other.

Pilgrim's Cranberry-Apple Crisp

1½ cups quick oats

½ cup plus 3 TB. all-purpose flour

½ cup light brown sugar

¼ cup unsalted chopped pecans

½ cup (1 stick) unsalted butter, melted

3 cups peeled, chopped Golden Delicious apples

2 cups fresh or frozen cranberries

1 cup granulated sugar

Makes 8 servings
Prep time: 20 minutes
Cook time: 45 minutes
Serving size: 3½×2¾-inch portion
Each serving has:
468.4 calories
6.2 mg sodium
6.4 g protein
16 g total fat
7.6 g saturated fat
30 mg cholesterol
76.8 g carbohydrate
6.1 g dietary fiber
33.6 mg calcium
242.7 mg potassium

1. Preheat the oven to 350°F, and grease an 11×7×2-inch non-stick baking pan with nonstick cooking spray with flour.

2. In a medium bowl, combine oats, ½ cup flour, brown sugar, and pecans. Stir. Drizzle in butter, and stir until well combined. Set aside.

3. In another medium bowl, combine apples, cranberries, sugar, and remaining 3 tablespoons flour. Stir to coat and then turn into the prepared pan. Sprinkle oat mixture over top. Bake for 45 to 50 minutes or until top is browned and fruit is tender.

 Pinch of Sage

If you're using frozen cranberries, just add them right to the mixture frozen. You don't need to thaw them before using.

Strawberry Double Crisp

Makes 6 servings
Prep time: 20 minutes
Cook time: 40 minutes
Serving size: 4×2½-inch square
Each serving has:
375.2 calories
8.4 mg sodium
6.1 g protein
14.5 g total fat
6.4 g saturated fat
25 mg cholesterol
57.6 g carbohydrate
6 g dietary fiber
40.2 mg calcium
296.1 mg potassium

3 cups sliced fresh strawberries

⅓ cup granulated sugar

⅔ cup quick oats

⅔ cup whole-wheat flour

½ cup firmly packed light brown sugar

¼ cup unsalted chopped pecans

5 TB. unsalted butter

1. Preheat the oven to 350°F. Spray the bottom of an 8×8×2-inch baking dish with nonstick cooking spray.

2. Place strawberries in a bowl, and sprinkle sugar over top. Set aside.

3. In a medium bowl, stir together oats, whole-wheat flour, brown sugar, and pecans. Using a pastry blender, two knives or your fingertips, cut in butter until crumbly and evenly distributed.

4. Spread 2 cups oat mixture over the bottom of the prepared dish. Stir strawberry mixture, pour into the dish, and spread remaining oat mixture over top. Bake for 40 minutes or until browned and bubbly. Serve warm or chilled.

Salt Pitfall

If you scoop on vanilla frozen yogurt or ice cream, that adds sodium. Don't forget to calculate the additional sodium the "extras" add.

Bubbly Blueberry Crisp

3 cups fresh blueberries

1 TB. fresh lemon juice

½ cup granulated sugar

¼ tsp. ground cinnamon

¼ tsp. ground nutmeg

¾ cup all-purpose flour

½ cup firmly packed light brown sugar

6 TB. unsalted butter at room temperature

Makes 6 servings
Prep time: 20 minutes
Cook time: 25 minutes
Serving size: 4×2½-inch portion
Each serving has:
330.4 calories
11.7 mg sodium
2 g protein
11.6 g total fat
7.1 g saturated fat
30 mg cholesterol
56.6 g carbohydrate
2.5 g dietary fiber
21.6 mg calcium
132.2 mg potassium

1. Preheat the oven to 350°F. In a large bowl, combine blueberries, lemon juice, sugar, cinnamon, and nutmeg, and stir to coat evenly. Turn into an 8×8×2-inch nonstick baking pan.

2. In another large bowl, combine flour and brown sugar. Cut in butter with a pastry blender, two knives or your fingertips until crumbly, and then evenly sprinkle over top of blueberry mixture. Bake for 25 minutes or until bubbly and golden brown. Serve warm or cold, as desired.

Salt Pitfall _____

Be sure to calculate the sodium and other nutritional data if you serve this crisp with frozen yogurt, ice cream, or whipped cream.

Topsy-Turvy Peach Cobbler

Makes 6 servings
Prep time: 15 minutes
Cook time: 55 minutes
Serving size: 4½×3-inch portion
Each serving has:
273.5 calories
17.7 mg sodium
3.4 g protein
7.8 g total fat
4.7 g saturated fat
20.6 mg cholesterol
48.9 g carbohydrate
1.8 g dietary fiber
113 mg calcium
331.3 mg potassium

4 TB. unsalted butter

1 cup all-purpose flour

2 tsp. sodium-free baking powder

¾ cup granulated sugar

¾ cup fat-free milk

2 cups peeled and sliced fresh peaches (about 1 lb. or 4 medium peaches)

1. Preheat the oven to 325°F. Place butter in a 9×9×2-inch non-stick baking pan. Melt in the preheating oven.

2. In a medium bowl, stir together flour, baking powder, and sugar. Pour in milk, and stir until blended. Pour batter into the prepared pan over bubbly butter.

3. Arrange peaches over batter without touching the edges of the pan. Do not mix. Bake for 55 to 60 minutes or until top is browned. Serve warm or cold with frozen yogurt, ice cream, or whipped cream, as desired.

 Pinch of Sage _____

To peel peaches, place them in a bowl and pour boiling water over them. Let the peaches stand for 1 minute and then plunge them into ice water. The skins can be removed easily.

Spiced Zucchini Cobbler

4 cups peeled, chopped
zucchini

⅓ cup fresh lemon juice

1½ cups granulated sugar

1 tsp. ground cinnamon

¼ tsp. ground nutmeg

2 cups all-purpose flour

¾ cup (1½ sticks) unsalted
butter

Makes 9 servings
Prep time: 25 minutes
Cook time: 51 minutes
Serving size: 3×3-inch portion
Each serving has:
371.1 calories
2.2 mg sodium
3.4 g protein
15.2 g total fat
9.4 g saturated fat
40 mg cholesterol
56.4 g carbohydrate
1.7 g dietary fiber
12.5 mg calcium
150 mg potassium

1. In a medium saucepan, combine zucchini and lemon juice. Cook over medium heat for 15 to 20 minutes or until zucchini is tender, stirring occasionally. Stir in ½ cup sugar, ½ teaspoon cinnamon, and nutmeg. Cook for 1 minute and then remove from heat.

2. Preheat the oven to 375°F. Grease a 9×9×2-inch baking dish with nonstick cooking spray with flour.

3. In a large bowl, stir together flour and remaining 1 cup sugar. Cut in butter with a pastry blender, two knives or your fingertips until crumbly. Stir ¼ cup flour mixture into zucchini mixture. Turn ½ remaining flour mixture into the prepared dish, and press in using your fingers. Spread zucchini mixture over top. Sprinkle remaining flour mixture over zucchini mixture. Sprinkle ½ teaspoon cinnamon over top. Bake for 35 minutes or until top is browned. Cool on a wire rack. Serve warm or cold.

Pinch of Sage

This recipe is a great way to use up your bountiful zucchini harvest—or your neighbor's. Serve it as you would an apple cobbler.

Part 7

'Tis the Seasoning

Many of the foods we enjoy wouldn't be worth eating without the condiments, dressings, and seasonings that contribute their flavor. If you love fish dishes because of the great taste of tartar sauce or order a taco because you're in the mood for salsa, then you'll appreciate the recipes that follow.

You may be restricting sodium, but you certainly don't want to hold back flavor. All your salads can be well dressed, and all your sandwiches spread with zest. Main dishes sing with the addition of a salsa or relish, and any savory recipe is more appetizing when spiced up with an aromatic seasoning blend. For more flavorful foods, turn the page!

Chapter 23

Classic Condiments

In This Chapter

- ◆ Enjoying your favorite condiments without excessive sodium
- ◆ Preparing your own low-sodium spreads and sauces
- ◆ Adding flavor without adding sodium
- ◆ Enhancing foods, not overpowering them

Do you find yourself craving fish because you fancy tartar sauce? Do people question if you'd like a little burger with your mustard? If so, you know how powerful a condiment can be in imparting delectable flavor to your favorite foods.

Many of the classic condiments are high in sodium. Maybe you've found suitable alternatives available at your local supermarket. Or perhaps you've discovered a mail-order supplier that keeps you stocked up on your favorites. If not, you do have options.

You can easily prepare many spreads and sauces at home. If you've been dying for a bowl of navy beans seasoned with a heaping teaspoon of horseradish or a finger-licking barbecue chicken leg, look no farther than the recipes in this chapter. Fresh, self-prepared condiments can tickle your taste buds into enjoying your favorite foods again—without ruining your low-sodium resolve.

Homespun Yum

Many of your favorite condiments are now available commercially in no-salt-added and low-sodium versions, but you may find it difficult to come by some of them, still. If you don't have access to sodium-responsible spreads and sauces, you don't have to forego them.

Pinch of Sage

If you can't convince your local supermarket to stock your favorite condiment in a no-salt-added, sodium-free, or low-sodium version, and you prefer not to make your own (but these recipes are easy, really!), check out Appendix B for more information on mail-order sources.

Making condiments in your own kitchen can be convenient. You can always have freshly prepared, great-tasting accompaniments when you need them. If you make fresh tartar sauce, you certainly won't be disappointed to find that the bottle of tartar sauce in the refrigerator expired 3 months ago. You can mix up what you'll use the very night you're cooking seafood.

Another benefit of homemade condiments is the savings. The ingredients are inexpensive. You'll be liberated from purchasing large quantities of a condiment to use only a quarter of it before it goes bad.

The top advantage, of course, is that you control the sodium. Homemade condiments allow you to enjoy the good taste without giving in to the temptation to eat too much sodium in favor of flavor.

Using a Light Hand

Adding spreads or sauces to your sandwiches, meats, soups, eggs, vegetables, and more should add flavor. Even if the condiments are low in sodium, you don't want to use a heavy hand, piling on additional calories and fat.

Be sure to note the serving sizes. A single serving of a condiment is intended to your enhance food, not overpower it. You *can* have too much of a good thing!

Home-Style Mustard

¼ cup white vinegar

3 TB. dry mustard

2 TB. water

6 TB. light brown sugar

1 large egg

1. In a small saucepan, combine vinegar and dry mustard. Whisk until blended. Add water, brown sugar, and egg. Whisk to combine.

2. Cook over high heat, whisking constantly. When mixture bubbles around edges, reduce heat. Gently simmer as you whisk for 10 minutes. Pour mustard into a clean jar. Let cool. Cover and refrigerate tightly covered for 3 to 5 days.

Salternative: If you want to gussy-up this mustard, add your choice of chopped fresh or dried herbs to taste. Try basil, dill, tarragon, cilantro, rosemary, for starters.

Makes ½ cup
Prep time: 5 minutes
Cook time: 15 minutes
Serving size: 2 teaspoons
Each serving has:
44.3 calories
8.1 mg sodium
1.2 g protein
1.2 g total fat
0.1 g saturated fat
17.7 mg cholesterol
7.2 g carbohydrate
0.1 g dietary fiber
12.9 mg calcium
28.8 mg potassium

Make-Your-Own Mustard

Makes ½ cup
Prep time: 5 minutes
Cook time: 10 minutes
Serving size: 1 teaspoon
Each serving has:
22.5 calories
2.8 mg sodium
0.7 g protein
0.8 g total fat
0.1 g saturated fat
8.9 mg cholesterol
3.3 g carbohydrate
0.1 g dietary fiber
4.6 mg calcium
5.9 mg potassium

¼ cup dry mustard

⅓ cup granulated sugar

⅓ cup cider vinegar

1 large egg

1. In the top of a double boiler, combine dry mustard, sugar, cider vinegar, and egg. Whisk together until very smooth.

2. Cook, stirring constantly, over simmering water for 10 minutes or until well thickened. Pour into a clean jar.

3. Cool completely. Cover with a tight-fitting lid, and store in the refrigerator for 3 to 5 days.

 Pinch of Sage ⎯⎯⎯⎯⎯⎯

If you don't have a double boiler, you can use two heavy pans if one sits nicely in the top of the other. Combine the mixture in the top pan off the heat while you bring the water in the bottom pan to a simmer on the burner. Keep the water in the bottom pan just at a simmer while cooking the mustard.

Kitchen Ketchup

3 (6-oz.) cans no-salt-added tomato paste

4 cups water

½ cup chopped yellow onions

½ cup chopped celery

½ cup cider vinegar

½ cup granulated sugar

2 TB. unsalted butter

1 TB. firmly packed light brown sugar

1 tsp. molasses

⅛ tsp. freshly ground black pepper

⅛ tsp. garlic powder

⅛ tsp. onion powder

⅛ tsp. dried basil

⅛ tsp. dried tarragon

⅛ tsp. ground cinnamon

⅛ tsp. ground cloves

Makes 3 cups
Prep time: 15 minutes
Cook time: 4 hours, 10 minutes
Serving size: 1 tablespoon
Each serving has:
23.7 calories
10.9 mg sodium
0.4 g protein
0.5 g total fat
0.3 g saturated fat
1.3 mg cholesterol
4.9 g carbohydrate
0.5 g dietary fiber
5.7 mg calcium
112 mg potassium

1. In a food processor, combine tomato paste, water, onions, celery, vinegar, and sugar. Process for 1 to 2 minutes or until smooth. (Process in batches if your food processor is not large enough to hold all the ingredients.) Pour mixture into a large saucepan.

2. Add butter, brown sugar, molasses, pepper, garlic powder, onion powder, basil, tarragon, cinnamon, and cloves to the saucepan. Bring to a simmer over medium heat. Reduce heat and gently simmer, uncovered, for 4 hours or until thickened, reduced, and deep red, stirring occasionally.

3. Pour ketchup into tightly covered containers, and refrigerate for up to 1 month.

Pinch of Sage

If you can't find no-salt-added tomato paste, you can use regular tomato paste. The difference in sodium content is negligible at about 15 milligrams of sodium per serving versus 20 milligrams in the regular stuff.

Sun-Up Tomato Gravy

Makes 5 servings
Prep time: 5 minutes
Cook time: 20 minutes
Serving size: ¼ cup
Each serving has:
45.2 calories
34.8 mg sodium
0.9 g protein
0 g total fat
0 g saturated fat
0 mg cholesterol
11 g carbohydrate
1.4 g dietary fiber
17.8 mg calcium
19 mg potassium

1 (14.5-oz.) can no-salt-added diced tomatoes

1½ TB. all-purpose flour

1½ TB. water

2 TB. firmly packed light brown sugar

1. In a medium saucepan, bring tomatoes to a boil over medium heat, stirring occasionally. When boiling, reduce heat to medium-low and stir. Return tomatoes to a boil.

2. Meanwhile, whisk together flour and water. When tomatoes are boiling, stir in flour mixture and brown sugar. Cook and stir for 10 to 15 minutes or until smooth and of desired consistency. Serve hot over fried potatoes or toast, as desired. Refrigerate any leftovers for up to 4 days.

Homemade Horseradish

1 cup pared, coarsely
chopped horseradish root

½ cup white vinegar

Makes 1 cup	
Prep time: 10 minutes	
Serving size: 1 teaspoon	
Each serving has:	
3 calories	
0.5 mg sodium	
0.1 g protein	
0 g total fat	
0 g saturated fat	
0 mg cholesterol	
0.6 g carbohydrate	
0 g dietary fiber	
5.3 mg calcium	
27.7 mg potassium	

1. In a well-ventilated area (gasmask optional), add horseradish root to a blender. Chop on high speed for a few seconds. Carefully tip up the lid's cap to pour in vinegar a little at a time while blending. Chop for 2 minutes or until mixture is creamy, stopping to scrape down sides as necessary.

2. Pack into small glass jars with tight-fitting lids and refrigerate for up to 3 or 4 months.

 Pinch of Sage _____
This is a quick, easy way to save on the salt and other added ingredients in many commercially prepared horseradish sauces. Use the amount of vinegar necessary to make the horseradish mixture creamy.

Like-So for Mayo

1 tsp. fat-free plain yogurt

1 tsp. fat-free sour cream

Makes 1 serving	
Prep time: 1 minute	
Serving size: 2 teaspoons	
Each serving has:	
12.1 calories	
5.3 mg sodium	
0.4 g protein	
0.8 g total fat	
0.6 g saturated fat	
3.4 mg cholesterol	
0.6 g carbohydrate	
0 g dietary fiber	
9.6 mg calcium	
7.5 mg potassium	

1. In a very small bowl, stir together yogurt and sour cream until blended.

2. Spread onto a sandwich as desired.

Pinch of Sage _____
This spread is tangier than mayonnaise, but it adds a nice zing to favorite sandwiches.

Easy BBQ Sauce

Makes 2¼ cups
Prep time: 15 minutes
Serving size: 2 tablespoons
Each serving has:
34.2 calories
3.7 mg sodium
0.4 g protein
1.4 g total fat
0.8 g saturated fat
3.3 mg cholesterol
5.5 g carbohydrate
0.3 g dietary fiber
7.7 mg calcium
75.8 mg potassium

1 cup no-salt-added ketchup

1 cup water

2 TB. firmly packed light brown sugar

2 tsp. fresh lemon juice

2 TB. unsalted butter, melted

2 TB. minced yellow onions

1 TB. minced green bell pepper

2 tsp. dry mustard

1 tsp. Salt-Shaker Substitute (recipe in Chapter 26) or other salt-free salt-substitute seasoning blend

1 tsp. celery seeds

1. In a medium stainless-steel or glass bowl, combine ketchup, water, brown sugar, lemon juice, butter, onions, bell pepper, dry mustard, Salt-Shaker Substitute, and celery seeds.

2. Whisk until well blended.

 Pinch of Sage _____

You can reduce or increase this barbecue sauce to use in your favorite recipes.

Dilly Tartar Sauce

Makes 7 servings
Prep time: 10 minutes
Serving size: 2 tablespoons
Each serving has:
14.4 calories
11.7 mg sodium
0.9 g protein
0.1 g total fat
0.1 g saturated fat
1 mg cholesterol
2.6 g carbohydrate
0.1 g dietary fiber
25.5 mg calcium
30.8 mg potassium

¼ cup fat-free plain yogurt

¼ cup fat-free sour cream

¼ cup minced yellow onions

3 TB. finely chopped fresh dill

¼ tsp. ground white pepper

1. In a small bowl, combine yogurt, sour cream, onions, dill, and white pepper.

2. Stir until thoroughly blended. Cover and chill if not serving immediately, using within 2 days.

Salternative: You may decrease or increase this recipe as needed.

Chapter 24

That's Salada Dressings!

In This Chapter

◆ Bidding high-sodium bottled dressings adieu!

◆ Whipping up homemade salad dressings

◆ Enjoying the natural taste of freshly made dressings

◆ Using discretion when drizzling on dressings

Salad dressing can make a good salad even better! A flavorful dressing can complement the salad ingredients and bring out their crisp, fresh taste. With just the right balance of a delightful salad dressing, a bowlful of greens transforms into a delicious endeavor.

Perhaps you're thinking: *Sure, I love salad dressings, so why are you torturing me with how great-tasting they are? I can't have bottled salad dressings now that I'm watching my sodium intake.* Hogwash! You can prepare a plethora of luscious dressings with little effort or fanfare. Salad dressing doesn't come from a bottle any more than bacon comes from a frying pan. With homemade salad dressings, you can go hog wild again!

Fast, Fresh, and Fabulous

If you enjoy your green salads without a dressing, then you don't have to concern yourself with the high sodium content of most bottled salad dressings. The same goes for tried-and-true vinegar-and-oil purists. However, if you're a lover of richly dressed greens, you may be heartbroken to discover the amount of sodium in a single serving of your favorite bottled dressing. If you've just got to have your salad dressing, you can buy a selection of sodium-free varieties.

Better yet, you can whip up your own fast, fresh, and fabulous salad dressings right in your own kitchen. You only need a few ingredients, a small bowl, and a whisk or a blender, and *violà!* You've created the perfect salad dressing to complement the salad you're ready to eat right now. If you have 5 to 10 minutes, you can take a naked green salad and dress it up in style.

> **Pinch of Sage**
>
> Whenever a recipe indicates that you should whisk dressing ingredients until blended, you can opt to combine the ingredients in a jar with a tight-fitting lid; instead of whisking, shake well until combined. Can cooking get any easier?

We've included a wide range of recipes here to cover an array of individual tastes, as well as any individual's taste on any given day. So whether you're a Balsamic Vinaigrette regular or a daily dressing swinger, you'll find these salad dressing recipes in good taste. Plus, we've included a flavorsome dressing for potato and macaroni salads, as well as a creamy dressing for fruit salads. All the dressings in this chapter are fresh and as bright-tasting as your lovingly selected salad fixings.

A Note on Oil

The salad dressing recipes in this chapter call for extra-virgin olive oil when needed. You can, of course, substitute your favorite oils or even experiment with subtle taste differences when employing different oils.

We've suggested olive oil because the Food and Drug Administration now allows olive oil labels to claim …

Limited and not conclusive scientific evidence suggests that eating about 2 tablespoons (23 grams) of olive oil daily may reduce the risk of coronary heart disease due to the monounsaturated fat in olive oil. To achieve this possible benefit, olive oil is to replace a similar amount of saturated fat and not increase the total number of calories you eat in a day.

So if you can help your heart health and enjoy a delicious dressing at the same time, can you beat that?

Getting Caught in a Downpour

You have a big, beautiful salad in front of you, full of crisp greens, a rainbow of veggies and maybe fruits, and unsalted nuts or seeds. It's a bowlful of nutritional benefits. It's time to add the dressing—but wait! Now is the time to show some constraint. Don't succumb to the temptation to drown those poor greens. A soggy salad doesn't taste good, and it's not good for you.

Most of the following dressings have a 2-tablespoon serving size. This amount is sufficient for a large salad. If you're eating a small side salad with your meal, cut back on the dressing to about 1 tablespoon or less. You should always use just enough dressing to make the taste of your salad pop and not any more.

Perhaps a downpour of dressing is your salad-eating downfall. To help you keep your salad dressing servings more reasonable, you can implement a few tactics. Some folks find it helpful to precisely measure. Knowing how much you're consuming is always a good idea, especially because a number of people are not as good at eye-balling the amount as they think. (You can test your accuracy, if you like. Pour the amount of dressing you would normally drizzle over your salad and then measure it. And don't be surprised if it measures a bit more than you thought.)

Another method that may help you control your portions is lightly dipping each forkful into a small container of measured salad dressing. Each bite has the perfect complement of dressing, and you won't eat a drop more than your salad requires.

A good, alternative device is time-proven. Salads aren't called tossed salads for nothing. After you assemble all your ingredients and add a small amount of dressing, toss it well to evenly coat the salad fixings. You'll get great taste without the puddle of surplus salad dressing at the bottom of the bowl.

Armed with a plan, you can dress up your favorite salads with great, complementary salad dressings and say bye-bye to bottles of sodium-laden salad dressings and hello to easy-to-mix-up, homemade yum!

Balsamic Vinaigrette

Makes 3 servings
Prep time: 10 minutes
Serving size: 2 tablespoons
Each serving has:
177.2 calories
2.9 mg sodium
0.4 g protein
18.4 g total fat
2.4 g saturated fat
0 mg cholesterol
3.2 g carbohydrate
0.1 g dietary fiber
8 mg calcium
14.2 mg potassium

¼ cup extra-virgin olive oil

2 TB. balsamic vinegar

1 tsp. ground dry mustard

1 clove garlic, minced

¾ tsp. granulated sugar

⅛ tsp. Salt-Shaker Substitute (recipe in Chapter 26)

⅛ tsp. freshly ground black pepper

1. In a small bowl, combine olive oil, balsamic vinegar, dry mustard, garlic, sugar, Salt-Shaker Substitute, and pepper. Whisk until well blended.

2. Cover and refrigerate for up to 2 weeks. Mix well before serving.

Pinch of Sage

Adjust this recipe for the amount you need, but don't mix up too much. Homemade dressings don't have the shelf life of commercial brands, being measured in days and weeks instead of months. But they do have a fresh, superior flavor.

Italian Dressing

¾ cup extra-virgin olive oil

¼ cup white vinegar

1 tsp. granulated sugar

¼ tsp. dried oregano

¼ tsp. dried basil

¼ tsp. onion powder

¼ tsp. garlic powder

¼ tsp. Salt-Shaker Substitute (recipe in Chapter 26)

⅛ tsp. freshly ground black pepper

Makes 8 servings
Prep time: 5 minutes
Serving size: 2 tablespoons
Each serving has:
183.2 calories
0.2 mg sodium
0.1 g protein
20.3 g total fat
2.7 g saturated fat
0 mg cholesterol
1.2 g carbohydrate
0.1 g dietary fiber
2.5 mg calcium
6.4 mg potassium

1. In a small bowl, combine olive oil, vinegar, sugar, oregano, basil, onion powder, garlic powder, Salt-Shaker Substitute, and pepper. Whisk until thoroughly blended.

2. Whisk again before serving. Refrigerate any leftovers tightly covered for up to 2 weeks.

Pinch of Sage _____

You may use another savory salt-free salt-substitute seasoning blend, if you prefer. You can't omit it altogether, though, because you'll lose a certain depth of flavor.

Golden Garlic Dressing

Makes 6 servings
Prep time: 10 minutes
Chill time: 30 minutes
Serving size: 2 tablespoons
Each serving has:
129.6 calories
8.8 mg sodium
0.8 g protein
13.5 g total fat
1.8 g saturated fat
0.3 mg cholesterol
2.1 g carbohydrate
0.1 g dietary fiber
23 mg calcium
10.3 mg potassium

6 TB. extra-virgin olive oil

6 TB. fat-free plain yogurt

2 tsp. fresh lemon juice

½ tsp. ground white pepper

4 cloves garlic, minced

1. In a small bowl, whisk together olive oil, yogurt, lemon juice, and white pepper until well combined and smooth. Whisk in garlic.

2. Cover and chill for at least 30 minutes to allow flavors to blend. Refrigerate any leftovers tightly covered for 3 to 5 days.

 Pinch of Sage

Garlic lovers will enjoy this creamy dressing. You may want to reduce the amount of garlic for others.

Vinegar-and-Oil French Dressing

Makes 9 servings
Prep time: 5 minutes
Chill time: 30 minutes
Serving size: 2 tablespoons
Each serving has:
160.9 calories
0.1 mg sodium
0 g protein
18 g total fat
2.4 g saturated fat
0 mg cholesterol
0.6 g carbohydrate
0.1 g dietary fiber
0.7 mg calcium
9.1 mg potassium

¾ cup extra-virgin olive oil

3 TB. white vinegar

½ tsp. paprika

¼ tsp. ground white pepper

1. In a small bowl, whisk together olive oil, lemon juice, vinegar, paprika, and white pepper until thoroughly blended.

2. Cover and chill for at least 30 minutes to allow flavors to mingle. Whisk again before serving. Refrigerate any leftovers tightly covered for up to 2 weeks.

Salternative: To make All-Thyme-Favorite French Dressing, add ½ teaspoon dried thyme to this recipe.

Citrus-Kissed Dressing

2 cups extra-virgin olive oil

¾ cup granulated sugar

1 cup fresh orange juice

¼ cup fresh lemon juice

3 TB. fresh lime juice

1 large pasteurized egg

1 large pasteurized egg white

2 TB. honey

Makes 4 cups
Prep time: 10 minutes
Serving size: 2 tablespoons
Each serving has:
198.2 calories
5.2 mg sodium
0.5 g protein
18.2 g total fat
2.5 g saturated fat
8.9 mg cholesterol
9.2 g carbohydrate
0 g dietary fiber
2.7 mg calcium
31.4 mg potassium

1. In a blender, combine olive oil, sugar, orange juice, lemon juice, lime juice, pasteurized egg, pasteurized egg white, and honey.

2. Blend for 30 seconds or until well blended. Refrigerate any leftovers tightly covered for 1 to 2 days.

Pinch of Sage _____

You must use pasteurized eggs in this recipe because it's uncooked. Regular eggs—even fresh, uncracked ones—leave you susceptible to food-borne illness. Look for egg cartons labeled pasteurized in the refrigerated case where you find regular eggs.

Sweet Onion Dressing

Makes 8 servings
Prep time: 5 minutes
Serving size: 2 tablespoons
Each serving has:
101.2 calories
0.3 mg sodium
0.1 g protein
10.2 g total fat
1.4 g saturated fat
0 mg cholesterol
2.7 g carbohydrate
0.1 g dietary fiber
3.1 mg calcium
11.3 mg potassium

6 TB. extra-virgin olive oil

4 TB. distilled white vinegar

¼ large sweet onion, coarsely chopped

1 small clove garlic

4 tsp. granulated sugar

¼ tsp. ground dry mustard

¾ tsp. Salt-Shaker Substitute (recipe in Chapter 26) or other salt-free salt-substitute seasoning blend

1. Place olive oil, vinegar, onion, garlic, sugar, dry mustard, and Salt-Shaker Substitute in a blender.

2. Blend on high speed for 10 to 15 seconds or until smooth. Refrigerate any leftovers tightly covered for up to 2 weeks.

 Pinch of Sage

To peel a garlic clove easily, smash it under a wide knife blade, such as that of a chef's knife (facing away from you, of course). The papery peel should slough off. Cut off and discard the woody root end.

Red Wine Ginger Dressing

Makes 11 servings
Prep time: 10 minutes
Serving size: 2 tablespoons
Each serving has:
143.2 calories
0.7 mg sodium
0.1 g protein
16 g total fat
2.2 g saturated fat
0 mg cholesterol
0.4 g carbohydrate
0 g dietary fiber
2.3 mg calcium
5.9 mg potassium

¾ cup plus 1 TB. extra-virgin olive oil

½ cup red wine vinegar

4 cloves garlic, minced

1 tsp. ground ginger

¼ tsp. freshly ground black pepper

1. In a small bowl, combine olive oil, red wine vinegar, garlic, ginger, and pepper.

2. Whisk until thoroughly blended. Refrigerate any leftovers tightly covered for up to 2 weeks.

Salternative: You can reduce the amount of red wine vinegar if you don't care for the tangy taste.

Creamy Herb Dressing

1 cup fat-free, sugar-free vanilla yogurt

2 TB. red wine vinegar

1 TB. extra-virgin olive oil

¼ heaping tsp. dried basil

¼ heaping tsp. dried oregano

1 clove garlic, crushed

Pinch freshly ground black pepper

Makes 9 servings
Prep time: 10 minutes
Serving size: 2 tablespoons
Each serving has:
27.4 calories
14.5 mg sodium
0.8 g protein
1.5 g total fat
0.2 g saturated fat
0.6 mg cholesterol
2.5 g carbohydrate
0.1 g dietary fiber
41.6 mg calcium
42.2 mg potassium

1. In a small bowl, combine yogurt, red wine vinegar, and olive oil. Whisk until blended. Whisk in basil, oregano, garlic, and pepper.

2. Serve immediately or cover and chill, whisking again before serving. Refrigerate any leftovers tightly covered for 3 to 5 days.

Salternative: You can use fresh herbs in this salad dressing if you prefer. Substitute 1 teaspoon fresh herb for both the basil and oregano in this recipe.

Hint of Lime Cucumber Dressing

¼ medium cucumber, peeled and chopped (about ¼ cup)

½ cup fat-free plain yogurt

½ tsp. fresh lime juice

1 small clove garlic, minced

¼ tsp. Salt-Shaker Substitute (recipe in Chapter 26) or other salt-free salt-substitute seasoning blend

⅛ tsp. ground white pepper

Makes 8 servings
Prep time: 10 minutes
Serving size: 2 tablespoons
Each serving has:
8.7 calories
8.5 mg sodium
0.8 g protein
0 g total fat
0 g saturated fat
0.3 mg cholesterol
1.7 g carbohydrate
0.1 g dietary fiber
21.9 mg calcium
18.8 mg potassium

1. In a blender, combine cucumber, yogurt, lime juice, garlic, Salt-Shaker Substitute, and white pepper.

2. Blend on high speed for 20 seconds or until well blended. Cover and chill if not serving immediately. Refrigerate any leftovers tightly covered for 3 to 5 days.

Salternative: If you prefer the taste of lemon juice, use it instead of the lime juice in this recipe.

Creamy Avocado Dressing

Makes 10 servings
Prep time: 10 minutes
Serving size: 2 tablespoons
Each serving has:
49.2 calories
6.1 mg sodium
0.7 g protein
4.4 g total fat
1.4 g saturated fat
5.3 mg cholesterol
2 g carbohydrate
1 g dietary fiber
7.9 mg calcium
135.8 mg potassium

1 ripe medium avocado, pitted

⅓ cup sour cream

2 TB. fresh lime juice

3 TB. water

1. Scoop avocado pulp out of rind and purée pulp in a blender. Add sour cream, lime juice, and water to blender.

2. Blend on high speed for 1 minute or until smooth, stopping to scrape down sides as necessary. Serve immediately or chill for 30 minutes, covering surface directly with plastic wrap to prevent discoloration.

 Pinch of Sage

This thick, creamy dressing can complement a fruit-studded green salad. Try it in the Creamy Avocado and Pink Grapefruit Toss recipe in Chapter 17.

Lemon-Pepper Balsamic Dressing

Makes 4 servings
Prep time: 5 minutes
Serving size: 2 tablespoons
Each serving has:
142.7 calories
5.2 mg sodium
0.1 g protein
13.5 g total fat
1.8 g saturated fat
0 mg cholesterol
5.9 g carbohydrate
0 g dietary fiber
8 mg calcium
27.2 mg potassium

¼ cup extra-virgin olive oil

¼ cup balsamic vinegar

1 TB. firmly packed light brown sugar

½ TB. fresh lemon juice

⅛ tsp. dried lemon peel

⅛ tsp. freshly ground black pepper

1. In a small bowl, combine olive oil, balsamic vinegar, brown sugar, lemon juice, lemon peel, and pepper.

2. Whisk until well blended. Refrigerate any leftovers tightly covered for up to 2 weeks.

Salternative: Substitute regular distilled white vinegar for the balsamic vinegar for an equally tasty salad dressing.

Honey Mustard Dressing

¼ cup fat-free plain yogurt   ¾ to 1 tsp. dry mustard

1 TB. honey   Pinch garlic powder

½ TB. fresh lemon juice   Pinch onion powder

1. In a small bowl, combine yogurt, honey, lemon juice, dry mustard, garlic powder, and onion powder.

2. Whisk until well blended. Cover and chill if not serving immediately. Refrigerate any leftovers tightly covered for 3 to 5 days.

Salternative: You can adjust the honey-to-mustard ratio to suit your taste from sweet to spicy dressing.

Makes 5 servings
Prep time: 5 minutes
Serving size: 1 tablespoon
Each serving has:
20.8 calories
6.9 mg sodium
0.7 g protein
0.2 g total fat
0 g saturated fat
0.3 mg cholesterol
4.6 g carbohydrate
0 g dietary fiber
16.4 mg calcium
4.6 mg potassium

Raspberry Fruit Salad Dressing

½ cup fat-free plain yogurt

¼ cup red raspberries

2 TB. honey

1. In a blender, combine yogurt, raspberries, and honey.

2. Blend on high speed for 10 seconds or until blended, stopping to scrape down sides as necessary. Cover and chill for up to 8 hours if not serving immediately.

Pinch of Sage _____

Drizzle this dressing over a medley of your favorite fruits.

Makes ⅔ cup
Prep time: 5 minutes
Serving size: 2 tablespoons
Each serving has:
35.9 calories
13 mg sodium
1.1 g protein
0 g total fat
0 g saturated fat
0.5 mg cholesterol
9 g carbohydrate
0.4 g dietary fiber
29.6 mg calcium
4 mg potassium

Classic Potato Salad Dressing

Makes 1¾ cups
Prep time: 20 minutes
Cook time: 8 minutes
Serving size: 2 tablespoons
Each serving has:
62.6 calories
14 mg sodium
1.4 g protein
1 g total fat
0.4 g saturated fat
31.3 mg cholesterol
12.3 g carbohydrate
0 g dietary fiber
14.6 mg calcium
8.9 mg potassium

¾ cup granulated sugar

¼ cup white vinegar

¼ cup water

2 large eggs, beaten

2 TB. all-purpose flour

1 tsp. unsalted butter

½ tsp. dry mustard

½ cup fat-free plain yogurt

1. In a small saucepan, combine sugar, vinegar, water, eggs, flour, butter, and mustard. Cook over medium heat for 8 minutes, stirring frequently, or until mixture thickens and is smooth. Remove from heat and cool.

2. Stir yogurt into the saucepan until mixture is well blended. Refrigerate any leftovers or salads made with this dressing tightly covered for 3 to 5 days.

 Pinch of Sage _____

You can use this mayonnaise-free mixture to dress your favorite potato salad. It yields enough salad dressing for about 4 pounds potatoes. You can also try it in the Homey Macaroni Salad recipe in Chapter 17.

Chapter 25

Salsas and Relishes

In This Chapter

- ◆ Choosing accompaniments low in sodium
- ◆ Stirring together fresh salsas and relishes
- ◆ Livening up meals with flavorful go-withs
- ◆ Adding more tasty fruits and veggies to your diet

Salsas and relishes can add the perfect zing to an otherwise ho-hum meal. Fish, meats, poultry, egg dishes, snacks, and more can benefit from a well-crafted blend of flavors.

What's more, accompaniments are most often easy to prepare. If you can chop and stir, you can whip up a fresh-tasting, meal-making medley. Nutrient-imparting ingredients; simple preparation; and big, zesty flavor will keep you craving these salsas and relishes.

Singing the Praises of Medleys

You may have been avoiding scooping on salsas or relishes because those jars available in supermarkets contain too much sodium for your needs.

Pinch of Sage

If you prefer ready-made salsas and relishes, some sodium-free, no-salt-added, and low-sodium varieties are available. Check the aisles of your local supermarket, or visit Appendix B for more information.

The good news is that these medleys of tasty vegetables, luscious fruits, and complementary flavorings are often quick, simple recipes to prepare, requiring little more effort than stirring together fresh ingredients.

The vegetables and fruits that make up mouthwatering medleys not only liven up ordinary meals but also add more healthful nutrients to your diet. And you did it effortlessly!

Relishing Accompaniments

Salsas and relishes can be the hit of your meal. Their fresh taste and bold flavors make a statement at the table. For an even bigger impact, why not have some fun with your accompaniments? Serve a salsa or relish in an appropriate container, such as a hollowed-out watermelon shell, pineapple rind, zucchini or cucumber boat, avocado peel, orange rind, bell pepper, or any other attractive and sturdy vegetable or fruit shell.

You can serve a salsa or relish at any meal because just about any food you find becomes even tastier with its addition. Fish and seafood, poultry, beef, pork, egg dishes, baked potatoes, and rice are good choices. Give these accompaniments a try on sandwiches, tacos, burritos, and burgers, too. Of course, you can always scoop up a salsa with a tortilla chip (a no-salt-added one, of course).

You'll find as many ways to serve salsas and relishes as there are recipes for them.

Fresh-Taste Tomato Salsa

1½ cups cored, diced
tomatoes (about 2 medium)

¼ cup finely diced sweet
onions

2 TB. minced jalapeño
peppers (about 1 medium)
or more to taste

1 tsp. fresh lime juice

1 tsp. dried cilantro or 1 TB.
chopped fresh cilantro

Makes 1½ cups
Prep time: 5 minutes
Serving size: 2 tablespoons
Each serving has:
7.6 calories
1 mg sodium
0.2 g protein
0.1 g total fat
0 g saturated fat
0 mg cholesterol
1.6 g carbohydrate
0.3 g dietary fiber
4.3 mg calcium
68.8 mg potassium

1. In a medium bowl, stir together tomatoes, sweet onions, jalapeño peppers, lime juice, and cilantro.

2. If not serving immediately, chill until serving time. Refrigerate any leftovers tightly covered for up to 1 week.

Salt Pitfall

Wash your hands carefully after cutting the jalapeño pepper (or at least before you rub your eye). The oil that gets on your hands is can burn.

Asian-Flavored Carrot Crunch Salsa

Makes 6 cups
Prep time: 30 minutes
Serving size: ¼ cup
Each serving has:
34.6 calories
6.5 mg sodium
0.9 g protein
2.5 g total fat
0.3 g saturated fat
0 mg cholesterol
2.5 g carbohydrate
0.8 g dietary fiber
8.6 mg calcium
90.5 mg potassium

2½ cups grated carrots

2½ cups grated zucchini

½ cup thinly sliced green onions

⅓ cup unsalted dry-roasted peanuts

2 TB. toasted sesame seeds

1½ jalapeño peppers, minced

1 (1-inch) section fresh ginger, peeled and minced

2 TB. extra-virgin olive oil

¼ cup sodium-free rice vinegar

1 tsp. granulated sugar

1. In a large bowl, combine carrots, zucchini, green onions, peanuts, sesame seeds, jalapeño peppers, and ginger.

2. In a small bowl, stir together olive oil, rice vinegar, and sugar. Pour over carrot mixture. Stir to coat. Refrigerate any leftovers tightly covered for 3 to 5 days.

Salternative: You can reduce this recipe as needed.

 Pinch of Sage _____

You can purchase toasted sesame seeds. If you need to toast them yourself, heat the sesame seeds in a dry skillet over medium heat for 2 to 5 minutes, shaking occasionally. Cool before using.

Flaming Watermelon Salsa

1 cup diced seedless
watermelon

¼ cup peeled, diced kiwifruit

3 TB. seeded, minced fresh
jalapeño peppers

2 TB. minced sweet onions

1 TB. balsamic vinegar

Pinch garlic powder

Makes 1½ cups
Prep time: 10 minutes
Serving size: ¼ cup
Each serving has:
16.4 calories
1.7 mg sodium
0.3 g protein
0.2 g total fat
0 g saturated fat
0 mg cholesterol
3.8 g carbohydrate
0.5 g dietary fiber
5.7 mg calcium
67.5 mg potassium

1. In a small glass bowl, combine watermelon, kiwifruit, jalapeño
   peppers, sweet onions, balsamic vinegar, and garlic powder.

2. Stir with a wooden spoon to mix well. Serve with grilled or
   broiled fish, eggs, cream cheese, or low-sodium crackers.
   Cover and chill if not serving immediately. Refrigerate any
   leftovers tightly covered for 1 to 2 days.

Caribbean Beach Fruit Salsa

1 (20-oz.) can crushed
pineapple, undrained

1½ cups peeled and finely
chopped mango

1 cup peeled and finely
chopped papaya

1 cup finely diced red onions

½ cup seeded, minced fresh
jalapeño peppers

Juice of 3 limes

¼ tsp. ground cayenne

Makes 6 cups
Prep time: 20 minutes
Chill time: 1 hour
Serving size: ¼ cup
Each serving has:
27.7 calories
0.9 mg sodium
0.3 g protein
0.1 g total fat
0 g saturated fat
0 mg cholesterol
7.2 g carbohydrate
0.7 g dietary fiber
7.7 mg calcium
80.2 mg potassium

1. In a medium bowl, combine pineapple, mango, papaya, red
   onions, jalapeño peppers, lime juice, and cayenne.

2. Gently stir until blended. Cover and chill for at least 1 hour
   before serving. Serve alongside grilled or broiled fish, chicken
   breast, pork, or steak, as desired. Refrigerate any leftovers
   tightly covered for 2 to 3 days.

 Pinch of Sage _____

Easily remove the seeds from a halved papaya by scooping them out with a metal spoon.

Tropical Breeze Pineapple-Orange Salsa

Makes 4 cups
Prep time: 15 minutes
Chill time: 1 hour
Serving size: ¼ cup
Each serving has:
23.7 calories
1.7 mg sodium
0.4 g protein
0.1 g total fat
0 g saturated fat
0 mg cholesterol
5.9 g carbohydrate
0.4 g dietary fiber
5.6 mg calcium
74.8 mg potassium

2½ cups bite-size fresh pineapple chunks

1 (15-oz.) can mandarin orange segments, drained and halved

½ cup finely diced red bell pepper

2 TB. seeded, minced jalapeño peppers

1 TB. fresh lime juice

1 tsp. finely chopped fresh cilantro

1. In a large bowl, combine pineapple chunks, mandarin orange segments, red bell pepper, jalapeño peppers, lime juice, and cilantro. Gently stir to mix.

2. Cover and chill for at least 1 hour to allow flavors to blend. Serve with chicken or white fish as desired. Refrigerate any leftovers tightly covered for 1 to 2 days.

 Pinch of Sage _____

To remove the crown of a fresh pineapple, twist the crown until it separates from the pineapple. Then you can cut the pineapple in half, cut around and discard the core, slice off the peel, and chop the flesh as needed.

Blushing Pear Salsa

2 ripe pears, cored and diced   Juice of 1 lime

½ cup minced red onions   2 TB. chopped fresh cilantro

1. In a medium glass bowl, combine pears and red onions. Drizzle lime juice over top. Stir to coat. Stir in cilantro until evenly distributed.

2. Cover and chill overnight. Stir again before serving. Refrigerate any leftovers tightly covered for 1 to 2 days.

Pinch of Sage

If you don't have time to chill this salsa for many hours, you can serve it after thoroughly chilling for a couple hours. The long chilling time allows for the flavors to mingle, as well as for the red onions to bleed onto the pears, causing the "blushing."

Makes 11 servings
Prep time: 15 minutes
Chill time: 8 hours
Serving size: ¼ cup
Each serving has:
22.1 calories
0.6 mg sodium
0.3 g protein
0.2 g total fat
0 g saturated fat
0 mg cholesterol
5.5 g carbohydrate
0.9 g dietary fiber
20.9 mg calcium
19 mg potassium

Cranberry-Apple Relish

Makes 14 servings
Prep time: 5 minutes
Cook time: 25 minutes
Serving size: ¼ cup
Each serving has:
80 calories
1.3 mg sodium
0.2 g protein
0.1 g total fat
0 g saturated fat
0 mg cholesterol
20.5 g carbohydrate
1.5 g dietary fiber
6.8 mg calcium
64.2 mg potassium

1 cup water

¾ cup granulated sugar

1 (12-oz.) pkg. fresh or frozen cranberries

1 cup peeled, diced Braeburn apples (about 1)

½ cup golden raisins

½ cup cider vinegar

¾ tsp. ground cinnamon

½ tsp. ground allspice

¼ tsp. ground cloves

¼ tsp. ground ginger

1. In a medium saucepan, combine water and sugar. Bring to a boil over medium heat. Add cranberries, apples, golden raisins, cider vinegar, cinnamon, allspice, cloves, and ginger. Stir. Return to a boil, and simmer for 10 minutes, stirring occasionally.

2. Turn relish into a serving bowl. Directly cover surface with plastic wrap, and cool to room temperature. Serve, or cover and chill, bringing relish to room temperature before serving. Refrigerate any leftovers tightly covered for 3 to 5 days.

Salternative: You can substitute your favorite apple in this spicy relish. Try Granny Smith, Golden Delicious, Red Delicious, Gala, Fuji, Jonagold, Pink Lady, or Cameo. You can also adjust the seasonings to taste, as it's a very spicy relish.

Southwestern Relish

½ cup frozen corn kernels,
thawed

½ cup diced avocado

1 cup Fresh-Taste Tomato
Salsa (recipe earlier in this
chapter)

Makes 2 cups
Prep time: 5 minutes
Serving size: ⅓ cup
Each serving has:
40.4 calories
3.2 mg sodium
0.8 g protein
2.1 g total fat
0.3 g saturated fat
0 mg cholesterol
5.2 g carbohydrate
1.2 g dietary fiber
7.1 mg calcium
166.6 mg potassium

1. In a medium bowl, stir together corn, avocado, and Fresh-Taste Tomato Salsa.

2. If not serving immediately, chill until serving time.

Pinch of Sage

To thaw corn kernels quickly, place the corn in a strainer or colander and run it under warm water.

Caraway-Beet Relish

Makes 10 servings
Prep time: 15 minutes
Cook time: 50 minutes
Serving size: ¼ cup
Each serving has:
43.9 calories
26.6 mg sodium
0.6 g protein
1.2 g total fat
0.7 g saturated fat
3 mg cholesterol
8.2 g carbohydrate
1 g dietary fiber
9.1 mg calcium
134.9 mg potassium

5 to 6 medium fresh beets (enough to yield 2 cups diced)

1 small yellow onion, minced

1 rib celery, minced

3 TB. granulated sugar

1 TB. distilled white vinegar

1 TB. unsalted butter

Juice of 1 orange

Zest of 1 orange

¼ tsp. caraway seeds

1. Fill a large stainless-steel saucepan with water and bring to a boil. Scrub beets and cut tops from beets, leaving at least 1 inch of stems. Reduce heat, add beets, and simmer for 20 to 25 minutes or until beets are fork-tender. Remove beets to a paper towel. Peel with your fingers under cold, running water, and cut off roots and stems. Dice to measure 2 cups.

2. Rinse out the saucepan and add 2 cups diced beets, onion, celery, sugar, vinegar, butter, orange juice, orange zest, and caraway seeds. Stir. Bring to a simmer over medium heat. Simmer over medium-low heat for 20 minutes. Cool. Cover tightly, and chill in a glass bowl for up to 1 month.

Salt Pitfall _____

Staining is a concern when cooking beets. Wash all surfaces immediately if splatters occur. Don't use a wooden cutting board or a wooden spoon, as they'll be purple when you're done! Instead, opt for materials that won't permanently stain.

Chapter 26

Slathers, Spreads, and Seasoning Blends

In This Chapter

◆ Adding bits of flavor without adding salt

◆ Sweetening each bite with fruit butters

◆ Spreading great taste with savory butters

◆ Shaking on seasonings without added salt

You, your family, and your guests all warmly welcome flavorful foods. And salt has been the greatest flavor enhancer throughout history. If now you're finding yourself without a good seasoning, don't despair. You can infuse flavor with just a little slather, spread, or seasoning blend.

Even better, butters and seasonings are easy to make. With just a little effort, you can whip up rich, complex flavors that will make you wonder why you were ever so dependent upon your salt shaker.

Wait 'Til You Smear!

Butters, both sweet and savory, are tasty additions to breads, rolls, buns, biscuits, quick breads, muffins, pancakes, waffles, French toast, and more. A once-plain food can take on new appeal when the smear is delicious.

Special butters can also make your guests feel special. The compliments you receive will easily outweigh the effort on your part as these butters are simple to make.

And any leftover savory butters are perfect for seasoning cooked vegetables. Perk up green beans, corn, baked potatoes, carrots, mushrooms, and more.

Shake It Up, Baby

Because you've put away the salt shaker, you may need to mix up your own seasoning blends to prepare your favorite foods again. Several commercially prepared seasoning mixes often include salt or even MSG as an ingredient. The recipes for chili powder and taco seasoning mix in this chapter should help you substitute for those most difficult to find without added salt. Many seasoning blends are available without salt, though. Check your local supermarket's spice aisle, or find a mail-order supplier of salt-free seasonings.

> **Salt Pitfall**
>
> When picking up seasoning blends from your supermarket's spice aisle, always read the labels carefully. Check vigilantly such seasoning mixes as chili powder, curry powder, garlic-pepper blend, lemon-pepper, poultry seasoning, seafood seasoning, salad seasoning, and any of the specialty seasoning blends. Often, salt is the primary ingredient. If you find salt listed as an ingredient, leave the seasoning on the shelf.

Even though the spice aisle is teeming with salt-free salt substitute seasoning blends in a wide variety of mixes, we've included a recipe here in case you want to mix up your own.

Making your own seasoning blends is an inexpensive alternative to the store-bought versions. Plus, if you have 5 minutes, you can create a flavor-imparting seasoning blend.

Sweet Strawberry Butter

1½ cups fresh strawberries, rinsed, hulled, and quartered

¾ cup (1½ sticks) unsalted butter, softened

1½ cups confectioners' sugar

Makes 2¼ cups
Prep time: 5 minutes
Chill time: 3 hours
Serving size: 2 tablespoons
Each serving has:
109.4 calories
0.2 mg sodium
0.1 g protein
7.4 g total fat
4.7 g saturated fat
20 mg cholesterol
10.8 g carbohydrate
0.3 g dietary fiber
1.9 mg calcium
21.2 mg potassium

1. Combine strawberries, butter, and confectioners' sugar in a blender. Blend on high speed for 1 to 2 minutes or until thoroughly blended, scraping down sides as necessary.

2. Pour strawberry butter into a storage container with a tight-fitting lid. Chill for at least 3 hours to firm up a bit. Store in the refrigerator tightly covered for up to 1 week.

Salternative: You can decrease this recipe as needed.

Pinch of Sage
Spread this scrumptious butter over your morning pancakes or waffles, and try it on biscuits or slices of sweet breads.

Overnight Spiced Pumpkin Butter

1 (29-oz.) can solid-packed pumpkin, not pumpkin pie filling

1¾ cups granulated sugar

1 tsp. pumpkin pie spice

Makes 3⅔ cups
Prep time: 5 minutes
Cook time: 13 hours
Serving size: 2 tablespoons
Each serving has:
56 calories
1.6 mg sodium
0.3 g protein
0.1 g total fat
0 g saturated fat
0 mg cholesterol
14.2 g carbohydrate
0.8 g dietary fiber
7.8 mg calcium
58.4 mg potassium

1. In a slow cooker, combine pumpkin, sugar, and pumpkin pie spice. Stir to blend. Cover and cook on high for 1 hour.

2. Reduce temperature to low, and continue to cook for 12 hours. Cool and store tightly covered in the refrigerator for up to 2 weeks.

Herb-Flecked Butter

Makes 12 servings
Prep time: 10 minutes
Chill time: 8 hours
Serving size: 1 teaspoon
Each serving has:
33.6 calories
0.3 mg sodium
0 g protein
3.7 g total fat
2.3 g saturated fat
10 mg cholesterol
0 g carbohydrate
0 g dietary fiber
1 mg calcium
3.5 mg potassium

4 TB. unsalted butter, cut into small pieces and softened

1½ TB. chopped fresh parsley

1 tsp. chopped fresh basil

¾ tsp. chopped fresh tarragon

1. In a small bowl, combine butter, parsley, basil, and tarragon. Stir until herbs are evenly distributed.

2. Spoon mixture onto a small sheet of waxed paper. Shape into a log, and wrap in the waxed paper. Chill overnight until firm and flavors are blended. Store in the refrigerator tightly wrapped for up to 1 week.

Salternative: You may decrease or increase this recipe as needed.

Lemon-Bright Cilantro Butter

Makes ¼ cup
Prep time: 10 minutes
Chill time: 1 hour
Serving size: 1 teaspoon
Each serving has:
33.8 calories
0.7 mg sodium
0 g protein
3.7 g total fat
2.3 g saturated fat
10 mg cholesterol
0.1 g carbohydrate
0 g dietary fiber
1.7 mg calcium
7.2 mg potassium

4 TB. unsalted butter, softened

¼ cup finely chopped fresh cilantro

½ tsp. fresh lemon juice

1. In a small bowl, cream together butter and cilantro until well blended. Stir in lemon juice.

2. Form mixture into a log on a small sheet of waxed paper. Roll up, and chill for 1 hour or until firm. Soften slightly to slice and serve. Store in the refrigerator tightly wrapped for up to 1 week.

Salternative: You may decrease or increase this recipe as needed.

Festive Green Pistachio Butter

½ cup (1 stick) unsalted
unshelled natural pistachios

4 TB. unsalted butter,
melted

2 drops green food coloring
(optional)

Makes ⅓ cup		
Prep time: 15 minutes		
Cook time: 5 minutes		
Serving size: 1 teaspoon		
Each serving has:		
47.8 calories		
0.4 mg sodium		
0.9 g protein		
4.6 g total fat		
2 g saturated fat		
7.5 mg cholesterol		
1.1 g carbohydrate		
0.4 g dietary fiber		
4.4 mg calcium		
41.7 mg potassium		

1. Fill a small saucepan with water, and bring to a boil. Add pistachios and remove from heat. Let stand for 1 to 2 minutes and then drain. Shell pistachios and peel off papery covering.

2. Turn pistachios into a sealable plastic bag and pound with a rolling pin or a meat mallet.

3. In a small bowl, blend together butter and pistachios with a spoon until evenly distributed. Add food coloring, and stir until evenly colored.

4. Pack butter into a serving crock. Cover tightly and chill for up to 1 week, softening slightly before serving.

Salternative: You can decrease or increase this recipe as needed.

Pinch of Sage

Some pistachios are still sold coated in their familiar bright red dye. The dye was once added because manufacturers wanted to mask the natural imperfections that mar the nuts' appearance. Because you'll be plunging the pistachios for this recipe into boiling water, you can't substitute the red-dyed pistachios for the natural nuts.

Salt-Shaker Substitute

Makes 2½ tablespoons
Prep time: 5 minutes
Serving size: ¼ teaspoon
Each serving has:
2.1 calories
0.3 mg sodium
0.1 g protein
0.1 g total fat
0 g saturated fat
0 mg cholesterol
0.3 g carbohydrate
0.1 g dietary fiber
3.4 mg calcium
6.5 mg potassium

1 TB. onion powder

1½ tsp. ground dry mustard

1½ tsp. dried basil

½ tsp. celery seeds

½ tsp. paprika

½ tsp. Firehouse Chili Powder (recipe later in this chapter) or other salt-free chili powder

1. In a small, airtight spice jar, combine onion powder, dry mustard, basil, celery seeds, paprika, and Firehouse Chili Powder.

2. Mix well.

 Pinch of Sage _____

Spice blends make a tasty alternative to place in your salt shaker. You can try this one or the many different commercial salt-free salt-substitute seasoning blends available.

Firehouse Chili Powder

⅓ cup crushed red pepper flakes

4 tsp. ground cumin

2 tsp. garlic powder

1 tsp. dried oregano

1 tsp. chipotle chili powder

Makes 5 tablespoons
Prep time: 10 minutes
Serving size: 1 teaspoon
Each serving has:
10.6 calories
3.5 mg sodium
0.4 g protein
0.5 g total fat
0.1 g saturated fat
0 mg cholesterol
1.7 g carbohydrate
0.9 g dietary fiber
9.6 mg calcium
47.8 mg potassium

1. Combine crushed red pepper flakes, cumin, garlic powder, oregano, and chipotle chili powder in a mini food chopper or food processor. Process for 2 to 3 minutes or until well combined and powdered.

2. Store in an airtight spice jar or other container.

Salt Pitfall

You can whip up this home-blended chili powder if you have difficulty finding a salt-free blend. Even if the label doesn't disclose salt, look for other sodium keywords, such as *monosodium glutamate,* or *MSG. Spices* or *natural seasonings* may be listed as an ingredient as well. You can contact the manufacturer to find out if the product includes salt or another sodium product.

Taco Seasoning Mix

Makes 1½ teaspoons
Prep time: 5 minutes
Serving size: 1½ teaspoons
Each serving has:
11.4 calories
3.2 mg sodium
0.5 g protein
0.5 g total fat
0.1 g saturated fat
0 mg cholesterol
1.9 g carbohydrate
1 g dietary fiber
17.8 mg calcium
45.8 mg potassium

½ tsp. Firehouse Chili Powder (recipe earlier in this chapter) or other salt-free chili powder

¼ tsp. freshly ground black pepper

¼ tsp. ground cumin

¼ tsp. dried oregano

¼ tsp. ground cayenne

1. Combine Firehouse Chili Powder, black pepper, cumin, oregano, and cayenne.

2. Use in a recipe or store in an airtight spice jar.

Salternative: The Firehouse Chili Powder recipe earlier in this chapter is a bit on the hot side. You can substitute a commercially prepared salt-free spice blend. If you like its flavor, you'll like the recipes you prepare with it.

 Pinch of Sage

This recipe makes enough seasoning mix to flavor 1 pound meat. Increase this recipe to keep a spice jar available for quick use.

Asian-Inspired Spice Blend

2 TB. ground ginger

2 TB. crushed red pepper flakes

2 tsp. ground black pepper

2 tsp. anise seeds

1½ tsp. ground cloves

1 tsp. ground white pepper

Makes 5 tablespoons
Prep time: 5 minutes
Serving size: 1 teaspoon
Each serving has:
7 calories
3 mg sodium
0.2 g protein
0.3 g total fat
0.1 g saturated fat
0 mg cholesterol
1.1 g carbohydrate
0.4 g dietary fiber
6.1 mg calcium
25 mg potassium

1. Add ginger, pepper flakes, black pepper, anise seeds, cloves and white pepper to a glass spice jar with a tight-fitting lid.

2. Combine thoroughly. Sprinkle dry into stir-fries or rice dishes, or mix with a little sesame oil. You may also try with the Grilled Asian-Spiced Chicken Thighs recipe in Chapter 13.

Pinch of Sage

If you don't care for the heat of this mix, try reducing the crushed red pepper flakes as desired. You can adjust all pre-mixed seasonings to taste.

Fast Fish Seasoning Blend

Makes 10 teaspoons
Prep time: 5 minutes
Serving size: ¼ teaspoon
Each serving has:
0.9 calories
0.2 mg sodium
0.1 g protein
0 g total fat
0 g saturated fat
0 mg cholesterol
0.2 g carbohydrate
0.1 g dietary fiber
4.1 mg calcium
3.6 mg potassium

1 TB. dried thyme

1 TB. dried chives

½ TB. dried basil

1 tsp. dried parsley flakes

½ tsp. garlic powder

½ tsp. dried lemon peel

¼ tsp. dried mint

⅛ tsp. ground cayenne

1. Combine thyme, chives, basil, parsley flakes, garlic powder, lemon peel, mint, and cayenne in a glass jar with a tight-fitting lid.

2. Shake well to blend.

Pinch of Sage

Combine ⅛ teaspoon seasoning blend with melted butter or oil and brush over a 3-ounce fish fillet. You can use it dry, too, if you prefer to cut the fat. Try it on chicken or pasta as well.

Appendix A

Glossary

acini de pepe A small pasta shaped like tiny beads commonly used in soups and cold salads. *See* pastina.

al dente Italian for "against the teeth." Refers to pasta (or other ingredient such as rice) that is neither soft nor hard, but just slightly firm against the teeth. This, according to many pasta aficionados, is the perfect way to cook pasta.

all-purpose flour Flour that contains only the inner part of the wheat grain. Usable for all purposes from cakes to gravies.

allspice Named for its flavor echoes of several spices (cinnamon, cloves, nutmeg), allspice is used in many desserts and in rich marinades and stews.

almonds Mild, sweet, and crunchy nuts that combine nicely with creamy and sweet food items.

arugula A spicy-peppery garden plant with leaves that resemble a dandelion and have a distinctive—and very sharp—flavor.

au gratin The quick broiling of a dish before serving to brown the top ingredients. The term is often used as part of a recipe name and implies cheese and a creamy sauce.

bake To cook in a dry oven. Dry-heat cooking often results in a crisping of the exterior of the food being cooked. Moist-heat cooking, through methods such as steaming, poaching, etc., brings a much different, moist quality to the food.

balsamic vinegar   Vinegar produced primarily in Italy from a specific type of grape and aged in wood barrels. It is heavier, darker, and sweeter than most vinegars.

barbecue   To quick-cook over high heat or to cook something long and slow in a rich liquid (barbecue sauce).

basil   A flavorful, almost sweet, resinous herb delicious with tomatoes and used in all kinds of Italian or Mediterranean-style dishes.

baste   To keep foods moist during cooking by spooning, brushing, or drizzling with a liquid.

beat   To quickly mix substances.

Belgian endive   A plant that resembles a small, elongated, tightly packed head of romaine lettuce. The thick, crunchy leaves can be broken off and used with dips and spreads.

black pepper   A biting and pungent seasoning, freshly ground pepper is a must for many dishes and adds an extra level of flavor and taste.

blanch   To place a food in boiling water for about 1 minute (or less) to partially cook the exterior and then submerge in or rinse with cool water to halt the cooking.

blend   To completely mix something, usually with a blender or food processor, more slowly than beating.

boil   To heat a liquid to a point where water is forced to turn into steam, causing the liquid to bubble. To boil something is to insert it into boiling water. A rapid boil is when a lot of bubbles form on the surface of the liquid.

bouillon   Dried essence of stock from chicken, beef, vegetable, or other ingredients. This is a popular starting ingredient for soups as it adds flavor (and often a lot of salt).

breadcrumbs   Tiny pieces of crumbled dry bread. Breadcrumbs are an important component in many recipes and are also used as a coating, for example with breaded chicken breasts.

brine   A highly salted, often seasoned, liquid that is used to flavor and preserve foods. To brine a food is to soak, or preserve, it by submerging it in brine. The salt in the brine penetrates the fibers of the meat and makes it moist and tender.

broil   To cook in a dry oven under the overhead high-heat element.

broth   *See* stock.

brown   To cook in a skillet, turning, until the food's surface is seared and brown in color, to lock in the juices.

brown rice   Whole-grain rice including the germ with a characteristic pale brown or tan color. Brown rice is more nutritious and flavorful than white rice but does take longer to cook.

bulgur   A wheat kernel that's been steamed, dried, and crushed and is sold in fine and coarse textures.

cake flour   A high-starch, soft, and fine flour used primarily for cakes.

caramelize   To cook sugar over low heat until the food develops a sweet caramel flavor. The term is increasingly gaining use to describe cooking vegetables (especially onions) in butter or oil over low heat until they soften, sweeten, and develop a caramel color.

caraway   A distinctive spicy seed used for rye bread as well as pork, cheese, and cabbage dishes. It is known to reduce stomach upset, which is why it is often paired with, for example, sauerkraut.

carbohydrate   A nutritional component found in starches, sugars, fruits, and vegetables that causes a rise in blood glucose levels. Carbohydrates supply energy and many important nutrients, including vitamins, minerals, and antioxidants.

cardamom   An intense, sweet-smelling spice, common to Indian and Scandinavian cooking, used in baking and coffee.

cayenne   A fiery spice made from (hot) chili peppers, especially the cayenne chili, a slender, red, and very hot pepper.

cheddar   The ubiquitous hard cow's milk cheese with a rich, buttery flavor that ranges from mellow to sharp. Originally produced in England, cheddar is now produced worldwide.

chilis (also **chiles**)   Any one of many different "hot" peppers, ranging in intensity from the relatively mild ancho pepper to the blisteringly hot habañero.

chili powder   A seasoning blend that includes chili pepper, cumin, garlic, and oregano. Proportions vary among different versions, but they all offer a warm, rich flavor.

Chinese five-spice powder   A seasoning blend of cinnamon, anise, ginger, fennel, and pepper.

chives   A member of the onion family, chives grow in bunches of long leaves that resemble tall grass or the green tops of onions. Chives provide a light onion flavor to any dish. They're very easy to grow and are often grown in gardens.

chop   To cut into pieces, usually qualified by an adverb such as "*coarsely* chopped," or by a size measurement such as "chopped into ½-inch pieces." "Finely chopped" is much closer to mince.

cider vinegar   Vinegar produced from apple cider, popular in North America.

cilantro   A member of the parsley family and used in Mexican cooking and some Asian dishes. Cilantro is what gives some salsas their unique flavor. Use in moderation, as the flavor can overwhelm. The seed of the cilantro is the spice coriander.

cinnamon   A sweet, rich, aromatic spice commonly used in baking or desserts. Cinnamon can also be used for delicious and interesting entrées.

clove   A sweet, strong, almost wintergreen-flavor spice used in baking and with meats such as ham.

coriander   A rich, warm, spicy seed used in all types of recipes, from African to South American, from entrées to desserts.

count   In terms of seafood or other foods that come in small sizes, the number of that item that compose 1 pound. For example, 31 to 40 count shrimp are large appetizer shrimp often served with cocktail sauce; 51 to 60 are much smaller.

couscous   Granular semolina (durum wheat) that is cooked and used in many Mediterranean and North African dishes.

croutons   Pieces of bread, usually between ¼ and ½ inch in size, that are sometimes seasoned and baked, broiled, or fried to a crisp texture. Popular in soups and salads.

cumin   A fiery, smoky-tasting spice popular in Mexican, Middle-Eastern and Indian dishes. Cumin is a seed; ground cumin seed is the most common form of the spice used in cooking.

curing   A method of preserving uncooked foods, usually meats or fish, by either salting and smoking or pickling.

curry   A general term referring to rich, spicy, Indian-style sauces and the dishes prepared with them. A curry will use curry powder as its base seasoning.

curry powder   A ground blend of spices used as a basis for curry and a huge range of other Indian-influenced dishes. All blends are rich and flavorful. Some, such as Vindaloo and Madras, are notably hotter than others. Common ingredients include hot pepper, nutmeg, cumin, cinnamon, pepper, and turmeric. Some curry can also be found in paste form.

custard   A cooked mixture of eggs and milk. Custards are a popular base for desserts.

dash   A few drops, usually of a liquid, released by a quick shake of, for example, a bottle of hot sauce.

deglaze   To scrape up the bits of meat and seasoning left in a pan or skillet after cooking. Usually this is done by adding a liquid such as wine or broth and creating a flavorful stock that can be used to create sauces.

devein   The removal of the dark vein from the back of a large shrimp with a sharp knife.

dice   To cut into small cubes about ¼-inch square.

dill   A unique herb that is perfect for eggs, salmon, cheese dishes, and, of course, vegetables (pickles!).

dollop   A spoonful of something creamy and thick, such as sour cream or whipped cream.

double boiler   A set of two pots designed to nest together, one inside the other, and provide consistent, moist heat for foods that need delicate treatment. The bottom pot holds water (not quite touching the bottom of the top pot); the top pot holds the ingredient you want to heat.

dredge   To cover a piece of food with a dry substance such as flour or cornmeal.

drizzle   To lightly sprinkle drops of a liquid over food. Drizzling is often the finishing touch to a dish.

entrée   The main dish in a meal. In France, however, the entrée is considered the first course.

essential fatty acids   A type of polyunsaturated fat that your body obtains from foods, the body being unable to make such fatty acids itself.

extra-virgin olive oil   *See* olive oil.

fillet   A piece of meat or seafood with the bones removed.

flake   To break into thin sections, as with fish.

floret   The flower or bud end of broccoli or cauliflower.

flour   Grains ground into a meal. Wheat is perhaps the most common flour. Flour is also made from oats, rye, buckwheat, soybeans, etc. *See also* all-purpose flour; cake flour; whole-wheat flour.

fold   To combine a dense and light mixture with a circular action from the middle of the bowl.

frittata   A skillet-cooked mixture of eggs and other ingredients that is not stirred but is cooked slowly and then either flipped or finished under the broiler.

fritter   A food such as apples or corn coated or mixed with batter and deep-fried for a crispy, crunchy exterior.

garbanzo beans (also **chickpeas**)   A yellow-gold, roundish bean that's the base ingredient in hummus. Chickpeas are high in fiber and low in fat, making this a delicious and healthful component of many appetizers and main dishes.

garlic   A member of the onion family, a pungent and flavorful element in many savory dishes. A garlic bulb, the form in which garlic is often sold, contains multiple cloves. Each clove, when chopped, provides about 1 teaspoon garlic. Most recipes call for cloves or chopped garlic by the teaspoon.

garnish   An embellishment not vital to the dish but added to enhance visual appeal.

ginger   Available in fresh root or dried, ground form, ginger adds a pungent, sweet, and spicy quality to a dish. It is a very popular element of many Asian and Indian dishes, among others.

grate   To shave into tiny pieces using a sharp rasp or grater.

grind   To reduce a large, hard substance, often a seasoning such as peppercorns, to the consistency of sand.

high-density lipoprotein (HDL)   The type of cholesterol mover that takes cholesterol to the liver to be passed from the body, a.k.a. good cholesterol.

hors d'oeuvre   French for "outside of work" (the "work" being the main meal). An hors d'oeuvre can be any dish served as a starter before the meal.

horseradish   A sharp, spicy root that forms the flavor base in many condiments from cocktail sauce to sharp mustards. It is a natural match with roast beef. The form generally found in grocery stores is prepared horseradish, which contains vinegar and oil, among other ingredients. Use pure horseradish much more sparingly than the prepared version, or try cutting it with sour cream.

hummus   A thick, Middle Eastern spread made of puréed chickpeas (garbanzo beans), lemon juice, olive oil, garlic, and often tahini (sesame seed paste).

Italian seasoning (also **spaghetti sauce seasoning**)   The ubiquitous grocery store blend of dried herbs—which includes basil, oregano, rosemary, and thyme—is a useful seasoning for quick flavor that evokes the "old country" in sauces, meatballs, soups, and vegetable dishes.

julienne   A French word meaning "to slice into very thin pieces" that are shaped like small matchsticks.

knead   To work dough to make it elastic so it will hold gas bubbles as it bakes; kneading is fundamental in the process of making yeast breads.

light or lite   In reference to sodium, this term labels a product that has less sodium than the regular version, usually 50 percent less.

lite salt   A blend of sodium chloride (salt) and potassium chloride in equal parts.

low-density lipoprotein (LDL)   The type of cholesterol mover that can contribute to arterial plaque deposits that can block the arteries, a.k.a. bad cholesterol.

low-sodium   The term used to label foods that contain 140 milligrams or less sodium per serving.

marinate   To soak meat, seafood, or other food in a seasoned sauce, called a marinade, which is high in acid content. The acids break down the muscle of the meat, making it tender and adding flavor.

marjoram   A sweet herb, a cousin of and similar to oregano, popular in Greek, Spanish, and Italian dishes.

medallion   A small round cut, usually of meat or vegetables such as carrots or cucumbers.

meringue   A mixture of sugar and beaten egg whites, often used as a dessert topping or as cookies when baked, or as a generic ingredient when added to a batter before cooking.

mince   To cut into very small pieces smaller than diced pieces, about ⅛ inch or smaller.

monosodium glutamate (MSG)   A flavor enhancer container about one-third the amount of sodium as in table salt.

mull (or **mulled**)   To heat a liquid with the addition of spices and sometimes sweeteners.

no-salt-added   A term used to label foods made without salt that's normally used, but still contains the sodium that's a natural part of the food itself.

nonreactive   A container that is glass, stainless steel, enameled ceramic, or other material that will not react with the acid in a food as aluminum or copper will.

nutmeg   A sweet, fragrant, musky spice used primarily in baking.

olive oil   A fragrant liquid produced by crushing or pressing olives. Extra-virgin olive oil is the oil produced from the first pressing of a batch of olives; oil is also produced from other pressings after the first. Extra-virgin olive oil is generally considered the most flavorful and highest quality and is the type you want to use when your focus is on the oil itself.

olives   The fruit of the olive tree commonly grown on all sides of the Mediterranean. There are many varieties of olives but two general types: green and black. Black olives are also called ripe olives. Green olives are immature, although they are also widely eaten.

oregano   A fragrant, slightly astringent herb used in Greek, Spanish, and Italian dishes.

orzo   A rice-shape pasta used in Greek cooking.

paprika   A rich, red, warm, earthy spice that also lends a rich red color to many dishes.

Parmesan   A hard, dry, flavorful cheese primarily used grated or shredded as a seasoning for Italian-style dishes.

parsley   A fresh-tasting green leafy herb used to add color and interest to just about any savory dish. Often used as a garnish just before serving.

pastina   a very small pasta, often shaped like stars, beads, rice grains, or alphabet letters.

pecans   Rich, buttery nuts native to North America. Their flavor, a terrific addition to appetizers, is at least partially due to their high unsaturated fat content.

peppercorns   Large, round, dried berries that are ground to produce pepper.

pesto   A thick spread or sauce made with fresh basil leaves, garlic, olive oil, pine nuts, and Parmesan cheese. Some newer versions are made with other herbs. Pesto can be made at home or purchased in a grocery store and used on anything from appetizers to pasta and other main dishes.

pickle   A food, usually a vegetable such as a cucumber, that has been pickled in brine.

pilaf   A rice dish in which the rice is browned in butter or oil, then cooked in a flavorful liquid such as a broth, often with the addition of meats or vegetables. The rice absorbs the broth, resulting in a savory dish.

pinch   An unscientific measurement term that refers to the amount of an ingredient—typically a dry, granular substance such as an herb or seasoning—you can hold between your finger and thumb.

pine nuts (also **pignoli** or **piñon**)   Nuts grown on pine trees that are rich (read: high fat), flavorful, and a bit pine-y. Pine nuts are a traditional component of pesto and add a wonderful hearty crunch to many other recipes.

pita bread   A flat, hollow wheat bread that can be used for sandwiches or sliced, pizza style. Pita bread is terrific soft with dips or baked or broiled as a vehicle for other ingredients.

polenta   Cornmeal mush.

portobello mushrooms   A mature and larger form of the smaller crimini mushroom, portobellos are brownish, chewy, and flavorful. They are trendy served as whole caps, grilled, and as thin sautéed slices.

preheat   To turn on an oven, broiler, or other cooking appliance in advance of cooking so the temperature will be at the desired level when the assembled dish is ready for cooking.

presentation   The appealing arrangement of a dish or food on the plate.

purée   To reduce a food to a thick, creamy texture, usually using a blender or food processor.

reduce   To boil or simmer a broth or sauce to remove some of the water content, resulting in more concentrated flavor and color.

reduced-sodium   A term used to indicate that a food's usual sodium level is reduced by at least 25 percent.

rehydrate   To cover a dried food with water to plump.

reserve   To hold a specified ingredient for another use later in the recipe.

rice vinegar   Vinegar produced from fermented rice or rice wine, popular in Asian-style dishes. Different from rice wine vinegar.

ricotta   A fresh Italian cheese smoother than cottage cheese with a slightly sweet flavor.

roast   To cook something uncovered in an oven, usually without additional liquid.

rosemary   A pungent, sweet herb used with chicken, pork, fish, and especially lamb. A little rosemary goes a long way.

roux   A mixture of butter or another fat and flour, used to thicken sauces and soups.

saffron   A famous spice made from the stamens of crocus flowers. Saffron lends a dramatic yellow color and distinctive flavor to a dish. Only a tiny amount needs to be used, which is good because saffron is very expensive.

sage   An herb with a musty yet fruity, lemon-rind scent and "sunny" flavor. It is a terrific addition to many dishes.

salsa   A style of mixing fresh vegetables and/or fresh fruit in a coarse chop. Salsa can be spicy or not, fruit-based or not, and served as a starter on its own (with chips, for example) or as a companion to a main course.

salt   Chemically, the compound sodium chloride (NaCl) and a major source of the sodium most people consume.

salt substitute   A sodium-free, potassium chloride replacement for salt.

salt-free   A term used to indicate foods that have had no salt added, but may still contain sodium.

salt-free herb and spice seasoning blends   Mixtures of various herbs and spices that are salt-free, MSG-free alternatives to salt.

scant   An ingredient measurement directive not to add any extra, perhaps even leaving the measurement a tad short.

Scoville scale   A scale used to measure the "hot" in hot peppers. The lower the Scoville units, the more mild the pepper. Ancho peppers, which are mildly hot, are about 3,000 Scovilles; Thai hot peppers are about 6,000; and some of the more daring peppers such as Tears of Fire and habañero are 30,000 Scovilles or more.

sesame oil   An oil, made from pressing sesame seeds, that is tasteless if clear and aromatic and flavorful if brown.

shallot   A member of the onion family that grows in a bulb somewhat like garlic and has a milder onion flavor. When a recipe calls for shallot, use the entire bulb. (It might or might not have cloves.)

shellfish   A broad range of seafood, including clams, mussels, oysters, crabs, shrimp, and lobster. Some people are allergic to shellfish, so care should be taken with its inclusion in recipes.

shiitake mushrooms   Large, dark brown mushrooms originally from the Far East with a hearty, meaty flavor. They can be grilled or used as a component in other recipes and as a flavoring source for broth. They can be used either fresh or dried.

shred   To cut into many long, thin slices.

simmer   To boil gently so the liquid barely bubbles.

skewers   Thin wooden or metal sticks, usually about 8 inches long, that are perfect for assembling kebabs, dipping food pieces into hot sauces, or serving single-bite food items with a bit of panache.

skillet (also **frying pan**)   A generally heavy, flat-bottomed metal pan with a handle designed to cook food over heat on a stovetop or campfire.

skim   To remove fat or other material from the top of liquid.

slice   To cut into thin pieces.

sodium   An essential mineral a body needs to regulate fluid balance.

sodium-free   A term used to label foods that contain less than 5 milligrams sodium per serving.

sodium-free baking powder   A compound containing no sodium used in place of regular baking powder.

sodium-free baking soda   A calcium carbonate product used to replace regular baking soda.

soft-set   A stage when eggs have started to firm but aren't yet solid.

steam   To suspend a food over boiling water and allow the heat of the steam (water vapor) to cook the food. Steaming is a very quick cooking method that preserves the flavor and texture of a food.

steep   To let sit in hot water, as in steeping tea in hot water for 10 minutes.

stew   To slowly cook pieces of food submerged in a liquid. Also, a dish that has been prepared by this method.

stir-fry   To cook small pieces of food in a wok or skillet over high heat, moving and turning the food quickly to cook all sides.

stock   A flavorful broth made by cooking meats and/or vegetables with seasonings until the liquid absorbs these flavors. This liquid is then strained and the solids discarded. Stock can be eaten by itself or used as a base for soups, stews, sauces, risotto, or many other recipes.

tamp   To tap a pan on a surface to release any air bubbles from a batter.

tarragon   A sweet, rich-smelling herb perfect with seafood, vegetables (especially asparagus), chicken, and pork.

thyme   A minty, zesty herb whose leaves are used in a wide range of recipes.

toast   To heat something, usually bread, so it is browned and crisp.

tofu   A cheeselike substance made from soybeans and soy milk. Flavorful and nutritious, tofu is an important component of foods across the globe, especially from East Asia.

turmeric   A spicy, pungent yellow root used in many dishes, especially Indian cuisine, for color and flavor. Turmeric is the source of the brilliant yellow color in many prepared mustards.

unsalted   A term used to label foods made without the salt that's normally used, but still contain the sodium that's a natural part of the food itself.

veal   Meat from a calf, generally characterized by mild flavor and tenderness. Certain cuts of veal, such as cutlets and scaloppini, are well suited to quick-cooking.

vegetable steamer   An insert for a large saucepan. Also a special pot with tiny holes in the bottom designed to fit on another pot to hold food to be steamed above boiling water. The insert is generally less expensive and resembles a metal poppy flower that expands to touch the sides of the pot and has small legs. *See also* steam.

very low-sodium   A term used to label foods that contain 35 milligrams or less sodium per serving.

vinegar   An acidic liquid widely used as dressing and seasoning. Many cuisines use vinegars made from different source materials such as fermented grapes, apples, and rice. *See also* balsamic vinegar; cider vinegar; rice vinegar; white vinegar; wine vinegar.

walnuts   Grown worldwide, walnuts bring a rich, slightly woody flavor to all types of food. For the quick cook, walnuts are available chopped and ready to go at your grocery store. They are delicious toasted and make fine accompaniments to cheeses.

water chestnuts   Actually a tuber, water chestnuts are a popular element in many types of Asian-style cooking. The flesh is white, crunchy, and juicy, and the vegetable holds its texture whether cool or hot.

whisk   To rapidly mix, introducing air to the mixture.

white mushrooms   Ubiquitous button mushrooms. When fresh, they will have an earthy smell and an appealing "soft crunch." White mushrooms are delicious raw in salads, marinated, sautéed, and as component ingredients in many recipes.

white vinegar   The most common type of vinegar found on grocery store shelves. It is produced from grain.

whole-wheat flour   Wheat flour that contains the entire grain.

wild rice   Actually a grass with a rich, nutty flavor, popular as an unusual and nutritious side dish.

wine vinegar   Vinegar produced from red or white wine.

without added salt   A term used to label foods made without the salt that's normally used, but still contain the sodium that's a natural part of the food itself.

wok   A wonderful tool for quick-cooking.

Worcestershire sauce   Originally developed in India and containing tamarind, this spicy sauce is used as a seasoning for many meats and other dishes.

yeast   Tiny fungi that, when mixed with water, sugar, flour, and heat, release carbon dioxide bubbles, which, in turn, cause the bread to rise. The yeast also provides that wonderful warm, rich smell and flavor.

zest   Small slivers of peel, usually from a citrus fruit such as lemon, lime, or orange.

zester   A small kitchen tool used to scrape zest off a fruit. A small grater also works well.

Appendix B

Resources

You can find most of the ingredients called for in the recipes in this book at your local supermarket. Others may be more difficult to find, perhaps depending on your location. In this appendix, we've listed a few sources we've found to help you in your search. Naturally, products and availability may change. Please keep in mind, too, that we are not endorsing these resources in any way; use your own best judgment in ordering from any of these sources.

The Baker
PO Box 528
60 Bridge Street
Milford, NJ 08848
908-995-4040
1-800-995-3989
Fax: 908-995-9669
askus@the-baker.com
www.the-baker.com
Salt-free whole-wheat bread.

Brownville Mills
PO Box 145
Brownville, NE 68321
1-800-305-7990
brownvillemills@alltel.net
www.brownvillemills-ne.com
Harder-to-find flours, grains, and more.

Healthy Heart Market
PO Box 459
Rogers, MN 55374
To order a printed catalog:
1-800-753-0310
Fax: 763-428-3926
For orders and questions:
763-428-3526 or 1-888-685-5988
orders@healthyheartmarket.com
www.healthyheartmarket.com
Baking supplies and staples, vegetables, rice and meal mixes, condiments and sauces, pasta sauces, packet mixes and seasonings, salad dressings, soups and broths, Southwestern/Mexican/chili, canned tuna and salmon, crackers and snacks, cereal, and more.

Heluva Good
6551 Pratt Road
PO Box 410
Sodus, NY 14551
1-888-611-4341
315-483-6971
Fax: 315-483-9927
consumeraffairs@heluvagood.com
www.heluvagood.com
Low-sodium cheddar cheese.

Manna Harvest
866-436-1390
www.mannaharvest.net
Organic low-sodium sprouted grain
bread.

Natural Ovens
PO Box 730
Manitowoc, WI 54221-0730
For customer service:
920-758-2500
1-800-558-3535
Fax: 920-758-2671
www.naturalovens.com
Breads naturally lower in sodium with
nutrition facts available for each product.

Trader Joes
www.traderjoes.com
More than 200 stores in Arizona,
California, Connecticut, Delaware,
Illinois, Indiana, Maryland,
Massachusetts, Michigan, Missouri,
Nevada, New Jersey, New Mexico, New
York, Ohio, Oregon, Pennsylvania,
Virginia, and Washington include bak-
ery, bars, beverages, candy, cereal, coffee
and tea, cookies, dairy, dried fruits,
fresh, refrigerated, frozen, grocery, nuts,
snacks, and supplements.

Nutrition Facts/Sodium Figures

NutritionData (ND)
www.nutritiondata.com
Get nutrition facts, calorie counts, and nutrient data for all foods and recipes.

Index

I

J

K-L

M

N

Q-R

T

W

X–Y–Z